Betsy Strathan 801

An Invitation from the Publisher

People who buy this guide have two things in common. They disdain the slick and the tacky, when it comes to lodgings. And they insist upon character and quality. You are evidently one such person, and we welcome you to the guide. You will benefit from the direct experience of thousands like yourself, travelers who spurned the Hiltons and the Holiday Inns, sought out delightful places to stay—and then were kind enough to write and tell us about them.

Will you in turn, as you travel, consider yourself an active member of this informal, beneficent fellowship and contribute your judgments to the existing treasury? Your letters to the guide, candidly reporting on hotels and inns that meet your standards—both those included here and new ones you may find—will greatly assist other travelers. They will also encourage those splendid people across the land, the new breed of hoteliers and innkeepers, who are rapidly giving America a reputation for superb hospitality.

In the back of the guide you will find forms on which you can make your reports. Use them, or compose as you will. The important thing is to write. To be vital, the guide needs fresh reports each year on every inn—to note the ones that have slipped and to affirm that the others are still wonderful.

We look forward to hearing from you.

Dunselina - Chatham
$120 a day
ocean.

Thomas Congdon
Publisher

States, Territories, and Canadian Provinces Covered in This Edition

UNITED STATES

Alabama
Connecticut
Delaware
District of Columbia
Florida
Georgia
Illinois
Indiana
Kentucky
Louisiana
Maine
Maryland
Massachusetts
Michigan
Minnesota
Mississippi
New Hampshire
New Jersey
New York
North Carolina

Ohio
Pennsylvania
Rhode Island
South Carolina
Tennessee
Vermont
Virginia
West Virginia
Wisconsin

U.S. TERRITORY

Puerto Rico

CANADA

New Brunswick
Nova Scotia
Ontario
Prince Edward Island
Quebec

Also in This Series

America's Wonderful Little Hotels and Inns

Eastern Region

Fourth Edition

Edited
by
Barbara
Crossette

Drawings by
Ron Couture
Assistant Editor
Jan L. Shannon

Congdon & Weed, Inc.
New York

Copyright © 1984 by Barbara Crossette
and Hilary Rubinstein Books Ltd.
Illustrations copyright © by Ron Couture

Library of Congress Cataloging in Publication Data

Main entry under title:

America's wonderful little hotels and inns, Eastern region.

Previous eds., covering both eastern and western regions, published as:
America's wonderful little hotels and inns.
Includes indexes.
1. Hotels, taverns, etc.—United States—Directories.
2. Hotels, taverns, etc.—Canada, Eastern—Directories.
3. Hotels, taverns, etc.—Puerto Rico—Directories.
I. Crossette, Barbara. II. Shannon, Jan L.
III. America's wonderful little hotels and inns.
TX907.A618 1984   647′.94701   83-23993
ISBN   0-86553-110-2 (pbk.)
ISBN   0-312-92021-0 (St. Martin's Press: pbk.)

Published by Congdon & Weed, Inc.
298 Fifth Avenue, New York, N.Y. 10001
Distributed by St. Martin's Press
175 Fifth Avenue, New York, N.Y. 10010
Published simultaneously in Canada by Methuen Publications
2330 Midland Avenue, Agincourt, Ontario M1S 1P7

Cover design by Krystyna Skalski
Cover illustration by Steven Guarnaccia
Maps by Donald Pitcher

_____ *Contents*

Preface

So large has been the response to earlier editions of *America's Wonderful Little Hotels and Inns* that this, the fourth edition, appears in two volumes, one for travelers east of the Mississippi, the other for those visiting the West. The reason for this surge of enthusiasm for these special places to stay is not hard to find.

America is caught up in an innkeeping revolution. From quiet Texas border towns or the California wine country through the Midwest to the oldest and largest East Coast cities, travelers of all kinds—business people as well as vacationers—are seeking, and now finding, small hotels of character with the kind of grace and personalized service that the age of the motel and big chain hotel had all but consigned to history. In a new age of restoration and rediscovery of our varied but uniquely American past, all kinds of interesting buildings are getting new lives as hotels and inns. Some of them were historic town houses or abandoned stately homes, a couple were general stores, several were boarding schools, at least one or two were brothels, hundreds were roadside taverns gone to seed.

Everyone seems to like these American classics: couples find romantic settings, business people value the quiet dignity and class, children can experience a kind of live-in history they will remember more vividly than a visit to any museum. Americans, innkeepers say, are more willing to make trade-offs to enjoy these old-fashioned luxuries. They are more willing to share bathrooms with other guests. They are content to put on a sweater and pull a chair closer to the fire if the heating becomes unreliable. They have found there is life without room service. "People want to see a little bit of how it used to be," said Harry Cregar, who rescued and restored the nineteenth-century canalside Riegelsville Hotel in historic Bucks County, Pennsylvania.

This new American innkeeping tradition, which is already challenging the reputation of European hotels, had its roots in the age of alternatives—the 1960s and 1970s—when Americans discovered restoration and urban renewal. Snatching up buildings that had been deserted or neglected in the rush to the suburban shopping malls, a new generation of innkeepers brought to these structures the fabrics, paints, and furniture that testify to the lead the United States has taken in interior design as well as in historic preservation. And they did more: they returned to cooking "from scratch," but with a sophistication that now supports a country full of fine food and wine shops. And the glorious breakfasts! There is probably nothing in the world of travel now to rival the best of the American inns' country-style breakfasts, with fresh fruit and juices, imaginative egg dishes, home-baked breads, and the best coffees and teas.

American innkeepers are as varied as the hotels and inns they run. Old people run inns; second-career people run inns; grown-up flower children run inns. Many successful innkeepers are women. Friends and couples of every description are in the business; sometimes whole families get into the spirit. Now and then the person who greets you at the door or brings you a cup of tea is a very small person indeed. The inn cat might spend the night in your armchair. Your innkeeper may be a musician, a painter, or the scion of the family in whose aristocratic home you are sleeping. At the Quimper Inn in Port Townsend, Washington, Paolo Wein and Mariii Lockwood are, among other things, jugglers. "On rainy days," Paolo says.

No state or Canadian province is without at least a handful of interesting places to stay, and the hotels are as diverse as the places they originally sprang up to serve. Want to sample a stagecoach stop? Try the 17-room Hotel Wolf in Saratoga, Wyoming. Want a college town hotel with Western glamour? Stay at Boulder, Colorado's ornate Boulderado. In Keosauqua, Iowa, there is the steamboat-stop Hotel Manning on the banks of the Des Moines River. In Natchez, Mississippi, you can stay in a former bawdy house in notorious Silver Street. Antebellum homes, gristmills, hunting lodges, spas, railway hostels, a lighthouse in Florida, a coffee plantation in Puerto Rico—the story of America is there to sample as you make your way around the country, eating and sleeping in local history instead of just looking at it from behind a velvet rope.

HOW TO USE THIS BOOK

Because *America's Wonderful Little Hotels and Inns* is a collection of places with special character and interest, it is not intended to be a comprehensive nuts-and-bolts guide; nor is it a guide with inspectors and a rating system. The "experts" who wrote this book are the travelers themselves, along with a few local historians, architects, and specialists in preservation and restoration who are aware of how important this boom in innkeeping is to keeping alive a traditional America, with all its regional differences.

Individualists choose individualistic hotels and inns, so your tastes and needs may differ from those of one or more of the books' contributors. If they do—or if a place you try seems no longer to meet the description you read here—please write, so that other travelers can learn from your experience. This book can only grow and change if you, the reader, join in. Inns that draw a number of complaints are removed from the book's next edition. A historical building is not much comfort to the weary if the service is poor; and one person's quirky or talkative innkeeper may be another person's bore.

Information at the foot of each entry is provided by the innkeepers, who may forget now and then to include a detail or two that would make the difference to you. Write or telephone and ask about it. Bar and dining room services vary considerably among small hotels and inns, sometimes in response to the plethora of state and local laws governing the serving of food and alcohol, sometimes because of the size of an inn or its staff. Many small inns and hotels, however, are very cooperative and will, with a little notice, make special provisions for people with special needs. An increasing number of innkeepers are, for example, providing vegetarian food and some facilities for the handicapped. And if a small inn or hotel does not accept credit cards, it will very frequently take personal checks.

Most hotels and inns in this book charge by the room—or, increasingly, for a room and breakfast, though the practice is still far from universal. Where the full or modified American plan is in operation, the charge, which includes meals, is usually per person. But this can vary, so be certain to confirm your plan when booking your room. Ask also about state or local taxes, or service charges that may be added to your bill. Many small hotels and inns, incidentally, require advance booking and may ask for a deposit. Some of the more popular inns can be booked up at peak holiday times—Christmas, for example—for months or even a year in advance.

Like their companion, *Europe's Wonderful Little Hotels and Inns*, these volumes that comprise *America's Wonderful Little Hotels and Inns* owe their existence to many people. Each year the loyal corps of contributors grows—some of them have followings of their own because they have become recognizable names to be trusted by other readers who share their tastes. Each new edition brings adjustments; in this fourth edition, a larger number of inns have been dropped than from any earlier edition. This testifies to both the increasing discrimination of American travelers and the larger choice of interesting places to stay. A few hotels and inns continue to be the subject of controversy, and sometimes conflicting views are presented here because not all of us react the same way to places not stamped from molds.

As always, this book is dedicated gratefully to the generous, wise, and witty people who wrote it.

Part One

New England

Connecticut
Maine
Massachusetts
New Hampshire
Rhode Island
Vermont

Griswold Inn,
Essex

Connecticut

East Haddam

Bishop's Gate Inn
Goodspeed Landing
East Haddam, Connecticut 06423
Telephone (203) 873-1677

"Julie Bishop, former president of the Goodspeed Opera Guild, has recently moved her inn into a new building in the center of East Haddam, just a short walk from the Opera House as well as shops and restaurants.

"There is something about inns that I realized when I was at Bishop's Gate. You are forced—and I don't mean that in a negative way—to be with people. You communicate. You say 'Good morning.' There is a big old table to sit around.

"Half the joy of the place is Julie. She stands back and doesn't intrude, but she is always there. If you are having a party, she will let you open her house to your guests—you can bring your own ham or chicken or roast. She's done a lot of research on how inns were run in the seventeenth, eighteenth, and nineteenth centuries. The atmosphere is wonderful. Some of the rooms have canopy beds and fireplaces. Julie and her antiques are exceptional."

—*George Herzog*

3

"Bishop's Gate is a place for people who know their antiques and appreciate good taste when they see it, as opposed to the hordes who thrill at phony quaintness. Every room is individually decorated with good stuff. We particularly admired an extraordinary set of late eighteenth-century Dutch marquetry furniture that is used in many of the rooms."   —*Tom Congdon*

Open all year.
6 rooms, including 1 suite with private sauna, 4 rooms with private
    bath, 4 with fireplaces.
Rates $60–$85, including breakfast.
No credit cards.
Innkeeper: Julie Bishop.

_____*Essex*

Griswold Inn
Main Street
Essex, Connecticut 06426
Telephone (203) 767-0991

"It's like a comfy old house slipper on a winter night—always a warm welcome, and better with age. We go back frequently; 'tis our favorite. The Griswold is a special sort of place in the wonderfully quaint but alive village of Essex, on the Connecticut River. You can lunch in the library or the Gun Room (guns date back to the fifteenth century) or dine in the Steamboat Room, where the mural floats gently up and down, giving one the feeling of dining on the river. The bar is unbelievable—a one-room schoolhouse with crackling fire, potbellied stove, and walls covered with old prints of steamships, posters, mast lights, ships' bells, and all sorts of impressive memorabilia. To top it off, there's an authentic antique popcorn machine on wheels that never gets a chance to rest.

"The inn dates back to 1776. The rooms are exactly as they should be—charmingly quaint and spotless. (We love climbing into the huge four-poster in Room 3.)

"There is a century-old railroad depot in Essex where one can take an antique steam train (the Valley Railroad) for an hour's nostalgic ride. Deep River, a village close by, has the annual Fife and Drum Muster in July. At East Haddam, a stone's throw away, there is the Goodspeed Opera House."   —*Chic Sciple-Cooper*

"It is fabulous, old and delightful."   —*Charles L. Garretson*

Open all year.
18 rooms, 3 suites, all with private bath.

Rates $48, suites $54–$56, including continental breakfast.
Credit cards: American Express, Diners Club, MasterCard, Visa.
Restaurant.
German spoken.
Amtrak train to Old Saybrook, taxi service to Essex.
Innkeeper: William G. Winterer.

_____*Greenwich*

The Homestead Inn
420 Field Point Road
Greenwich, Connecticut 06830
Telephone (203) 869-7500

"I discovered the Homestead by accident, having arrived in Greenwich on a business trip and finding all the local motels booked. Like that rare blind date that winds up at the altar, my first visit was the beginning of a long love affair with this charming hostelry. From first glimpse—etched against the evening sky, a wonderful chocolate brown and homesteadish place, with a cupola and a wide, welcoming porch—to the last great cup of coffee (part of the inn's complimentary continental breakfast), it was a take.

"In the first place I was warmly greeted, not simply admitted. Then, on the way to my room, I had the fun of learning a bit about the inn's history. Built in 1799, it was originally the home of one of Greenwich's earliest settlers. It opened as an inn in 1859, during that colorful era when guests arrived in horse-drawn carriages, and the railroad and car were decades away. My room (for all of its modern appointments: air conditioning, TV, telephone, private bath) took me straight back to those tranquil times. Furnished with antiques (including sleigh beds of glowing mahogany, the last word in comfort) and with handsome paintings on its freshly painted walls, 'my room' (I've been asking for this one ever since) is like a tree house. The first thing I see in the morning, and the last thing on a moonlit night, is a magnificent old tree at my window. Even if the meals were merely passable, 'my room' would keep bringing me back.

"But those meals! Beautifully served in a big, festive room with a chestnut-beamed ceiling and wide brick fireplace, the food, like everything at this inn, is noble. If this reads like a love letter, forgive. In a way, it is."
—*Jean Martine*

Open all year.
11 rooms, 2 suites, all with private bath.

Rates $65–$125, including continental breakfast.
Credit cards: American Express, Diners Club, MasterCard, Visa.
Restaurant and chocolate bar.
French and Spanish spoken.
Greenwich is on the Metro North train line, New Haven division, from Grand Central Terminal, New York City. Limousine service to La Guardia Airport; taxis to Westchester Airport.
Innkeepers: Lessie Davison and Nancy Smith.

_____*Ivorytown*

Copper Beech Inn
Main Street
Ivorytown, Connecticut 06442
Telephone (203) 767-0330

"I was so surprised and so very disappointed not to see the Copper Beech Inn in your guide. It's a marvelous inn with five rooms (all with private bath) in a most tranquil setting. It is run by a most friendly group. By itself, it's idyllic, but its gourmet dining rooms make it paradise."   —*Victoria A. Nugent*

Open all year, except Christmas and New Year's Day.
5 rooms, all with private bath.
Rates $55–$95, including continental breakfast.
Credit cards: American Express, Diners Club, MasterCard, Visa.
Restaurant.
French spoken.
Amtrak trains to Old Lyme, airports at New Haven and Hartford.
Innkeepers: Paul and Louise Ebeltoft.

_____*Litchfield*

The Litchfield Inn
Route 202
Litchfield, Connecticut 06759
Telephone (203) 567-4503

"Just opened in January 1983. A lovely Early American inn with some Victorian furnishings. I enjoyed an excellent breakfast in a gardenlike room."   —*Mary Pagnovo*

Open all year.
12 rooms, all with private bath.

Rates $55–$65 summer, lower off-season rates. Continental break-
fast included Monday through Friday.
Credit cards: American Express, MasterCard, Visa.
Knowledge of sign language. Special equipment for the handi-
capped.
Innkeeper: Rose Marie Irwin.

_____ *Mystic*

Charley's Harbor Guest House
Edgemont Street (RFD 1, Box 398)
Mystic, Connecticut 06355
Telephone (203) 572-9253

"From this small house, you can walk to town or seaport. Charley
is very congenial. While we were there he took one of his single
guests to see the local tourist attractions."
                                        —*Mr. and Mrs. James Haldeman*

Open all year.
4 rooms, 2 with private bath, and a 3-room cottage.
Rates $20–$65, including use of dock, laundry facilities, and
kitchen.
No credit cards.
Greek spoken.
Guests can be met at train, bus, airport, or marina.
Innkeeper: Charley Lecouras, Jr.

_____ *New Milford*

Homestead Inn
5 Elm Street
New Milford, Connecticut 06776
Telephone (203) 354-4080

"Just off the village green of this lovely New England town, about
eighty miles north of New York City, the Homestead Inn offers two
choices. You can stay in the main house, which was built around
1817, or in the adjoining motel rooms. The rooms are immaculate.
A number of restaurants are within a mile or two of the inn—there
is a good choice of fresh seafood. Many executives visiting local
branches of their national organizations find the inn a relaxing stop.
I continue to recommend this delightful place in a most interesting
area of Connecticut."   —*Paul R. Hatch*

Open all year.
15 rooms, all with private bath.
Rates $26–$28 single, $32–$34 double.
Credit cards: American Express, MasterCard, Visa.
Reached by Bonanza Bus Lines from New York.
Innkeepers: Barbara and Donald McPherson.

_____*New Preston*

Boulders Inn
Lake Waramaug (Route 45)
New Preston, Connecticut 06777
Telephone (203) 868-7918

Nestled in the Berkshires of northwestern Connecticut, Boulders Inn has been welcoming guests for forty years. The building itself is almost a century old; it was constructed in 1895 as a private mountain home. The inn is in an area frequented by music lovers —the Berkshire String Quartet has a summer residence nearby— and by outdoors people, too: there is canoeing on the Housatonic, Bantam, and Shepang rivers and hiking and biking at Litchfield's White Memorial Foundation.

"I first went to Boulders Inn with my four young children (ages ranging from about seven to fifteen) at the enthusiatic recommendation of a close friend. There I found lovely surroundings conducive to both a quiet time and a social life. The children were safe— able to enjoy swimming, hiking, camping, and many other sports. In fact, we liked the summers so much, we went back in the winters to enjoy the skating and sledding. Now my children are grown, but we still return to Boulders to enjoy the delicious food."

—*Jenny Lee Hanson*

Open all year.
14 rooms, all with private bath.
Rate $54 per person, including breakfast and dinner.
Credit cards: MasterCard, Visa.
Restaurant and bar.
Greyhound bus to Marbledale; Bonanza bus to New Milford. Trains from Grand Central, New York City, to Brewster, New York, with connecting Kelly buses on weekends. Taxi service can be arranged in advance from Marbledale, New Preston, and New Milford.
Innkeepers: Carolyn and Jim Woollen.

Hopkins Inn
Hopkins Road
New Preston, Connecticut 06777
Telephone (203) 868-7295

"Eating out alone is, like good whiskey, an acquired pleasure. You can eavesdrop, scribble verse on a napkin or, if you are a stranger in town, fish out a copy of the local newspaper and see who has been making a noisy disturbance on Main Street. All too often, alas, solitary eaters, like blind men with begging bowls, are shunted to one side, nuisances getting in the way of real people—groups of two and up. Let it be said right at the start that at the Hopkins Inn the reverse was the case. The youngish staff were attentive, but tactfully avoided stomping over my daydreams. Someone had made them wear Austrian costumes, but that was not their fault.

"The restaurant was calm—you can also eat outside under tall trees if you like—without that frantic feeling that disturbs so many meals eaten alone.

"The upstairs is chock-full of rambling staircases and corridors. You can borrow the books on the shelves—Solzhenitsyn back to back (a little awkwardly, one presumes) with *The Hunchback of Notre Dame.* The Hopkins is a handsome house, with its yellow exterior and black shutters, sitting high up over the broad silvery expanse of Lake Waramaug."   —*David Wigg*

Open May through October (rooms), April through December
   (apartment)
11 rooms, 8 with private bath, 1 apartment.
Rates $29–$42.
No credit cards.
French and German spoken.
Innkeepers: Franz and Beth Schober.

The Inn on Lake Waramaug
North Shore Road
New Preston, Connecticut 06777
Telephone (203) 868-0563

"The inn, built as a home in 1795 and used as a guesthouse since 1860, has been in the same family since the 1890s when it was bought as a summer home. At that time, it was known as Lakeview. In 1951, Richard Combs bought out his grandfather's interest and renamed it The Inn. He has operated it ever since with the help of his family. The original building has only five guest rooms and an intimate living room. There are no telephones in the rooms. The inn is immaculately clean and the food is traditional American and very good.

"The area around Lake Waramaug is picturesque and private (there are only three public inns on the twenty-mile lake coastline; the rest of the area is taken up by private homes). It is perfect for leisurely bicycling on the road around the lake or for canoeing or sailing. The inn provides both bicycles and boats for a small charge, as well as a free tennis court and 150 acres for strolling around or just sitting in one of the many lounge chairs scattered over the lawns. Nearby are several state parks, horseback-riding stables, local museums, antique shops, and charming New England countryside and small towns.

"The Combs have kept the inn decorated in colonial style and filled the rooms with eighteenth-century pine and cherrywood antiques. They added an indoor pool and bar adjacent to the old building, built two separate guest lodges to accommodate a growing clientele, and provided a boat dock and lakeside snack bar."

—*Phillip and Debbie Fretz*

"This is not your perfect little inn. It sprawls, and a lot of people pour through. Some of the furniture is terrific and some not so great. But it's pleasant and serviceable, at the least. Better than many." —*Tom Congdon*

Open all year.

25 rooms, all with private bath, 8 with fireplaces.

Rates $60–85 per person, including breakfast and dinner. Special midweek discounts November through June.

Credit cards: American Express, Diners Club, MasterCard, Visa.

Restaurant and bar.

French spoken.

Bus service daily from New York City by Greyhound to New Preston and by Bonanza to Southbury, New Milford, or Kent. Train from Grand Central to Brewster, New York, on Friday meets connecting bus to New Preston; return trip on Sunday. For a fee, the inn will meet guests at Bradley Airport, in Windsor Locks, 45 miles away.

Innkeeper: Richard Bonynge Combs.

Turn to the back of this book for pages inviting *your* comments.

_____*Norfolk*

Mountain View Inn
Litchfield Road (Route 272)
Norfolk, Connecticut 06058
Telephone (203) 542-5595

"The inn is in historic Litchfield County in the foothills of the Berkshires. Norfolk, full of Early American history, exemplifies a quiet New England town complete with village green and steepled church. Activities and facilities within a short driving distance include shopping for antiques, swimming, boating, fishing, golf, and downhill and cross-country skiing. Excellent music is available across the road at the Yale Summer School of Music, and at Tanglewood, one hour away." —*Dr. Richard A. Susskind*

Open all year.
11 rooms, 5 with private bath.
Rates $52–$57 double, including breakfast bar.
Credit cards: American Express, MasterCard, Visa.
Restaurant and bar.
Bonanza Bus Lines connects Norfolk and nearby Canaan and Winsted to New York and Boston. Inn will meet guests.
Innkeepers: Mr. and Mrs. Hodge.

_____*Norwalk*

Silvermine Tavern
Silvermine and Perry Avenues
Norwalk, Connecticut 06850
Telephone (203) 847-4558

The area of Silvermine dates its settlement to the mid-seventeenth century. Over the years it has become known as a center of art and craft work. A 200-year-old inn, the Silvermine Tavern is only an hour from New York City and a short distance from the American Shakespeare Theater at Stratford and the Westport Summer Theater.

"There is a quaint dining room furnished with antiques. In summer, meals are served outside on a terrace amid trees and above a running brook. The food is tasty and well prepared."
—*Ann Rosenberg; also recommended by Patricia Lievow*

Open all year; closed Tuesdays October through May.
10 rooms, all with private bath.

Rates $37–$57, including continental breakfast.
Credit cards: American Express, Diners Club, MasterCard, Visa.
Restaurant and bar.
Bus and rail service to Norwalk.
Innkeeper: Frank J. Whitman, Jr.

_____*Old Lyme*

Bee and Thistle Inn
100 Lyme Street (Route 1)
Old Lyme, Connecticut 06371
Telephone (203) 434-1667

Old Lyme, founded by sea captains where the Connecticut River meets Long Island Sound, has remained conscious of both its natural setting—there are marshlands and beaches—and its colonial past. There are museums to visit, and there is the Old Lyme Historic District for walking and bicycling. On a five-and-a-half-acre plot in the district is the Bee and Thistle Inn, built as a judge's home in 1756 and renovated in 1920. It has been an inn since 1941.

"The inn sits back from the road amid the towering trees that surround it. The yellow color with its white trim and the little circular porch off the front door somehow bid you welcome even from a distance. Inside, the feeling is casual, relaxed, as though you already lived there and a few old friends dropped by to spend the weekend. There are two parlors with a roaring fire in each, and another fire blazes in the main dining room down the hall. Classical music comes from the stereo in the offices off the hall. Upstairs the tubs are so large you can actually submerge your whole body."

—*Jay B. Teasdel*

"The Bee and Thistle is not cozy. It has been stripped down for commerce. There's nothing in it. It has its charms, but the idea is to hold people. You get the idea that the restaurant business matters more than the overall inn experience. Still, somehow it's a nice place in an attractive setting."   —*Tom Congdon*

"The Bee and Thistle provided precisely the inn we were looking for as an Easter weekend retreat: an Early American house of character, set well back from the road on five acres overlooking the river, a prosperous village well endowed with several good antique shops. The owners, who took over in June 1982, are amiable. The rooms were furnished with decent period pieces and the whole place had a welcoming air. There were, as everywhere, small details to grumble about—inadequate bedroom lighting, lack of shelves in the bathroom, ever-crowded public rooms in the evening—but overall the hotel scored high marks. It didn't surprise us to learn that the place was already booked in April for the summer.

"We didn't sample the restaurant, but it was clearly doing a thriving business, with a harpist on Saturday evenings. The printed menu promised a general selection of fairly elaborate French dishes."   —*Hilary, Helge, and Felicity Rubinstein; Andre, Leina, and Natilya Schiffrin; also recommended by Dorothy M. Konley*

Open all year.
10 rooms, 8 with private bath.
Rates $48–$68.
Credit cards: American Express, MasterCard, Visa.
Amtrak and Metro North trains to Old Saybrook, New Haven, and New London; taxis from stations.
Innkeepers: Bob and Penny Nelson.

Old Lyme Inn
85 Lyme Street (P.O. Box 208)
Old Lyme, Connecticut 06371
Telephone (203) 434-2600

"The atmosphere is pleasant, serene, efficient, and slightly merry. The food, in my opinion, is the best that can be found between New York City and Boston. The wine list provides a range and quality not usually found in American restaurants."   —*Lee Hall*

"The dining room is gracious, the food imaginative, with choices like seafood sausages and duck and raisin ravioli. The chef does lean heavily on the brandy and raisin sauce, though."

—*JLS*

Open all year
5 rooms, all with private bath.
Rates $45–$50, including continental breakfast.
Credit cards: American Express, Carte Blanche, Diners Club, MasterCard, Visa.
Restaurant.
Amtrak rail service to Old Saybrook; taxis at station.
Innkeeper: Diana Field Atwood.

Do you know a hotel in your state that we have overlooked? Write *now.*

_____*Ridgefield*

Stonehenge
Route 7 (P.O. Box 667)
Ridgefield, Connecticut 06877
Telephone (203) 438-6511

"We always said that one day we would spend the night at Stonehenge. For many years it had been one of our favorite restaurants. On many a Sunday afternoon we would go out for a ride through the countryside of Rhode Island and Connecticut and end up there for an enjoyable dinner. Let me tell you about one particular experience. On one Sunday they were serving a 'floating island' dessert. This had been a favorite in my boyhood home: my family had brought the recipe with them from their homeland in the Portuguese Azores. I asked the waiter if he knew the dessert was Portuguese. He replied that he was Italian and that he had also been raised on 'floating islands.' He offered me a second helping.

"When we finally made reservations to stay at Stonehenge we were lucky to get a room in the main house. When we entered our room, we were surprised to find blue cheese, crackers, and apples waiting for us, along with a half-bottle of wine. The evening was a wonderful, relaxing one. We thought the inn was a little expensive, but it was well worth the price."   —*Arthur and Dolores Raposo*

Open all year.
8 rooms, all with private bath.
Rates $58.50–$70.
Credit cards: American Express, Diners Club, MasterCard, Visa.
Restaurant and bar.
French, German, Italian, Spanish, and Portuguese spoken.
Managers: David Davis and Douglas Seville.

_____

West Lane Inn
22 West Lane (Route 35)
Ridgefield, Connecticut 06877
Telephone (203) 438-7323

"The drive from mid-Manhattan to the old New England town of Ridgefield takes little more than an hour. Main Street is wide, tree-lined, and lovely. The homes are a combination of pre-Revolutionary and Victorian architecture. Just off Main Street, next to the

imposing Inn at Ridgefield, known for its dining, is the West Lane Inn, a nineteenth-century mansion that has been remodeled into fourteen guest rooms. The decor is impressive; the rooms are spacious. Continental breakfast is served in a cheery room. Guests gather in the reception area at night for cheese, fruit, and coffee.
—*Kay Wilder*

"This beautifully restored house is the best place for an overnight stay in town. It has large rooms—individually furnished, each with its own bath, some with fireplaces. The breakfast is more substantial than just 'continental.' "
—*Mildred Gilman*

"Fruit, cheese, and coffee are not served every night. We arrived at 8:30 P.M. and no such offer was made. Nonetheless, the room was terrific, the breakfast wonderful."
—*Geoffrey Lawrence*

"We had some trouble finding West Lane because there was no street sign. Guests should look for Route 35, which is clearly marked."
—*JLS*

Open all year.
20 rooms, all with private bath.
Rate $90 double, including continental breakfast.
Credit cards: American Express, MasterCard, Visa.
Restaurant and bar.
Spanish spoken.
Train service to New Canaan or Katonah, New York. Buses to Ridgefield from New York City.
Innkeeper: Maureen M. Mayer.

_____ *Riverton*

Old Riverton Inn
Route 20 (P.O. Box 6)
Riverton, Connecticut 06065
Telephone (203) 379-8678

"The Old Riverton Inn is located in the northwestern part of Connecticut at the foot of the Berkshire Hills on the Farmington River. The inn was originally opened in 1796 by Jesse Ives, as Ives' Tavern, on the post route between Hartford and Albany. It was later owned by the Yale family and was known as the Yale Hotel. In 1937 the inn was restored to its earliest possible state. In 1954, because of increased business, the Grindstone Terrace was added. The floor of this room is made of grindstones that, according to records, were quarried in Nova Scotia and shipped to Long Island Sound and then up the Connecticut River to Collinsville to be used in the making of axes and machetes.

"There is an attractive Hobby Horse cocktail lounge and ten rooms for overnight guests. The upper lounge is filled with family pieces of furniture, many of them antique treasures. The dining room is furnished with Hitchcock chairs and tables, made in the factory across the river.

"The inn's cooking is American style, with specialties of baked stuffed pork chops, veal in cream and brandy, and baked stuffed shrimp. The fish—sole and scrod—is all fresh. The atmosphere of the inn is relaxing, and its location excellent—ten miles from the Yale Summer Music School (Norfolk), less than an hour's drive from Tanglewood, and of course across the river from the famous Hitchcock chair factory and museums."   —*Ruth Katzin*

"What you always thought an old-fashioned inn should be—simple, unpretentious, true to itself, picking up no false or faddish new styles. A reflection of the tiny community in which it has served since 1796, a town that time has passed by and is the better for it."
—*David Halberstam*

"One small cavil: one of the rooms upstairs has been made into a shop, complete with loud music. Consequently, the landing at times may be as busy as Grand Central Terminal—annoying if you are staying in one of the rooms a few yards away."   —*David Wigg*

"Another inn that has been overwhelmed somewhat by its restaurant and tourist business. The dining room, though rather attractive, throngs with a Howard Johnson sort of crowd seeking the mediocre food, and the innkeeper rather grimly tries to deal with it all, with mechanical charm. The Hobby Horse lounge was not a good idea. Upstairs, though, it's quite nice, and Riverton is a sweet little town."   —*Tom Congdon*

"Very nice accommodations. Our room had a fireplace and private bath. Excellent food. Quaint town—home of the Hitchcock chair."
—*Ora and Phil Beilock*

Open all year. Dining room and lounge closed first two weeks in January.
10 rooms, all with private bath.
Rates $40–$56 double per person, including breakfast.
Credit cards: American Express, Carte Blanche, Diners Club, MasterCard, Visa.
2 restaurants; bar.
Spanish spoken.
Innkeeper: Mark A. Telford.

Salisbury

Ragamont Inn
Main Street
Salisbury, Connecticut 06068
Telephone (203) 435-2372

"The food is still great. The ambience is still warm. The Ragamont Inn, owned by Barbara and Rolf Schenkel, is still a great place to recharge your batteries. The Schenkels have recently expanded the place because of its increasing popularity. They have also added a chef, Alice Stefanisko. Much of the food still comes, fresh, from the garden behind the inn. Guests now have a choice of the original rooms or new rooms with color TV and air conditioning. The rooms are intimate, with a colonial motif. Antique furniture abounds—take a look at the old wooden chest from the 1700s that stands near the front entrance.

"Some of the places in the area are worth noting. The Sharon Playhouse offers professional productions of popular plays and musicals. You can also walk to an art gallery and enjoy the striking paintings and sculptures."   —*Danny Fiore*

"If the interior decor were as good as the facade, this would be a fine inn. But, except for the main dining room—which is attractive and has good food—the taste is very uneven. This is a place where you really have to know what room to ask for. The reception room is barnlike and cheerless. But the Ragamont is worth a stay. The exterior is really handsome."   —*Tom Congdon*

Open May 1 to November 1.
12 rooms, 9 with private bath (3 are motel-style units).
Rates $18–$30 single, $38–$58 double.
No credit cards.
Restaurant.
German spoken.
Innkeepers: Barbara and Rolf Schenkel.

Woodbury

Curtis House
508 Main Street South (U.S. 6)
Woodbury, Connecticut 06798
Telephone (203) 263-2101

"Our room at Curtis House was attractively and comfortably furnished. It was clean and of good value. The four-poster beds in all the rooms seemed a bit pretentious, but the style was tasteful. The traffic on Route 6 was a little bothersome throughout the night, in spite of the fact that our room did not face the street—in fact, our room was at the back of the inn—but we did manage to sleep fairly well.

"The food at Curtis House was an enormous disappointment. First of all, the menu was far too ambitious. There were four categories of entrée, and four or five selections within each category. No one can do that many things well—probably not even acceptably. Most serious of all, though, was that, in spite of the fact that we were visiting in August and had seen roadside fruit and vegetable stands every few miles throughout our trip, the first-course fruit cup at Curtis House was basically canned fruit cocktail, and the vegetables served with dinner were right out of the can. Such shortcuts seemed inexcusable and even insulting. The dessert menu listed about ten choices, and the pies and puddings were billed as 'homemade.' Upon inquiry, I was told that they were made from packaged pie crust, canned pie filling, and packaged pudding mix. These abominations may be accurately labeled 'home assembled,' but please, not 'homemade.'"
—*Phyllis Faber Kelley*

Open all year. Restaurant closed Christmas Day.
18 rooms, 11 with private bath.
Rates $26–$42, including continental breakfast.
Credit cards: MasterCard, Visa.
Restaurant.
Bus transportation available to Southbury, 4 miles away. Taxi service to inn.
Innkeeper: Chester C. Hardisty.

American hotels and inns generally list rates by the room, assuming one person in a single, two in a double. Extra people in rooms normally incur extra charges. Where rates are quoted per person per day, at least one meal is probably included under a Modified American plan (MAP). A full American Plan (AP) would include three meals.

Captain Lord Mansion,
Kennebunkport

Maine

Bar Harbor

Clefstone Manor
92 Eden Street (Route 3)
Bar Harbor, Maine 04609
Telephone (207) 288-4951

"The Jackson family devote themselves to making their guests comfortable. They serve home-baked breads in the morning with fresh-brewed coffee or tea, 'high tea' at 4 P.M., and wine and cheese in the evening. No full dining service is available but menus and recommendations are offered. The inn is beautifully decorated with wonderful rooms, a hallway library, fireplace in the front room, and a lovely sun porch with wicker furniture. This inn is a 'must-see.'"
—*Linda Rogers*

"The Jackson children own Omawki Balloon Adventures, a hot-air balloon service. After an early morning flight, guests are treated to a champagne landing and then breakfast at Cleftstone Manor."
—*JLS*

Open May 15 through October 15.
15 rooms and 3 suites, 13 with private bath.

Rates $30–$80, including full breakfast, afternoon tea, and evening wine and cheese.
Credit cards: American Express, MasterCard, Visa.
Dining room for guests only.
Innkeepers: The Jackson family.

_____

Town Guest House
12 Atlantic Avenue
Bar Harbor, Maine 04609
Telephone (207) 288-5548

"My husband and I had been traveling along the East Coast, following your handbook. While in Bar Harbor, we stayed in a lovely establishment, the Town Guest House, which much to our surprise was not listed in your guide. The Guest House is a small Victorian hotel in a quiet neighborhood, though not far from the center of Bar Harbor."
—*Mrs. N. N. Furbush*

"For the past five years my husband and I have gone to Bar Harbor for vacation, and for the past five years we have stayed here. You will not find any nicer people than Joe and Paulette Paluga."
—*Helene E. Fye*

Open May 1 through October 20.
9 rooms, all with private bath.
Rates $30–$70.
Credit cards: American Express, MasterCard, Visa.
French spoken.
Bus and air service to Bar Harbor.
Innkeepers: Paulette and Joe Paluga.

_____*Boothbay Harbor*

Howard House Motor Lodge
Route 27
Boothbay Harbor, Maine 04538
Telephone (207) 633-3933

"A delightful spot, away from the waterfront of Boothbay, but quiet and very homelike. The innkeepers are well traveled and friendly. Breakfast is continental, with fresh baked goods each morning. A mile from town, the inn has seven spacious rooms with private baths and country furnishings."
—*Kristin Kennell*

Open all year.
7 rooms, all with private bath and outdoor deck.
Rates $24–$40 double, including continental breakfast.
No credit cards.
No pets, but the innkeepers will make reservations for pets to be
    boarded with local veterinarian.
Bus to Wiscasset, 13 miles away.
Innkeepers: The Farrins.

_____ *Camden*

The Owl and Turtle Bookmotel
8 Bay View
Camden, Maine 04843
Telephone (207) 236-4769

"The Owl and Turtle Bookmotel, located at the public landing
where many of the windjammers embark, is surely one of the most
beautiful bookstores anywhere. One of the guest rooms has been
converted into a tearoom that adds to the attraction of the place.
The tearoom has a rack of good reading—*The New York Review of
Books, The New York Times Book Review,* and so on. Pictures of Maine
authors decorate the walls. They have two motel rooms at the back,
both of which look out on the bay. This is a most unusual combination—guests enjoy browsing amid the thousands of books—and
excellent for someone who is staying one night only. Breakfast
comes with the room."   —*Patricia Lievow*

"The description I read in an early edition of this book, though
interesting enough to whet one's curiosity, gave but a limited idea
of what this unique place is all about. For an unusually low price,
I had expected a small room with a 'no frills' type of atmosphere.
I was pleasantly amazed. This motel maintains the quiet, homey
feeling so sought after by lovers of country inns, while at the same
time providing a large, modern, tastefully decorated room. Carpeting extends not merely from wall to wall, but also into the bathroom. Sliding glass doors reveal a private balcony, which overlooks
the harbor. For those who do not spend all their time investigating
the beautiful town of Camden, color television is also provided.
There is complimentary tea in the charming tearoom, where guests
are surrounded by autographed photos of authors. Perhaps the
nicest touch is having breakfast delivered to one's room."
                                              —*Vincent J. Kish*

Open all year.
2 double rooms, both with private bath.

Rates $40–$50, including continental breakfast and afternoon tea.
Credit cards: MasterCard, Visa.
French spoken.
1 block from bus, 10 miles from Rockland airport.
Innkeepers: Rebecca Gene Conrad and Bill Conrad.

_____*Centre Lovell*

Westways on Kezar Lake
Route 5 (P.O. Box 175)
Centre Lovell, Maine 04016
Telephone (207) 928-2663

"My husband and I discovered the inn on Columbus Day of 1980
when the foliage of the White Mountains was at its peak. We were
stunned by the view and enchanted by the inn. It was built in the
1920s as a retreat for the Diamond Match Company. The master
bedroom, with its carved furniture, is a place we hope to stay once
a year until we're ninety."   —*Anna Kasabian*

"Westways was wonderful. The people couldn't have been nicer.
We have never been anywhere we enjoyed so much—we're dis-
tressed only that anyone else would discover it."
                                      —*Merle and Barry Stern*

Open all year, except November and April when open only for
   special reservations.
21 rooms, 12 with private bath.
Rate $55 per person, MAP double occupancy.
Credit cards: MasterCard, Visa.
Restaurant.
Pick-up service from Portland.
Innkeeper: Nicholas Wylde.

_____*Deer Isle*

Goose Cove Lodge
Post Office
Deer Isle, Maine 04627
Telephone (207) 348-2508

Goose Cove is a group of basic cabins scattered in a wooded area
in view of Penobscot Bay. A main lodge serves meals and acts as a
gathering place for visitors. Goose Cove was owned for many years

by Dr. Ralph Waldron, a naturalist and author, and his wife, Florence.

"The lodge preserves an informal atmosphere, offers quite good food, and continues to draw a group of attractive guests with a common bond—a love of nature. Aside from their varied interesting occupations, many guests are competent amateur botanists, ornithologists, and photographers, as well as artists and musicians. Nature walks, slide shows, and concerts are offered, and there are opportunities to make very satisfying friendships."

—Jean Whitehill

"I think it is crucial that your readers have a more complete picture of the place before electing to stay there. The cabins are a good hike from the main lodge. There are stall showers but no bathtubs. Breakfast is served only from 7 to 8 A.M. and dinner is promptly at 6 P.M. The innkeeper scolds guests who don't show up for dinner and fail to notify her in advance, yet the site of the lodge, though rustic and beautiful, is so remote and the surrounding roads such slow going, that it is difficult to go anywhere to sightsee for the day and still be back in time for dinner." *—Linda Fitzpatrick*

Open May 1 through October 15.
11 cottages, 10 suites, all with private bath.
Rates $300–$400 per person per week, including breakfasts and dinners. Daily rates between May 1 and June 18, September 10 and Columbus Day: $50–$60, including breakfast.
No credit cards.
French, German, and Spanish spoken.
Air service to Bangor, where there are rental cars and taxis.
Innkeepers: George and Eleanor Pavloff.

Pilgrim's Inn
Deer Isle, Maine 04627
Telephone (207) 348-6615

"Squatting on a gentle rise of land, Pilgrim's Inn faces the unpredictable Northwest Harbor, which can fling its surf high over the rocks or feign contentment with the soft murmur of its relentless tides. A quiet millpond provides another kind of watery view from the back of the late Georgian house, and is a place where children might take turns in a rowboat. The deep-red clapboard inn, once the home of Squire Ignatius Haskell, a sawmill owner and politician who helped frame Maine's constitution, has accommodated summer lodgers since the early twentieth century. Architecturally there is nothing similar to the imposing structure anywhere on Deer Isle, and the interior has undergone extensive renovations.

"Although guests are treated royally, life is essentially simple. Bedrooms are all equipped with woodburning stoves but all do not have private baths. Interesting local art is displayed everywhere. Cocktails are served in the common room, which is the heart of the inn. Dominated by massive colonial fireplaces replete with Dutch ovens, it is furnished with sinfully comfortable furniture and lined with bookshelves. Enhanced by candlelight, small tables, and waitresses in colonial costumes (music on weekends), dinner is elegant and artistic."   —*Marion Laffey Fox*

Open May to October.
12 rooms, 3 with private bath.
Rates $55–$60 per person, including breakfast and dinner. Weekly rates $330–$360 per person. Four-night minimum stay required in August.
No credit cards.
Restaurant.
Guests met by arrangement at Bangor or Bar Harbor airport.
Owners: Jean and Dud Hendrick.

Kennebunkport

The Captain Jefferds Inn
Pearl Street (P.O. Box 691)
Kennebunkport, Maine 04046
Telephone (207) 967-2311

"This charming inn, across the street from the Captain Lord Mansion, has been redecorated in antiques and charm. Our huge, comfortable room had a Victorian wicker daybed with matching table and side chairs—plus fine, unusual lamps. The innkeepers served a fine breakfast with Maine blueberries in the pancakes. Collections of old baskets, shellwork, and pottery delight the eye."
                                                    —*Mary Lou Johns*

Open all year.
13 rooms, 7 with private bath.
Rates $55–$68, including complete country breakfast.
No credit cards.
Innkeepers: Warren Fitzsimmons and Don Kelly.

Captain Lord Mansion
P.O. Box 527
Kennebunkport, Maine 04046
Telephone (207) 967-3141

"Nestled about three blocks from the main square of Kennebunk-port, overlooking a large expanse of lawn and marina, is the Captain Lord Mansion. The mansion is a beautiful old house built during the War of 1812 that remained in the Lord family until 1874. The charm of the house has been maintained throughout by using many of the original pieces of furniture and other furnishings of the period. The owners, Beverly Davis and Rick Litchfield, are a delight-ful couple who are extremely helpful and offer a tour of the mansion to all arriving guests. The tour revealed large, comfortable rooms, many of which have working woodburning fireplaces.

"Breakfast is included with lodgings. During the summer, the breakfast includes, among other things, fresh strawberries picked on the grounds, as well as freshly baked zucchini bread and muffins that are out of this world. The inn attracts very interesting guests and breakfast is a great way to meet them and to engage in interest-ing and lively conversations.

"A great place to overindulge in lobster is Nunan's Lobster Shack on the road to Cape Porpoise. Its decor is simple, and the atmo-sphere is very casual. The lobsters were the best that we had in Maine. You can phone a few days in advance for large lobsters."
—*Jon H. Manchester*

Open all year.
16 rooms, all with private bath, 11 with fireplaces.
Rates $54–84, including breakfast.
No credit cards.
Restaurant.
No pets. No children under 12.
Bus depots in Kennebunk and Portland. Airport in Portland; pickup at bus terminal or airport may be arranged in advance.
Innkeepers: Beverly Davis and Rick Litchfield.

If you would like to amend, update, or disagree with any entry, write *now*.

Old Fort Inn
Box 759
Kennebunkport, Maine 04046
Telephone (207) 967-5353

"The Old Fort Inn has all the charm of the 1880s and all the amenities of the 1980s, blending in a most unique way: solar-heated swimming pool, homemade fruit bread, original oak and pine furniture, down quilts, color TV, stenciled wall decor, wall-to-wall carpeting. The experience is not as dichotomous as the elements. This is the cleanest hotel or inn I have ever stayed at, without being sterile in feeling.

"The environment has a direct impact on the behavior and mood of individuals, as reflected in the consistently pleasant interchanges with other guests, the owners, the housekeepers. The innkeepers were as unobtrusive as they were available."   —*Jan Lendman*

Open May through October.
12 rooms, 1 suite, all with private bath.
Rates $50–$60 single, $60–$90 double, including continental
   breakfast.
Credit cards: American Express, MasterCard, Visa.
Innkeepers: Sheila and David Aldrich.

Ogunquit

Sea Chambers Motor Lodge
37 Shore Road
Ogunquit, Maine 03907
Telephone (207) 646-9311

Though the Sea Chambers is a newer place than many that travelers to New England recommend, its location at the edge of the water, its intent to remain true to an innkeeping tradition, and its integration into the town of Ogunquit make it worth mentioning. The lodge is built around a gray cape-style house dating to about 1800. The house, the Sea Bell, had been a tearoom and lodging place for sea captains who docked their schooners and walked up Wharf Lane, past fishing shacks and cottages. The Sea Bell now serves as the breakfast room of the Sea Chambers Motor Lodge.

"The Sea Chambers is in the center of Ogunquit, a beautiful place by the sea, with a three-mile sandy beach and a picturesque rocky shore to the south. The Marginal Way footpath leads from the Sea Chambers to Perkins Cove. There is a summer playhouse and a large artists' colony in Ogunquit.

"The rooms are all modern, with excellent housekeeping. There is a very fine view of the ocean and beach. The lodge has a heated pool and several sundecks facing the Atlantic Ocean. Attached is the lovely old Sea Bell, with the charm and hospitality of old New England."   *—Eric H. Boyer*

Open March through October.
43 rooms, all with private bath.
Rates $26–$80 according to season, including breakfast.
No credit cards.
French spoken.
Ogunquit bus station 2 blocks away. Lodge will pick up and return guests.
Innkeeper: John H. Bullard.

Poland Spring

Poland Spring Inn
Route 26
Poland Spring, Maine 04274
Telephone (207) 998-4351

The waters of Maine's Poland Spring area have been praised—and transported—far and wide for more than a century, and the pleasant land from which they come has been a resting-place for travelers for almost a century longer than that. First a stagecoach stop before Maine became a state (it was part of Massachusetts), Poland Spring grew by the turn of the twentieth century into a community of hotels, a glittering resort—indeed something of a spa—frequented by the rich and famous. Its recent history has been less happy. By the time the present owner of the complex took over in 1972, many of the old buildings were in shambles and only a newer (albeit well-appointed) inn built in 1963 and a nearby motor hotel remained usable. So the owner, Mel Robbins, started with these. A grand Victorian building, the Presidential Inn, was added to the collection in 1980. Mr. Robbins says he runs the place in the tradition of a country inn. There is no menu. You eat "what's for supper."

"We spent a lovely vacation at the inn at Poland Spring. It's a unique type of family hotel owned by a very friendly couple. The host, Mel Robbins, is a remarkable man, intelligent, witty, and an extremely warm individual who makes everyone feel very special! The inn is situated on lovely grounds with beautiful scenery.

"There are a lot of activities if you want to get involved, or you can just relax and watch. The villages nearby are fascinating with their boutiques and flea markets."   —*Edith and Alex Scheffer*

Open May through October, weekends only in spring and fall.
143 rooms, all with private bath. No single rooms.
Rates: Weekends: $25–$79 per person for 2–3 nights, MAP, double occupancy. Summer midweek: $59–$99 per person, MAP, double occupancy. Rates vary according to season and special activities as well as length of stay.
No credit cards.
Restaurant.
Innkeepers: Mel and Cyndi Robbins.

_____ *Rangeley*

Davis Lodge
Route 4 (Box 289)
Rangeley, Maine 04970
Telephone (207) 864-5569

"I have spent most relaxing and pleasant hours at various times of the year at the Lodge, and find that every season casts its own charm. The fall and winter bring robust, friendly fires in the two huge stone fireplaces. The spring and summer sunshine find the Lodge wrapped in green, with the full glory of the lake and the mountains capturing your thoughts. No matter what the time of year, the food is delicious and plentiful. The rooms are simple and spacious, and give one the feeling of the old days, when times were good and uncluttered."   —*Jan Pelletier*

Open May 30 through October 15, December 26 through April 1.
5 rooms, all with adjacent bath.
Rate $23 per person, including breakfast.
Credit cards: MasterCard, Visa.
4 dining rooms; bar.
Innkeepers: Fred Slayter and Joyce Martin.

All inkeepers appreciate reservations in advance; some require them.

_____*Southwest Harbor*

The Claremont
Southwest Harbor, Maine 04679
Telephone (207) 244-5036

"Located not far from the harbor and high above the southern end of Somes Sound—the only fjord on the East Coast—the Claremont commands magnificent views of the sound and of the mountains of Mount Desert Island. These are the mountains seamen watch for in navigating these waters. The hotel, now nearly a century old, has been entered on the National Register of Historic Places; but it is no relic, no outworn shell. The original building has been carefully and expertly restored, and a beautiful dining room with huge picture windows on three sides added at the back of the building. Also a new kitchen and laundry.

"The food is delectable; the beds the best we have ever encountered away from home. The public rooms are pleasant and comfortable. There is a well-stocked library. The wide and spacious lawns surrounding the hotel are carefully tended. Tetherball, croquet, and tennis are played. One notices a hammock suspended between two shade trees—apple trees, I think. It is obviously a good place for children and young people, and there are many of these. Down the hill, near the water and the hotel's dock, is the boathouse, where older guests may gather in late afternoon for refreshment and talk of the day's activities—mountain climbing, golf, sailing, exploring. Some of us consider it the most beautiful and interesting little island in the U.S.A. (See Samuel Eliot Morison's book *The Story of Mt. Desert Island;* Boston: Little, Brown and Company)."

—*Richard McClanahan*

Open mid-May to mid-October.
32 rooms, 30 with private bath; 9 cottages.
Rates $52–$99, including breakfast and dinner. EP also available.
Restaurant and service bar.
No credit cards.
French and Spanish spoken.
Delta Airlines to Bangor, 50 miles away; Bar Harbor Airlines to Hancock County airport, 10 miles away. Guests can be met. By road, take I-95 from Boston to Augusta, Route 3 from Augusta to Belfast, Route 1 north to Ellsworth, Route 3 again to Mt. Desert Island, and Route 102 to Southwest Harbor.
Owner: Gertrude McCue; manager: John Madeira, Jr.

Turn to the back of this book for pages inviting *your* comments.

_____ _____ *Tenants Harbor*

The East Wind Inn
P. O. Box 149
Tenants Harbor, Maine 04860
Telephone (207) 372-6366

The inn was built in 1870 in a small fishing village that was once an important shipbuilding center. Originally the building was part of a shipyard complex; sails were made in it. After many years of standing vacant, it was restored in 1975 by Tim Watts.

"The small, comfortable lobby invites you to stay awhile, share the excellent dining room fare and watch the fishing boats and yachts in the harbor across the broad expanse of lawn. The food is delicious and the fresh lobsters and other seafood make the short journey down the St. George peninsula well worth anyone's time. Conversely, if at times a tiny New England hamlet seems to be lacking in urban affairs, then a few minutes' drive takes you to numerous art galleries and studios, craft shops or to the museum (with all the Wyeths represented), or to crowded Camden Harbor and its windjammer fleet. Port Clyde and Monhegan Island are only a short distance away."   —*Henry and Bettie Miller*

Open all year.
16 rooms, 2 with private bath.
Rates $32 single, $38 double; $46 room with bath; slightly lower
    November through April.
Credit cards: MasterCard, Visa.
Greyhound bus to Thomaston and Rockland, where there are taxis.
    Bar Harbor Airlines from Boston to Owls Head airport. Taxis at
    Owls Head.
Innkeepers: Tim Watts and Ginnie Wheeler.

_____ *Wiscasset*

Squire Tarbox
Route 144 (RFD 2, Box 2160)
Wiscasset, Maine 04578
Telephone (207) 882-7693

"Westport Island is hardly an island at all. It's a turn off the road toward the Atlantic, between the Bath drawbridge that overlooks the old town's shipyards and the town of Wiscasset, whose sea captains' and merchants' houses of the eighteenth century are worth a detour in themselves. The inn is some three miles from U.S. Route 1, an elegant reminder of Maine's past, which grew rich on whaling and then felt the wealth slip away toward the more economically convenient centers of southern New England. The inn is a square, white clapboard Federal house, furnished with antiques from the families of the owners. Its ample bedrooms each have a fireplace, and the good beds are covered with handsome quilts. As it should be, though, the two dining rooms and the kitchen are the center of the house. Anne McInvale is a superb cook with a special gift for the vegetable dishes that accompany and enhance the choice of dinner between a meat and fish course: tomato pudding, minted carrots, ratatouille or summer squash, depending on the season and harvest from the inn's own and other gardens. Elsie White makes an excellent dry martini, and both the red and white house wines, en carafe, are good. The bread and breakfast muffins are fresh-baked at the inn. Elsie and Ann are both from Mississippi and, in choosing Maine for their venture into the inn business, are an exception to the trend of Americans migrating toward the Sunbelt."

—Patricia H. Painton

"The Squire Tarbox Inn is about two fabulous women who take extraordinary care of travelers. It's about their incredible home cooking (don't diet here), their graciousness, warmth, and respect for your privacy, the ambience of the public rooms and bedrooms —either the simplicity of the rooms in the old barn or the charm and elegance of the main house.

"The surroundings are beautiful. One can sit on the terrace and sip morning coffee or linger over afternoon drinks, surrounded by honeysuckle and wild flowers and smells of the nearby ocean, which mix and mingle with the incredible smells wafting from the kitchen. It's a place to bring your bruised and weary body and soul to."

—Mr. and Mrs. Alan H. Bomser; also recommended by Camilla Tanner

Open Memorial Day to mid-October.
8 rooms, 2 with private bath.
Rates $40 single, $45 double, including continental breakfast.
No credit cards.
Dining room for guests only.
Greyhound bus to Wiscasset.
Innkeepers: Anne McInvale and Elsie White.

Where are the good little hotels in Boston? Philadelphia? Omaha? Dallas? If you have found one, don't keep it a secret. Write *now*.

_____ *Yarmouth*

Homewood Inn
Drinkwater Point (P.O. Box 196)
Yarmouth, Maine 04096
Telephone (207) 846-3351

Homewood Inn is a cluster of buildings on the shorefront of
Maine's Casco Bay. Centerpiece of the cottages and houses is the
1742 Maine House, one of the Yarmouth area's historic buildings.

"My husband and I vacationed at the Homewood for several years.
The food is delicious. The accommodations are very comfortable.
We usually take a room in the guesthouse, overlooking the bay. The
room is decorated with rustic furniture and charming prints and has
a working fireplace. Since we usually take our vacation in October,
we use the fireplace at least once a day.

"The lodge itself is very homey (complete with woodburning
stove), and we like to take a half hour every morning or evening to
chat with whoever is running the desk—or just sit and read the
books or magazines.

"The Homewood is located in a very untouristy area—and that's
what we especially like about it. The place is relaxed. The more
active types can play tennis, shuffleboard, or swim—but we prefer
to walk on the beach with our dog (yes, they do allow animals), or
just through one of the Homewood's pastures or around the beautiful houses next to the inn."   —*Phyllis Schneider*

Open early June to mid-October.
44 rooms, including suites and cottages, all with private bath.
    Housekeeping facilities available.
Rates $36–$65 rooms, $90–$184 suites and cottages, higher for
    1984.
Credit cards: American Express, MasterCard, Visa.
Restaurant.
Greyhound local bus via Portland. Nearest airport: Portland. Inn
    recommends car rental for sightseeing in area.
Innkeepers: Fred and Colleen Webster, Doris and Ted Gillette.

_____ *York*

Dockside Guest Quarters
Harris Island Road (P.O. Box 205)
York, Maine 03909
Telephone (207) 363-2868

"I loved the scenery and the setup at Dockside. My room was great, and its balcony overlooked the harbor. I bought my own dinner at an adjoining seafood restaurant. The inn served me, at no-charge, a simple breakfast. I am impressed by innkeepers who don't charge the top price—that's part of hospitality, too."   —*Camilla Tanner*

"We approached Dockside expecting to see a seaside motel. Imagine our surprise to arrive at a beautiful wooded setting and an old sea captain's home constructed in the 1700s. Dockside, a unique combination of the picturesque, historic, modern, and comfortable, offers a constantly changing panorama of natural beauty and activity. There are views not only of the harbor, but also of the Atlantic Ocean. The traffic of fishermen and yachtsmen in their vessels is always interesting. Some of the sunrises we have watched from our favorite room—14—were so spectacular that we will never forget them.   —*Kenneth F. Kniskern*

"Cleanliness abounds at this very delightful and peaceful old house. A very nice continental breakfast is served to guests."
    —*Dorothy M. Konley*

"York and the surrounding area are most interesting. Indians, who called the area Agamenticas, were hard-hit by a plague and deserted the neighborhood by 1623. In 1630 settlers from Bristol, England, moved in and, in 1683, when permission was granted for them to trade with their home city, they named the area Bristol. In 1640 Sir Fernando Georges made Bristol a chartered city and gave it the name Georgeana, though he never did come to the New World. In 1652 the colony of Massachusetts took control of the province of Maine, and Georgeana was reduced to town status and renamed York.   *Joyce and Ken Tuddenham;*
    also recommended by Linda Fitzpatrick

"The Dockside was a splendid retreat. We stayed in one of the lovely cottages—perfectly situated for watching the sailboats or sitting on the balcony with a good book. We will definitely return, and have already passed on our recommendation to friends."
    —*Valerie Thorner*

Open Memorial Day to Columbus Day.
20 rooms, 18 with private bath. Efficiency suites available.
Rates $21–$71.50. Special weekly rates and rates for families.
Credit cards: MasterCard, Visa.
Restaurant.
Greyhound bus to York.
Innkeepers: The Lusty family.

Wheatleigh,
Lenox

_____ *Massachusetts*

Boston

Copley Plaza
138 St. James Avenue
Boston, Massachusetts 02116
Telephone (617) 267-5300

"Great hotels may have a second flowering. Since 1912 the Copley Plaza has shared Copley Square with some of America's architectural gems. From the start it has had great public rooms, spacious private rooms, and a superb location. For many years Sheraton's flagship, it was abandoned in that chain's relentless pursuit of formula commercialism. Enter Hotels of Distinction and a multiyear renovation program. The rooms are again flawless. The restaurant is superb, except the courtyard breakfast. Copley's is the loveliest grown-up bar in Boston. And desk service has copied all the correctness of the Ritz yet added its own touch—friendliness. Though not little, you couldn't ask for a more wonderful hotel."

—George Herzog

Open all year.
417 rooms, including 25 suites, all with private bath.
Rates $95 single, $110 double for standard rooms; $105 single,

34

$120 double for superior rooms; $115 single, $130 double for deluxe rooms; $175–$500 for suites. Two-night weekend package at $155 includes continental breakfast.
Credit cards: American Express, Carte Blanche, Diners Club, Visa.
Managing Director: A. Tremain.

The Ritz-Carlton
15 Arlington Street
Boston, Massachusetts 02117
Telephone (617) 536-5700

"Though not small, the Ritz-Carlton offers such attentive service that one feels in the care of a small hotel. The white-gloved elevator operators are solicitous in inquiring how you are. The best rooms have fireplaces and overlook the Public Garden with its swan boats. Decor is restrained, elegant but comfortable. The dining room is undoubtedly Boston's finest restaurant, offering a superbly executed, ambitious menu, knowledgeable service, and piano or chamber music under the best of crystal chandeliers. In sum, this is one of the world's great hotels."   —*George Herzog*

"A delightful establishment—charming atmosphere, excellent food, friendly and helpful service. It is very handy for the theaters and shops."   —*H. C. Beddington*

Open all year.
257 rooms and suites, all with private bath.
Rates $105–$145 single; $120–$145 double.
Credit cards: American Express, MasterCard, Visa.
French and Italian spoken.
Manager: James Bennett.

Brewster

Bramble Inn
2019 Main Street (Route 6A)
Brewster, Cape Cod, Massachusetts 02631
Telephone (617) 896-7644

"On historic Route 6A in Brewster, the Bramble Inn offers good food and comfortable lodging as well as a gallery of local artwork. Restoration of this Civil War-period home revealed the wide and mellow pine floorboards and the narrow staircases. Many antique furniture pieces grace the foyer and dining room areas. Candles burning on small tables in the gallery lend warmth to the intimate dining atmosphere and invite patrons to linger over both paintings and such tempting dishes as Cape Cod chowders, quiches, crêpes, and fruit-and-cheese trays.

"The rooms on the upper floor are spacious and sunny, and accented with antiques. It is delightful to discover a pot of coffee and a tray of doughnuts in the hallway each morning. The inn's location allows easy access to any spot of interest on the Cape. Brewster itself has a fascinating old general store, a fine needlework shop, and uncrowded beaches, all within walking distance of the inn. Nearby are the Cape Cod Museum of Natural History, the New England Fire and History Museum, and the Stony Brook gristmill."

—Jean Driver

"We found the Bramble Inn to be exactly as Jean Driver described it. The rooms are quaint and comfortable, enhanced by the warm hospitality shown us by the innkeepers. Absolutely delicious was the baked stuffed fillet of sole, and all the other food we enjoyed at the inn. Endorsed with enthusiasm."

—Victoria H. Stevens

Open May to October.
8 rooms, 2 with private bath.
Rates $46–$62, including continental breakfast.
Credit cards: MasterCard, Visa.
Restaurant.
French and Russian spoken.
Bus stops 5 buildings away. By car, take Exit 10 from Route 6. Follow Route 124 to the intersection of Route 6A (4 miles). Turn right, 1/10 mile to inn. Airport ½ hour away.
Innkeepers: Elaine Brennan and Karen Etsell.

_____ *Concord*

The Colonial Inn
48 Monument Square
Concord, Massachusetts 01742
Telephone (617) 369-9200

For students of American literature and history, Concord has always held a special rank among towns. Here, today's pilgrim finds the Old North Bridge, Walden Pond, and the cemetery where Emerson, Thoreau, Hawthorne, and the Alcotts are buried. Together the towns of Lexington and Concord—where that "shot heard 'round the world" was fired—like to think of themselves as the starting point of the Revolutionary War.

"For over thirty years my wife and I and our three children have visited the Colonial Inn. The inn is at the end of Concord Green, presenting an authentic colonial front to the beautiful expanse of grass and trees. Apart from being ideally situated for visits to Concord and its environs, it is a base for the short trip by car or frequent rail service into Boston. The north and south shores are also readily accessible. Several interesting dining rooms and bars at the inn have always added to our pleasures."   —*Stuart C. Henry*

"My wife and I had been quite pleased with our stays at the Colonial Inn until this year. We found faucets that would not completely shut and produced a continuous banging noise, an inoperative sink stopper and exhaust fan in the bathroom, a window shade that wouldn't stay lowered, filthy drapes, and dirty dresser drawers. The quality of the Colonial Inn has deteriorated substantially."

—*John Vourtsis*

"We loved the main dining room and had delicious food. Our room, however, was small and ordinary. We found it was part of the newer addition. I peeked into two rooms in the original part of the inn and they were darling—big, full of antiques, a fireplace. I would definitely specify these next time.   —*Melanie Omohundro*

"Having never been to Concord before, my husband and I had high hopes. The Colonial Inn exceeded even our most vivid expectations. Spending time in Concord with all its remarkable history and having the inn to call 'home' was like turning the clock back 200 years. As the snow silently fell, the warmth of both the inn's fireplaces and its truly cordial staff made our first vacation together without children picture-perfect. I highly recommend the dining room, Thoreau's, and compliment the chef on his old-fashioned New England chicken pot pie."   —*Patricia Bailey*

Open all year.
60 rooms, 54 with private bath.
Rates $50–$70.
Credit cards: American Express, Carte Blanche, Diners Club, MasterCard, Visa.
Restaurant and bar.
German spoken.
Innkeeper: Paul M. Barry.

Hawthorne Inn
462 Lexington Road
Concord, Massachusetts 01742
Telephone (617) 369-5610

"The inn, in Concord's historic district, is across the street from
The Wayside, Nathaniel Hawthorne's home on the battle road between Lexington and Concord. The inn is furnished with antiques,
and each bed has a homemade quilt on it. Our room had a bay
window that looked out on well-kept grounds with many trees. The
innkeeper and owner, a delightful young artist named Gregory
Burch, was a marvelous host. He joined us at breakfast, which consisted of fruit and juice, homemade baked goods, coffee and tea. All
this was included in the price of a room, which was very reasonable."
                                        —*Mrs. Meredith Szostek*

Open February through December.
5 rooms, no private baths.
Rates $50 single, $70 double, including breakfast.
No credit cards.
Commuter train service connects Concord to Boston.
Innkeepers: Gregory Burch and Marilyn Mudry.

East Orleans

Nauset House Inn
141 Beach Road (Box 774)
Beach Road
East Orleans, Cape Cod, Massachusetts 02643
Telephone (617) 255-2195

"To spend a few fleeting days at the Nauset House out in East
Orleans on Cape Cod is a delectable experience not soon to be
forgotten. Where else can one enjoy breakfast coffee in the pleasant
ambience of a greenhouse filled with bougainvillea, ferns, and hundreds of lush floral creations? There is Nauset Beach, perhaps the
most beautiful sandy stretch along our Eastern Seaboard, which is
almost within a stone's throw of the inn. Add to this the lovely decor
of Nauset House itself, so exceedingly well run. My wife and I
cherish the thought of it even while off on a trip to Hawaii."
                                        —*Folke B. Lidbeck*

Open April 1 to January 1.
14 rooms, 7 with private bath.
Rates $30–$35 single, $42–$60 double.
Credit cards: MasterCard, Visa.
Innkeepers: Albert and Diane Johnson.

Ship's Knees Inn
Beach Road (Box 756)
East Orleans, Cape Cod, Massachusetts 02643
Telephone (617) 255-1312

"For the uninitiated to Cape Cod's historic landmarks, its winding two-lane roads like Route 6A (bypass the mid-Cape Highway 6, as you'll never see the real Cape this way), the beautiful hydrangeas everywhere and the roses of Falmouth, a quiet, small distinctive place to spend the night—and preferably several days—is East Orleans' Ship's Knees Inn, an old sea captain's house on Beach Road about a mile from Route 28. It is only a matter of several minutes' walk to Nauset Beach, one of the loveliest on the East Coast.

"Distances are so short on the Cape. Fifteen minutes away is the Salt Pond Visitor Center of Cape Cod National Seashore, with Nauset Marsh trail. A bit beyond that is the site of the French cable station built in 1890 to house the trans-Atlantic cable from Brest. Provincetown is a mere half-hour drive beyond that. To the west of East Orleans are the captivating towns of Chatham, Harwich Port, Falmouth, and Woods Hole, the home of the Oceanographic Institute and Marine Biological Laboratories."   —*Marion Jacques*

"The tree-filled town of East Orleans is a mixture of all that is New England, from the rambling dwellings to the picket fences, white clapboard New England churches, and Cape Cod and Victorian homes. East Orleans has maintained its idyllic country look. Ship's Knees is a charming and neat clapboard country inn.

"As for the inn itself, I am completely taken by the colorful individuality of each room. The inn abounds with Early Americana, from braided rugs to antique furniture and wall arrangements. The atmosphere and feeling of Ship's Knees is unquestionably the best of Cape Cod and New England.

"A wide variety of restaurants to suit all tastes and discriminating palates are close by. The area abounds with local artisans and shops that would tempt even the strongest. Their pottery, paintings, glass

(Sydenstricker in particular), weaving, and jewelry are unique. Of course the antique shops are nonpareil." —*Roseanne Donovan*

Open all year.
27 rooms, 12 with private bath.
Rates $35–$65 in-season, $30–$50 off-season, including breakfast.
No credit cards.
Innkeepers: Ken and Louise Pollard.

_____*Edgartown*

Charlotte Inn
South Summer Street
Edgartown, Massachusetts 02539
Telephone (617) 627-4751

"I'd like to recommend the Charlotte Inn, near the center of Edgartown on Martha's Vineyard. Each room there is furnished with the most fabulous antiques. The food is wonderful, and the personal service impeccable. I can't think of a more charming, luxurious inn." —*Phyllis Grann*

Open all year.
22 rooms, 20 with private bath, 3 suites.
Rate $98 average in-season, including breakfast.
Credit cards: MasterCard, Visa.
Martha's Vineyard is reached by ferry or air. Shuttle buses to inn, which is centrally located in Edgartown.
Innkeeper: Gerrett Conover.

The Edgartown Inn
North Water Street (Box 1211)
Edgartown, Massachusetts 02539
Telephone (617) 627-4794

"The inn is situated one block up from Edgartown harbor on Martha's Vineyard. Its location puts it within easy walking distance of the shops and restaurants as well as the ferry that takes five minutes to reach the island of Chappaquidick. Because of its popularity during the summer, we return year after year right after Labor Day to find the pace much less hectic. There are geranium-filled flower boxes and comfortable lounging furniture on the open porch and inside. The shelves are filled with books and magazines and there is a lot of original art. All the breads and cakes served for breakfast are made daily, filling the inn with tantalizing aromas. You can eat in the dining room with its whaling artifacts and antiques, as well as on the enclosed patio."   —*Fran Bergere*

Open April 1 to November 1.
18 rooms, 12 with private bath.
Rates $24–$85 depending on location and season.
No credit cards.
French spoken.
Public bus from ferry to Edgartown. Taxis from airport and ferry.
Innkeeper: Catherine Scopecchi.

_____*Falmouth*

Elm Arch Inn
Elm Arch Way
Falmouth, Cape Cod, Massachussetts 02540
Telephone (617) 548-0133

"The Elm Arch Inn is in the center of historic Falmouth, in a quiet area convenient to everything, including several beautiful beaches and the excellent Cape Cod restaurants in the vicinity. Woods Hole is only a few miles away, with daily steamers to Martha's Vineyard and Nantucket Island. The Elm Arch Inn, built in 1812 for Silas Jones, was bombarded by the British frigate *Nimrod* in 1814; the wall in the former dining room still carries the scar of the cannonball. The inn and the Richardson House have a variety of fine accommodations, all in charming Early American decor. A swimming pool surrounded by beautiful old trees and spacious lawns is right next to the inn. There is a homelike atmosphere in this truly old Cape Cod inn, a fine place to stay and enjoy the tranquillity of the Early American tradition."   —*Eric H. Boyer*

"Harry Richardson and his wife, Flossie, carry on a family tradition that happily began over fifty years ago. Their hospitality, warmth, and friendliness create an atmosphere that is congenial, relaxing, and most conducive to an enjoyable change of pace, any season of the year. No two rooms in the inn are exactly alike; each one has been thoughtfully and creatively decorated in colonial fashion. The Richardsons have a boundless knowledge of Cape Cod and an unending list of fascinating and interesting things to do and see.

Although meals are not served, several fine restaurants are located within a very short walking distance."

—*Mr. and Mrs. James F. Donovan;*
also recommended by Harold and Ruth Maxton

Open all year.
24 rooms, 12 with private bath.
Rates $25 single, $30–$42 double, including coffee.
No credit cards.
Bonanza Bus Lines links Falmouth to major cities. Nearest airport: Hyannis.
Innkeepers: Harry C. and Florence Richardson.

Mostly Hall
27 Main Street
Falmouth, Cape Cod, Massachusetts 02540
Telephone (617) 548-3786

"At Mostly Hall both the grounds and the house are very well taken care of. This was a first experience with an American bed-and-breakfast and my expectations were more than satisfied. The elegance of Mostly Hall made me wary of the price but when I was told the rate, I thought it was per person and was more than willing to pay it. We chose the least expensive room because it was our favorite—the widow's walk on the third floor, a small room surrounded by ten windows that look over the lovely grounds. Ginny Austin's breakfast was an experience in itself—elegant just like the inn, with delicious coffee, fresh grapefruit, wonderfully seasoned scrambled egg rolled in a light crêpe, and homemade zucchini bread. I think what impressed me most about Mostly Hall, however, was the warmth of the owners, Ginny and Jim Austin, who went out of their way to make us feel welcome and at ease. We borrowed their bicycles and took the bike path to Woods Hole. I loved not having to use my car until it was time to go home." —*Nancy Kelly*

"I think the best description of Mostly Hall is 'comfortable elegance.' This is a bed-and-breakfast that will allow you to turn your day upside down, for with Ginny's fabulous gourmet breakfasts, you can easily do with simple fare the rest of the day. Jim and Ginny are the kind of friendly innkeepers who make guests feel welcome and comfortable, offering tips on things to do and see and places to eat on the Cape and beyond." —*JLS*

Open all year except a few weeks in "the worst of the winter."
7 rooms, 5 with private bath.
Rates $30–$55 depending on room and season, including full
   breakfast.
No credit cards.
Innkeepers: Jim and Ginny Austin.

_____*Harwich Port*

Dunscroft Inn
24 Pilgrim Road
Harwich Port, Cape Cod, Massachusetts 02646
Telephone: (617) 432-0810

"Dunscroft is a large house well worth a visit. Bill and Maureen
Houle are warm and friendly people who make you feel at home.
They have a lovely enclosed porch to read or relax or sun yourself
on. Only 300 feet away is a private beach. Within walking distance
is the little town with restaurants, stores, and a small movie theater.
                                                    —*Dorothy M. Konley*

Open March 1 through New Year's.
6 rooms, 2 efficiencies, 1 cottage, all with private bath.
Rates $50–$57, including continental breakfast. Deduct $10 off-
   season.
No credit cards.
Innkeepers: William and Maureen Houle.

The Melrose Inn
601 Main Street
Harwich Port, Cape Cod, Massachusetts 02646
Telephone (617) 432-0171

"The Melrose Inn welcomes visitors to Cape Cod from lilac time to
the cranberry season. Redwood chairs and benches on flagstones
beneath lovely shade trees front the white, yellow, and green
wooden building. Flowering shrubs encircle the inn; a wide green
lawn is on one side. In a garden setting, at the end of a flagstone
path, is a heated swimming pool. A short walk along a pine-edged
road leads to the inn's lovely beach house, on a sea-rose–bordered
sandy Nantucket Sound beach. In both the inn and the beach house,

crackling log fires glow in fieldstone fireplaces on spring and autumn evenings.

"The Cape cranberry from the nearby bogs is featured in many forms on the menu. Charming floral arrangements in unusual vases grace each table, and ruffled white Cape Cod curtains dress the dining room windows. Magnificent tall ships, cruising on a smooth sea at sunset or plunging into whitecapped waves, adorn the walls of the dining room and the guest rooms. These paintings are T. Bailey's oil translations of Masefield's 'Sea Fever.'

"Owned and managed since 1921 by the Smith family, the Melrose Inn radiates warmth, charm, and hospitality. Choice objects from the family's European, Asian, and African travels are of special interest. Personal attention and interest are traditional."

—*Katherine Tucker*

"After Labor Day, the bar is closed except on Friday and Saturday nights. Our room had not been dusted for some time, perhaps because we went in off-season, but we also found sheets torn and towels worn out years ago. Furnishings included a card table for the table in our room. Families should be warned that children and teenagers are not allowed in the pool between 10:30 A.M. and 4 P.M. The dining room was well maintained and the food and service above average."　　　　　　　　　　　—*Charles H. Henrie*

Open mid-June to mid-October.
75 rooms, 65 with private bath.
Rates $20–$46.
Credit cards: MasterCard, Visa.
Restaurant and bar.
Plymouth and Brockton bus to Harwich Port. Driver will stop at inn on request.
Innkeepers: Gladys E. Smith, Betty Smith Blum, Jane Smith Lynch.

Holyoke

Yankee Pedlar Inn
1866 Northampton Street
Holyoke, Massachusetts 01040
Telephone (413) 532-9494

"The Yankee Pedlar Inn is a combination of Victorian charm and modern commercial efficiency. The Main House, which was the original inn, now houses the dining rooms, the oyster bar and Gilded Cage lounge, as well as the office, kitchen, and upstairs guests rooms. Other guest rooms are located in adjacent houses:

the 1850 House, the Carriage House, the Mansion House, the Lodge. The Opera House is a newer addition to the Main House, built to blend with the architecture of the other buildings. With its stained-glass windows and crystal chandelier, it is used for parties, banquets, and Sunday brunch.

"Unfortunately, on a recent inspection, I found that the commercial had begun to outweigh the personal touches. Guests were left standing while the help went about their business. The food at the Sunday brunch was definitely not what I remembered. It was arranged attractively and there were some good dishes, but overall it was uninspired. The breads were dry, the eggs overcooked, the meats somewhat tasteless. The more ambitious the dish, the less appetizing.

"But the inn is still worth a visit if you are looking for something conveniently located near the interchange of the Massachusetts Turnpike and Interstate 91. It is in the heart of the Pioneer Valley near Amherst, Smith, Mount Holyoke, and Hampshire colleges and the University of Massachusetts as well as historic Deerfield."

—JLS

"A slightly commercial feel, but still well done. I had a wonderful second-story porch, lots of windows, canopied bed, and wing chairs. There was a large bath with clawfoot tub and an even larger shower."   *—Karen Bresenhan*

"It was here that I slept in a canopy bed for the first time. The room was furnished in antiques and golden oak. Traveling as a 'single' and unknown, I was concerned that I would be given the least desirable room in the place, but this was definitely not the case. There was even a complimentary bottle of wine waiting for me."

—Stephanie Jatlow

Open all year, except Christmas Day.
47 rooms, all with private bath.
Rates $36–$59.
Credit cards: American Express, Carte Blanche, Diners Club, MasterCard, Visa.
Restaurant and bar.
French, Spanish, and Polish spoken.
Located at the corner of Routes 202 and 5, which is off Exit 4 of I-90, and Exit 16 of I-91. Two blocks from Holyoke bus terminal, 30 minutes from Bradley International Airport.
Innkeepers: Frank and Claire Banks.

Turn to the back of this book for pages inviting *your* comments.

_____*Lee*

The Morgan House
33 Main Street
Lee, Massachusetts 01238
Telephone (413) 243-0181

"Our first visit was on a Memorial Day weekend, and we were Beth and Bill Orford's first reservation. We went back the next month and it was even better. We wanted to book for the July 4th weekend, but they were already full! From the moment we first arrived, we were treated with pure, sincere, natural friendliness—a friendliness I must say permeated through the other members of the staff. At first I didn't cherish the idea of sharing bathrooms, but when I saw how clean they were, my thoughts immediately changed. Even though there are six rooms on each floor, with two shared baths, we never waited.

"The Morgan House is right on Main Street, but don't let that 'Main Street' dismay you: it is a very quiet road. The village green is diagonally across the street from the inn, as is the Lee Congregational Church, with chimes that mark the hour. We enjoyed having our before-dinner cocktails on the second-floor porch, while watching the townspeople below going about their business. The food was super! There was a do-it-yourself breakfast buffet, with boiling water to make as many eggs as you could eat." —*Arthur and Dolores Raposo*

"This nice little inn is simple but pleasant. The food in the dining room is very good; the menu is varied and includes at least one entrée for vegetarians. On weekends the piano and singer in the bar appear to be the center for local entertainment, and the sound carries upstairs to the rooms, not unlike inns in colonial America, I imagine." —*JLS*

Open all year.
11 rooms with shared baths.
Rates $25–$35 weekdays, $30–$55 weekends. Two-night minimum stay on summer weekends.
Credit cards: American Express, MasterCard, Visa.
Restaurant and bar.
Buses stop at drugstore next to inn.
Innkeepers: Beth and Bill Orford.

Do you know a hotel in your state that we have overlooked? Write *now*.

_____*Lenox*

Lenox is the site of Tanglewood, which means summer music to people throughout the Northeast and beyond. The many inns in Lenox and nearby villages add to the ambience and enjoyment of the sunny days and warm evenings filled with music. The area can be equally enjoyable, however, when covered with new-fallen snow, brought to life by spring flowers or putting on a show of autumn color.

_____

The Village Inn
16 Church Street
Lenox, Massachusetts 01240
Telephone (413) 637-0020

"The setting is strictly New England inside and out. Accommodations, with or without bath, are cozy and comfortable."
—*Vincent C. Daniel; also recommended by Joe L. Wells*

Open all year.
27 rooms, 7 with private bath, 4 with fireplaces.
Rates $45–$95, according to room and season.
Credit cards: MasterCard, Visa.
Restaurant and bar.
French, Spanish, and German spoken.
Bus service by Bonanza or Greyhound from New York, Boston, Providence, Springfield, or Hartford.
Innkeepers: Clifford Rudisill and Ray Wilson.

_____

Wheatleigh
Box 824
Lenox, Massachusetts 02140
Telephone (413) 637-0610

The Wheatleigh is a 33-room Italian-style palazzo built in 1893 by Henry H. Cook, who had accumulated a fortune in railroads and banking. He bequeathed his 22-acre country estate to his daughter, the wife of Count Carlos de Heredia. It remained the home of the Countess de Heredia until her death.

"The Wheatleigh is a most unusual hostelry. This mansion has magnificent rooms with decorations of the period in which it was built. The surrounding Berkshire countryside is one of the most beautiful parts of New England, with forests and rolling hills. Tanglewood is less than a mile away. Stockbridge, Williamstown, and other historic and cultural centers are not far."   —*Earl Morse*

Open all year.
17 rooms in summer, 16 in winter, all with private bath, 9 with fireplaces.
Rates $95–$215, including breakfast.
Credit cards: Diners Club, MasterCard, Visa (restaurant only).
Restaurant and bar.
Bonanza or Greyhound buses to Lenox; Precision Airlines to Pittsfield, 7 miles away.
Innkeepers: Susan and Linfield Simon.

Whistlers Inn
5 Greenwood Street
Lenox, Massachusetts 01240
Telephone (413) 637-0975

"I go back every summer to Whistlers Inn. I enjoy opening those great Dutch doors that admit one to this rambling Victorian mansion.

"Whistlers Inn is about a century old and was the home of a nephew of the painter James Whistler. It is perched on a hill across from an old cemetery and an old church—should you wish to reflect on the past and the future! There are eleven rooms in the mansion —a few small, most large and roomy, furnished in the old style, but with all the modern amenities (except TV). A curved staircase leads to the rooms, which are all one flight up. The inn is only a short walk to several Lenox restaurants.

"Ah, yes, the irresistible library—it's a veritable plum pudding of books, old and new, hundreds of them, on almost every conceivable subject from mysteries to medieval philosophy, and especially rich in literature, history, and political science. Lots of soft chairs and soft lighting, and classical music playing from the music room next door. If you're not careful, the library could seduce you away from the many other cultural attractions of Lenox and the surrounding area."   —*Terrence Dewhurst*

Open May through October.
11 rooms, all with private bath.
Rates $45–$100, including continental breakfast.
Credit cards: MasterCard, Visa.
French, Polish, and Spanish spoken.
Innkeepers: Mr. and Mrs. Richard C. Mears and family.

Nantucket

Nantucket, thirty miles off the coast of Cape Cod, is an old whaling center, now become a quaint vacationland between April and November. The island offers windswept beaches, good boating and windsurfing, marvelous boutiques, and a great choice of inns and guesthouses.

Jared Coffin House
29 Broad Street
Nantucket, Massachusetts 02554
Telephone: (617) 228-2405

"Nantucket Island is blessed with some of the finest warm-water beaches in the northwestern United States, blissful bicycling, and an overabundance of good restaurants. Nantucket is also blessed with a number of hostelries that merit inclusion in an anti-motel guide, and paramount among them is the Jared Coffin House.

"The origins of the Jared Coffin House date back to whaling days, when the original building (1845) was an opulent private home. That building, embellished by a number of small additions, was restored at tremendous expense by the Nantucket Historical Trust, with the goal of recreating the aura of a bygone age. The restoration achieved its goal.

"A number of the hotel's rooms (but by no means all) are furnished with priceless antiques. Most noteworthy are the rooms with elegant, finely carved four-poster canopy beds, adorned with fabrics of crewel embroidery done by island ladies. The public areas are graced with Oriental rugs and works of fine art. Accompanying these surroundings (lest you fear you have intruded into a plutocrat's private museum) is an atmosphere of extraordinary warmth and friendliness, not to mention courtesy, extending from chambermaids to waitresses to the front desk and to the owners themselves.

Phil and Peg Read (Peg is a native Nantucketer) are committed to maintaining 'the Jared' as a very special place.

"Let there be no mistake, the Coffin House has been discovered by those who value fine personal hotels. Reservations are a must, and for the summer season and other peak holiday periods, they must be made well in advance. We found the hotel especially delightful off-season. In an age of crass commercialism, however, it is a truly civilized place at any time of year."

—*Richard Hugh Linden*

"The Jared Coffin House is a great old place, especially from the outside, but no one should expect perfection. It's geared to the general, affluent tourist trade, people who can't tell antiques from reproductions, and they pour through, goggling with uncritical admiration. The parlors are furnished with a hodgepodge of stuff, most good but some very out of keeping; the rugs are getting quite threadbare. The dining room, though pleasant, is nothing special, and that goes for the food as well. All this said, one still gets a kick out of walking up the stone steps, through the great, brass-knockered door, and into the high-ceilinged majesty of a Nantucket whaler's mansion . . . and realizing that this is where Herman Melville stayed when he came to Nantucket during the writing of *Moby Dick.*"

—*Tom Congdon*

Open all year.
58 rooms, all with private bath.
Rates $70–$110.
Credit cards: American Express, Diners Club, MasterCard, Visa.
Spanish and French spoken.
Restaurant and bar.
Innkeepers: Philip Whitney Read, Margaret Gibson Read.

La Languedoc and 10 Hussey Street
24 Broad Street
Nantucket, Massachusetts 02554
Telephone (617) 228-2552; 228-9552

"Two guesthouses at 10 Hussey Street and the inn and restaurant called La Languedoc comprise this complex, located very conveniently in the village of Nantucket. The main inn, across the street from the Jared Coffin House, is a cheerful blue and white inside and out. The guesthouses are just a block away."

—*JLS*

Open April through October.
25 rooms in 3 buildings, 6 with private bath.
Rates: $35–$85, depending on season.
Credit cards: American Express, MasterCard, Visa.
Innkeeper: Rosalie Grennan.

The Ships Inn
13 Fair Street
Nantucket, Massachusetts 02554
Telephone (617) 228-0040

"The most important thing about Nantucket is just being there, though getting there and finding moderately priced accommodations can be trying. This island offers more to the senses than any other sea-trapped sand hillock you could imagine. Fifty square miles of beaches, dunes, moors, ponds, and even forests (you may spend years on the island and never suspect their existence, much less visit one) surround one of the largest collections of lovely old dwellings in the United States. Ships Inn was built in 1912 by Captain Obed Starbuck—as in *Moby Dick*. It stands on the site of the house where Lucretia Mott, the abolitionist and early feminist, was born. Across the street is the Episcopal church and, beyond it, on Orange Street, is the Unitarian church where Ishmael heard Father Mapple preach the night before he signed on for the last voyage of the *Pequod*.

"But the inn's charm is contemporary as well as antiquarian. It is a typical whaler's mansion—center entrance, two windows on either side, two full stories. Its twelve rooms are neatly and adequately if plainly furnished. Some of the rooms do contain furniture of the period. In the basement, which you may enter from the outside through a tiny but lovely planted patio garden, is the Captain's Table, where Nantucket standbys are prepared with more than usual care and imagination. Steaks, lobster in season, duck, swordfish, and lamb are other frequent menu items."

—John Ravage

Open Easter through Thanksgiving.
12 rooms, 10 with private bath.
Rates $20–$30 single, $50–$70 double, including continental breakfast.
Restaurant and bar.
Credit cards: American Express, MasterCard.
Innkeepers: Bar and John Krebs.

_____*Newburyport*

Morrill Place
209 High Street
Newburyport, Massachusetts 01950
Telephone (617) 462-2808

The house itself was built by Captain William Hoyt in 1806, when Newburyport was a major shipping center. The Federal house has a hanging staircase and the cornices, mantels, and balustrades that made its era architectually distinct. Among the house's owners was a junior law partner of Daniel Webster, and Webster was a frequent visitor. One of the inn's rooms is named for him; the other rooms bear other names from Newburyport history. Morrill Place became an inn in 1979.

"The same people who once ran the smaller Benjamin Choate House are now operating Morrill Place, close by. This is an elegant home with a most unusual staircase. Very formal. We can recommend it."   —*Wolfgang and Karin Kutter*

Open all year.
10 rooms with shared baths.
Rates $38–$48 double, including breakfast.
Credit card: American Express.
Innkeeper: Rose Ann Hunter.

_____*Princeton*

The Country Inn at Princeton
Mountain Road (Box 342)
Princeton, Massachusetts 01541
Telephone (617) 464-2030

"Sometime in the eighteenth century, when the fear of the Indian frontier had reasonably subsided, a Bostonian known as the Reverend Dr. Prince resigned from his Congregational congregation and pushed west and north some sixty bird-flight miles to the slopes below Mount Watuschett. There he bought up several hundred acres and founded a village named for himself: Prince-ton, no kin to the one in New Jersey. Princeton, Massachusetts, has been attracting runaway Bostonians and other New Englanders ever since.

"Princeton is a lovely weekend or stopover village for motorists on their way to or from Maine, say, who wish to avoid the vast traffic problems of Boston. From the south or west one ignores the Massachusetts Turnpike after Sturbridge. Route 31 winds interestingly about thirty-two miles to Princeton—and the getaway route to Maine leads east, later. In Princeton the place to sleep, dine, and breakfast is the Country Inn, half a mile or less up the slope from the post office."   *—John Tibby*

"Everywhere you look there is something lovely to see: glance into a charming dining room, spread over several parts of the downstairs, and on outside to a patio by the garden in summer, a living room with fireplace that is for 'living' as well as for admiring, a gift shop that evokes nothing of the standardized hotel. On the stairs you pass a Victorian dollhouse, a show-treasure to come back and back to."   *—David Mallery; also recommended by Dianne M. Foster*

Open all year, Wednesday through Sunday.
6 rooms, all with private bath.
Rate $95, including continental breakfast.
Credit cards: American Express, MasterCard, Visa.
Bus service from Boston to Worcester and Fitchburg. Airport at Worcester.
Innkeepers: Don and Maxine Plumridge.

_____*Provincetown*

Bradford Gardens Inn
178 Bradford Street
Provincetown, Cape Cod, Massachusetts 02657
Telephone (617) 487-1616

"The visitor traveling to the tip of Cape Cod and the Bradford Gardens Inn goes along the Cape's rocky spine at the end of a sandy spit and reaches Provincetown where trees live buried up to their 'chins' in the dunes. The town, with its harbor and surrounding dunes, cliffs on multicolored sands and grassy moors, imparts a feeling of tranquillity. I visit Bradford Gardens Inn frequently and during all seasons. In summer, after an early run or swim, there is a grand breakfast served in the rose garden, where I usually can pick up a backgammon game. In the winter the Cape is quiet and isolated —travelers are few—a different feeling from the summer season. I arrive with my books and find the fire lighted in my room."
                                                                —Joan Lang

"My first reaction to Bradford Gardens was warmth. You feel at home when you meet the innkeeper, Jimmy Logan. He is young, charming, and eager to answer all your questions. When you live at the inn, which was built in 1820, you find it has a quiet atmosphere surrounded by New England grandeur. There are interesting paintings by Provincetown artists. You see antiques from all over the globe because Jimmy is an avid traveler. You can lounge by the fireplace in his living room, where a gourmet breakfast is served. Each of his rooms has a character of its own, like the Jenny Lind bedroom which has a spool bed. What moved me most was the presence of fresh flowers each day from his garden, and sometimes a goody on your pillow at night. You can relax in his rose garden or swing in his blue swing."

—Mary Meehan

Open April 1 to December 1.
8 rooms, 4 suites, all with private bath.
Rates $64–$95, including breakfast.
Credit cards: American Express, MasterCard, Visa.
Off-Cape bus stops at the inn door.
Innkeeper: James Logan.

Land's End Inn

Land's End Inn
22 Commercial Street
Provincetown, Cape Cod, Massachusetts 02657
Telephone (617) 487-0706

"Located at the very tip of the Cape, Land's End Inn is a treasure trove of Victorian furnishings, Art Deco, charm, and ghostly legend. David Schoolman, the owner, and his crew have delightfully outfitted this citadel—built by a mysterious, reclusive Boston merchant in the late 1800s—with Tiffany lamps, Victorian sofas, stained-glass windows, grandfather clocks, and Oriental urns. Try the Tower Room, an octagonal, glass-encompassed room overlooking the harbor, where the ghosts of the merchant and his wife (or daughter or maid, depending on which version of the legend you accept) are still known to wander. Within easy walking distance is the Provincetown art colony, to which we strolled through Londonlike pea-soup fog one late October evening."

—Thomas M. Elliott

Open all year.
15 rooms, 10 with private bath.
Rates $37–$65, including continental breakfast.
No credit cards.
Taxi from bus, plane, or summer ferry from Boston.
Innkeeper: David Schoolman.

_____*Salem*

The Coach House Inn
284 Lafayette Street
Salem, Massachusetts 01970
Telephone (617) 744-4092

"The Coach House looks more like a house than today's more conventional inns and motels. The antique-furnished hallways and winding stairway give an atmosphere of warmth. The room in which I stayed was clean and spacious, with plenty of closet space, and was simply but adequately furnished. It gave out the same homey warmth I experienced at the entrance to the inn. The private bath I had was also very clean and large, with a small refrigerator. The room had a TV, but no phone. I appreciated the literature I found in my room about the town and its many historical sites, in addition to the pamphlets listing all the restaurants in Salem."

—Leila Dabbagh

Open all year.
12 rooms, 10 with private bath.
Rates $40–$101.
Credit cards: American Express, MasterCard, Visa.
Train and bus service from Boston, 30 minutes away.
Innkeeper: Patricia Kessler.

_____*Sandwich*

Daniel Webster Inn
149 Main Street
Sandwich, Cape Cod, Massachusetts 02563
Telephone (617) 888-3622

"After a three-week stay in Plymouth, we started to venture down Cape Cod along the seaboard and soon came across the quaint town of Sandwich, of glass fame. The inn is new—it was rebuilt after a fire —but the theme is very much New England. Our room had deep shag rugs and furnishings that lent an almost family atmosphere. All in all, our weekend stay has since become the highlight of our month in the area.

"The village of Sandwich has a beautiful park area with all trees and shrubs labeled with their Latin and common names. There are excellent restaurants nearby, where fresh seafood is superbly cooked."

—Andree Zeritsch

Open all year.
27 rooms, 4 suites, all with private bath.
Rates Summer: $57.50–$103, MAP, double occupancy; fall and winter: $40.50–$75.50.
Credit cards: American Express, MasterCard, Visa.
20 minutes by taxi from Hyannis, where there is air and bus service.
Innkeeper: Steven Catania.

_____ *Sheffield*

Ivanhoe Country House
Undermountain Road (Route 41)
Sheffield, Massachusetts 01257
Telephone (413) 229-2143

"This wonderful inn has a large library, parlor with piano and huge fireplace, meeting rooms. It is located at the foot of Mount Rice just across from Lake Berkshire. Our room was a complete efficiency. Breakfast, left at the door, was homemade muffins and coffee ready to be plugged in.   —*David Einbinler and Felicia Sileo*

Open all year.
9 rooms, 6 with private bath.
Rates $35–$85, including continental breakfast. Dogs $10.
No credit cards.
Innkeepers: Carole and Dick Maghery.

_____ *South Sudbury*

Longfellow's Wayside Inn
Wayside Inn Road
South Sudbury, Massachusetts 01776
Telephone (617) 443-8846

"If you have a good imagination you can almost feel the eighteenth-century stagecoaches on the Boston Post Road that passes the Wayside Inn. This fine seventeenth-century hostel, once called the Red Horse Inn, played a part in the making of colonial history during Revolutionary days. It was immortalized in Longfellow's poem 'Tales of a Wayside Inn' and still contains a special exhibit to his memory. The dining is great, with a wide variety of items and special 'Revolutionary War' drinks for stouthearted individuals. Dinner is served in one of many period rooms often lit only by candles and presided over by the innkeeper, Frank Koppeis. A stroll around the grounds or the town of Sudbury will reward you with sights and pleasures seldom available outside museums: an operating grist-mill, the schoolhouse from 'Mary Had a Little Lamb,' a typical New England church, and many other sights blended into the colorful landscape all year round." —*Calvin P. Otto*

"In nearly 300 years this impressively tranquil, architecturally pure masterpiece has served generations of people who have cherished it. After a fire in 1955, the inn was completely restored (with a Ford Foundation grant) in line with modern building codes but retaining the indefinable feeling of the original. From the antique furnishings in the guest rooms to the excellent cuisine, to the exceptionally devoted staff, one cannot leave the property without being profoundly affected." —*Eleanor W. Lambert*

Open all year, except Christmas Day.
10 rooms, all with private bath.
Rates $32.50 single, $37.50 double.
Credit cards: American Express, Diners Club, MasterCard, Visa.
No public transport. By car 22 miles from Boston or Worcester on Route 20.
Innkeeper: Frank Koppeis.

_____*Stockbridge*

The Red Lion Inn
Main Street
Stockbridge, Massachusetts 01262
Telephone (413) 298-5545

The inn was built in 1773 as a stagecoach stop on the route linking Albany, Hartford, and Boston, and the year after was the site of a convention of protesters from the Berkshire country towns, angered by the use of articles imported from England. After a disastrous fire in 1896, the inn was rebuilt, and since then there has been extensive restoration.

"Stepping into the Red Lion Inn is like stepping into a Currier and Ives print—a nostalgic return to the past with all of its charm, warmth, and history. The inn was completely restored a few years ago, but many of its antique furnishings and fixtures were retained to keep its authenticity, even to the rope-operated elevator. Old hat collections, comb collections, pictures, pewter, china, mirrors, and clocks fill the nooks and crannies, halls and walls. History buffs will be delighted to realize that they may be sitting at a table where William Thackeray, Charles Dickens, or Abraham Lincoln dined and that they are staying at the same inn where Nathaniel Hawthorne, Henry Wadsworth Longfellow, William Cullen Bryant, and five presidents laid their weary heads.

"Nearby are Stockbridge, Tanglewood, Norman Rockwell's Corner House Museum, Jacob's Pillow, Chesterwood Gallery, and other spots of interest in the Berkshires. The courtyard in the rear is a delightful place to meet and eat with friends in the summer. The other dining areas are always filled with eager and satisfied guests. Skiing, antiquing, gift shopping, and browsing are but a few of the many activities one can enjoy before returning to the inn to sit in wonderful old rocking chairs on the large veranda in summer or before the open fireplace in winter."   —*Betty G. Mower*

"The inn was everything I thought it would be—old, warm, charming. I loved all the porches, antiques, nooks and crannies. Our room was cute and small—bathroom down the hall, though, which we didn't like. Also, the inn is at a busy intersection with trucks stopping at the corner all night. It was pretty noisy. Loved the dining room and the food. Next time I'll get a room away from the corner and with a bathroom."   —*Melanie Omohundro*

Open all year.
114 rooms in summer, half with private bath.
Rates $30–$125, depending on season and room size. Pets $10.
Credit cards: American Express, Carte Blanche, Diners Club, MasterCard, Visa.
Restaurant.
From Massachusetts Turnpike, Exit 2, follow Route 102 to Stockbridge. Bus service from New York.
Innkeeper: Betsy M. Holtzinger.

_____ *Ware*

The Wildwood Inn
121 Church Street
Ware, Massachusetts 01082
Telephone (413) 967-7798

"The inn is located between historic Deerfield and Old Sturbridge Village. The famous Salem Cross Inn and Amherst are minutes away, and leisurely country drives through autumn foliage are part of the allure of the place.

"The inn is furnished in comfortable country charm. Not untouchable antiques, but lovely, old, livable, usable pieces. In the evening, we would all sit by the fireplace in the living room, with its great old spinning wheel, resting ourselves on the couch in front of a shoemaker's bench filled with books about the area."

—*Rhonda Smith*

"This charming Victorian house is set up comfortably and feels much more like a home than a hotel. The large living room has a fascinating collection of antique toys and contemporary games. The proprietress produced a marvelous breakfast prettily served in the sunny dining room the next morning. A small loaf of homemade bread and a crock of the best apple butter I've ever tasted graced each table. We slept in a handsome colonial bed in a room decorated in keeping with the period. If we enjoyed a bleak weekend in February this much, the experience in spring, summer, or fall must be even more wonderful."

—*Kay Bentley*

"For my daughter there were special firsts that a child born and raised in Hawaii misses: swinging on a swing on a big old wraparound porch (she now wants a porch swing for her dollhouse), climbing over a stone wall on a hike, seeing all those antique cradles in the sitting room, sleeping under a lovely old quilt on pillows with eyelet-trimmed cases, and sitting in an antique sleigh on the front lawn to have her picture taken. Probably best for all of us was an invitation for Jenny to join the Lobenstines for dinner while my parents and I enjoyed a grownup night out at a local restaurant."

—*Kristina Dyer*

"I felt like part of the family. In fact, the evening I arrived the dog and I were the only ones around for several hours."

—*John Doxy*

"The handmade quilts on the beds are lovely to look at, especially for me, since my hobby is quilting. I had brought my sewing basket with me and enjoyed sitting by the fire in the evening working on a quilt square."

—*Zita E. McCabe*

As in all the best country inns, the warmth of the innkeeper makes this a special place. Margaret Lobenstine is the kind of person who loves to share with others. As a way of sharing her expertise, her successes and failures, she runs an apprentice program for potential innkeepers. If you are fantasizing about opening an inn or a bed-and-breakfast, call Margaret for details. She may be able to help.

—*JLS*

Open all year.
5 rooms with shared baths.
Rates $25–$45, including continental breakfast.
No credit cards.
Innkeepers: The Lobenstine family.

_____ *West Harwich*

Barnaby Inn
36 Main Street (Route 28, Box 151)
West Harwich, Cape Cod, Massachusetts 02671
Telephone (617) 432-6789

"This is a brief note of excitement to share the discovery of a lovely little inn. On a recent trip back to the East Coast, I discovered the Barnaby Inn on Cape Cod and spent three nights at this little spot, enjoying the delicious breakfasts and dinners. The innkeepers, Susan and Steven Esons, and their baby Amanda made us feel at home. Their chef's reputation is apparently widespread on the Cape."
—*Freda Depoy*

Open mid-May to mid-October.
5 rooms, 3 with private bath.
Rates $25–$40, including breakfast.
Credit cards: American Express, MasterCard, Visa.
Restaurant and bar.
Danish spoken.
Hyannis bus stops in front of the inn.
Innkeepers: Susan and Steven Esons.

_____ *Whitinsville*

The Victorian
583 Linwood Avenue
Whitinsville, Massachusetts 01588
Telephone (617) 234-2500

"Whitinsville is gracefully off all main roads, some fourteen miles southeast of Worcester and some thirty-six road miles from Boston —a wonderful weekend or trip-breaking place for those driving northeast or southwest and seeking to avoid the Lost World of Boston traffic. In Whitinsville the place to stay is the Victorian mansion overlooking a clean-looking little river and one of the town's original mills; astonishingly, it is still a busy mill. Astonishingly, too, for those who have read about the decline of New England mill towns, Whitinsville nowadays carries the air of a rather sparkling and prosperous place: some Greek Revival houses among the Victorian and a proudly spreading building belonging to its historical society."
—*John Tibby*

"Being from San Francisco, we both were dubious that any place outside of that area could truly lay claim to an authentic Victorian atmosphere. How mistaken (and vain) we were—and how royally pleased! The Victorian, built originally in the 1880s as a private home by the founder of Whitinsville, is richly decorated with antiques and furnishings that made us feel as if we had left the twentieth century at the front door and briefly stepped into the adornments of the Victorian nineteenth century. Our favorites were the commanding center staircase of luxuriously oiled wood, the library dining room (where we were at liberty to browse and borrow at will among valuable old volumes), the original brass chandeliers throughout the inn, and the Armour Room (the room we had)—complete with functioning fireplace, high arched windows with window seats, tooled leather wall coverings, king-size bed with brass headboard, and fresh apples on a crystal platter to greet us each evening.

"The surrounding countryside well illustrates the reputation New England has for autumn foliage. Old Sturbridge Village is an easy drive and should not be excluded from a day's outing."

—*Scott and Luree Miller*

Open all year.
8 rooms, all with private bath.
Rates $67–$82, including continental breakfast.
Credit cards: American Express, MasterCard, Visa.
Restaurant.
French spoken.
ABC buses from Worcester or Providence stop on request. For a fee, guests can be met at Boston or Providence airport.
Innkeeper: Martha Flint.

Where are the good little hotels in Boston? Philadelphia? Omaha? Dallas? If you have found one, don't keep it a secret. Write *now*.

New Hampshire

Bristol

The Pasquaney Inn
Star Route 1, Box 1066 (Route 3A)
Bristol, New Hampshire 03222
Telephone (603) 744-2712

"The inn is on Newfound Lake; I was quite frankly astonished to find such a clean, clear body of water in New England. My children couldn't spend enough time on the inn's beach. Older children can water-ski and canoe or sail with equipment provided by the inn."

—_Judy Toland_

"We spent eight days of our wedding trip here. We were especially impressed with the quality of the inn's dining room and cooking. The view of Newfound Lake is splendid. Swimming in those very cold waters is a bracing tonic for the hot traveler. Also close by are Audubon trails and public beaches. During our stay we enjoyed a climb of Stinson Mountain in Rumney. Our only problem on the hike was that the box lunch prepared by the inn staff was so large, we were almost unable to make the summit!"

—_David and Cynthia Stinson_

Open May 15 through October 15, December 25 through April 1.
28 rooms in main house, 10 with private bath.
Rates $35–$48 per person, MAP.
Credit cards: MasterCard, Visa.
Plane to Laconia or bus to Plymouth. Pickup from bus available.
Innkeepers: Marge and Roy Zimmer.

_____ *Chocorua*

Stafford's-in-the-Field
Chocorua, New Hampshire 03817
Telephone (603) 323-7766

"I had always wanted to see the three northern New England states.
I was traveling alone and had only seven days, so I purposely selected inns as small as possible, and not too far apart. The smaller
inns provided built-in companionship at the end of the day's drive.
This was especially true of Stafford's-in-the-Field (and Squire Tarbox in Maine), where the guests really seemed to mingle. Stafford's
had gourmet-type meals."   —*Camilla Tanner*

"You drive up a long driveway and approach a large comfortable
house with a front porch that has rocking chairs on it. The tone is
set by the host, Fred Stafford, originally a farmer from California.
He and his wife, Ramona, who supervises the fantastic food served
at Stafford's, have been running Stafford's-in-the-Field for more
than fifteen years. There is a large main house, which has a dining
room, Fred's office, a sitting room, a library, and one bedroom.
More bedrooms (some with baths, some without) are on the second
and third floors. Next to the house there is a large barn, beautifully
preserved. Behind the house are three cottages, one of which we
occupied on an October visit. That cottage has two bedrooms; it was
very clean, with rustic decor, a nice-size living room with a fireplace,
which we enjoyed, and one full bathroom. The house in which we
stayed during our July visit had a tremendous amount of charm: the
decor took us back about 150 years. On the July visit, we saw Fred
and his two sons stenciling a room.

   "Dinner is soup, a main course, sometimes salad, and your choice
of incredible desserts. The guests mix before dinner. Fred might
have several tables together or a long table of twelve to fourteen
people."   —*Fred and Nancy Weil*

Open all year.
13 rooms, 7 with private bath; 3 cottages.

Rates $55–$70 per person, MAP.
Credit cards: American Express.
Trailways and Green Mountain buses to North Conway. Car rental
   recommended for sightseeing.
Innkeepers: Fred and Ramona Stafford.

Eaton Center

Rockhouse Mountain Farm Inn
Eaton Center, New Hampshire 03832
Telephone (603) 447-2880

"This is a working farm in the White Mountains, purchased by the
Edge family in 1936 to be run as an inn. The setting is spectacular
and the view breathtaking in every direction—mountains, lakes,
rivers, ponds, and fields. Most people take day trips, but my husband refuses to leave the farm, commenting that there is no more
beautiful vista anywhere. Children find it a paradise too—there are
horses and ponies to ride; geese, turkeys, ducks, and pigs to feed;
milking to watch; hayrides, swimming, and boating. The farmhouse
is filled with family antiques, not things acquired to impress. The
evening meal is always an occasion, with fresh flowers and candlelight and the most superb food served beautifully. Then there are
the Edges themselves—Libby, John, Johnny, Betsi Edge Ela and her
husband, Bill—an intellectual family, well read, widely traveled,
interested in everything and delighting in physical work."

—*Elinor Evangelist*

Open mid-June to November 1.
16 rooms, 4 with private bath.
Rates $38–$42, MAP.
No credit cards.
French and German spoken.
Guests met at Trailways buses in Conway; travel to and from Port-
   land, Maine, airport can be arranged by the inn.
Innkeepers: The Edge family.

Exeter

Exeter Inn
90 Front Street
Exeter, New Hampshire 07833
Telephone (603) 772-5901

"The Exeter Inn has been traditionally affiliated with Phillips Exeter Academy, but the inn welcomes other guests as well. Attractively decorated with traditional furniture, the inn has a large cheerful dining room that features daily buffet breakfasts, a sumptuous brunch on Sundays, and regular luncheon and dinner menus. The staff is friendly and helpful. We brought our two young children for a weekend and were given two spacious rooms, each with bath and television. We even had our own private hall. The inn is apt to be full during academy events such as parents' day, reunions, and graduations. Be sure to book well in advance."   —*Michelle Rhum*

Open all year.
48 rooms, all with private bath; 2 suites.
Rates: $46–$52 single, $58–$64 double, $65–$115 suites.
Credit cards: American Express, Carte Blanche, Diners Club, MasterCard, Visa.
Restaurant and bar.
Innkeeper: John Hodgins.

_____*Fitzwilliam*

Fitzwilliam Inn
Fitzwilliam, New Hampshire 03447
Telephone (603) 585-9000

"The Fitzwilliam Inn—set in what must be the most beautiful village in New England, or at least a heavy contender for the title—is modest and charming, inexpensive and restful. It is a good inn, and could be an exceptional one if a little imagination were used. For example, the landlord could invest in a few small, inexpensive electric fans for guests on those still August nights, especially in the smaller rooms. Also, the menu could benefit from lightening, and by the use of local fruit and vegetables in season. There is local corn, and there are spectacular berries—but not on the menu. Why not a good New England specialty now and then—a good boiled dinner is very good indeed; real baked beans are a revelation to those who haven't had them, and inexpensive, too. Otherwise, a splendid place. Nice square dancing on Saturday night; apart from that, just peace and quiet. Worth noting that Vermont Transit buses go to the door."   —*Linda and David Murray*

"This atmospheric old place badly needs a coat of paint, and could also use a more imaginative chef. By asking, we were moved to a bedroom less sparse than our reservation, but unfortunately over a drunken party that the management did nothing to restrain. The public rooms are cozy, though, and the town has a lovely green surrounded by old churches."   —*Dr. Jeanne M. Safer*

"If you like antiques, you'll love this inn; they are all over. Two large parlors with working fireplaces, small lounge and bar also with fireplace, and a dining room with very good food. We stayed here over Thanksgiving, and on a table in the front entrance was a large cornucopia filled with fruits, vegetables, and nuts, which was a very nice touch."   —*Ora and Phil Beilock*

Open all year.
21 rooms, 12 with private bath.
Rates $22–$26 single, $26–$30 double.
Credit cards: American Express, Carte Blanche, Diners Club, MasterCard, Visa.
Dining room and bar.
Vermont Transit bus stops at inn.
Innkeepers: Barbara and Charles Wallace.

--- *Francestown*

The Inn at Crotched Mountain
Mountain Road
Francestown, New Hampshire 03043
Telephone (603) 588-6840

"This brick colonial house, with a wing built in 1822, faces intimate mountains, excellent for hiking or skiing. On the other side there is an unimpeded forty-mile view of rolling hills and meadows. Later we were told that our elevation was a pleasant 1,300 feet. On arriving at the inn, we were greeted by a delightful young man, who introduced us to our lovely New England room. He proved to be the host and owner. The next day, after a pleasant night's rest, we found the swimming pool, a wading pool, and two tennis courts. We had been told they were championship courts, and indeed they were. At that time of year we found the inn ideal for rest, healthy recreation, and excellent food. I am sure that other times of year are equally delightful."   —*Kenneth J. Cooper*

Closed from the last weekend in October to Thanksgiving Day, and from the end of the ski season to Memorial Day.
14 rooms, 5 with private bath.
Rates $25–$40 single, $30–$45 double.
Dining room and bar.
No credit cards.
Chinese and Spanish spoken.
Innkeepers: John and Rose Perry.

Franconia

Franconia Inn
Easton Road (Route 116)
Franconia, New Hampshire 03580
Telephone (603) 823-5542

"The rooms are immaculate and each time we returned from out-ings we found that little elves had straightened up our vacationers' mess. Fresh fruit in the room, fresh flowers daily, beds turned down at night, and thick, thirsty fresh towels are the most visible signs of the attitude that prevails. The food is excellent and attractively served. The members of our group are addicted to tennis and we found the four clay courts in excellent condition. The location of the inn makes it ideal for day trips into the beautiful White Mountains. We did some walking, some climbing, and some driving through spectacular countryside. We are not skiers, so I do not know what the inn is like during its peak season. I can only say that as an off-season autumn respite our stay was thoroughly enjoyed."
—*Phoebe Liss*

"Our stay at the Franconia Inn left much to be desired. We stayed in Room 27, with a lock on the door that stuck so badly that even my muscular 200-pound husband had great difficulty opening it. In case of fire, it would have been very dangerous. The worst part concerned misleading advertising. We made reservations for a room with 'connecting bath,' which turned out to be down the hall. When I inquired about this, I was told, 'That's what we call a con-necting bath. There are about three families sharing it with you.'"
—*Mrs. Sig Richardson*

Open December 18 to March 21, Memorial Day to October 18.
30 rooms, 12 with private bath.
Rates $45–$55, MAP.
Credit cards: MasterCard, Visa.
2 dining rooms; rathskeller.
Continental Trailways bus to Franconia.
Innkeepers: The Morris family.

Rates quoted were the latest available. But they may not reflect unexpected increases or local and state taxes. Be sure to verify when you book.

Lovett's Inn
By Lafayette Brook
Profile Road
Franconia, New Hampshire 03580
Telephone (603) 823-7761

"More extraordinary than ever."
—*David Mallery*

"Lovett's has made few concessions, thank goodness, to the onward march of mediocrity and sameness that today characterize so many of the lodging places in this country. Charlie Lovett with his wife, Red, has directed the destiny of this charming North Country inn for some thirty years.

"Changes at Lovett's through the years have been relatively few and, for the most part, well advised. For several years now guests have been offered the alternative of bathing in a small swimming pool filled with solar-heated water instead of being compelled to indulge their aquatic whims in the pond across the road, which is fed with icy springwater from Lafayette Brook. A few years ago Charlie Lovett attended an auction of the furnishings of one of the great Newport cottages, and returned to Franconia with a magnificent curved marble bar, the focal point of the charming and intimate barroom at Lovett's.

"Lovett's food demands special mention in any description of the inn. There is no more savory cuisine to be encountered anywhere. At dinner the guest is confronted with a choice of seven or eight tempting entrées, ranging on a typical evening from broiled fresh swordfish to 'heavy western sirloin.' The salads are simple, but without peer, being made with lettuces and herbs gathered that very day from the salad garden just outside the kitchen. What can one say about Lovett's desserts? Simply that they will break down the resistance of the most iron-willed dieters. I think that a reasonable rule of thumb for the guest at Lovett's would be to figure on two to three added pounds of weight for each week spent in residence!"
—*A. Wells Pettibone*

"Tucked in a small valley in the splendor of the White Mountains is this unpretentious country inn. The surrounding towns of Franconia and Sugar Hill are unspoiled villages with examples of well-maintained and charming eighteenth- and nineteenth-century homes and farms. The fall foliage season offers magnificent color, harvests, fairs, and fetes. Downhill ski areas abound, and newly created cross-country trails lead the adventurous into lovely winter woodlands. In the summer the state and national parks provide hiking, camping, climbing, and swimming. Scenic wonders for the photographer or painter—gorges, flumes, mineral caves, and a cog railway to the top of Mount Washington—are nearby. Arts and crafts shops welcome visitors. Historic spots include one of the first successful iron forges in New England.

"Accommodations at the inn vary from private rooms in the restored farmhouse to separate motel units to simple 'barn' accommodations for singles and teenagers who share baths and showers and enjoy a special camaraderie. Charlie Lovett presides in the attractive cocktail lounge, introducing guests and mixing a superb martini."   —*Mrs. James H. Cannon*

This was a delightful place, with the best food we have ever eaten anywhere."   —*Harold and Ruth Maxton;*
also recommended by Eric H. Boyer

Open December 26 to April 1, July 1 to Columbus Day.
7 rooms, 2 with private bath; 14 cottages, all with private bath.
Rates $36–$54, MAP.
Credit cards: American Express, MasterCard, Visa.
Continental Trailways bus to Franconia.
Innkeepers: Mr. and Mrs. Charles Lovett, Jr.

_____*Hancock*

The John Hancock Inn
Hancock, New Hampshire 03449
Telephone (603) 525-3318

"Surrounded by mountains, Hancock is a thriving community of friendly people, and the John Hancock Inn is truly the heart of this community. In the many visits we have made to the inn in the last several years, we have made many friends among the people of the town and surrounding areas. We feel very much at home, and of course much of this feeling is due to the warm, welcoming atmosphere created by Pat and Glynn Wells and their children. And one can't overlook the great meals prepared for us by chef Dick Doucette and the staff.

"For anyone interested in early New England towns this is the area to visit—time and progress have not brought ugly structures of metal, glass, and neon. Hancock is much as it was before the turn of the century. The beautiful old buildings are treasured and maintained. The inn itself has been in operation since 1789. Norway

Pond and the old cemetery, both within two minutes' walk of the inn, will appeal to camera buffs and historians."

—*Marjorie S. Burns*

"I found this inn rather worn at the edges, the food ordinary, and the room (at the front) noisy and public, although it did sport a lovely old canopy bed. The only place really worth staying in here is the wonderful room with the primitive murals, a Rousseauesque delight. The staff is most gracious."   —*Dr. Jeanne M. Safer*

"The best thing about the Hancock Inn is the food. We spent Thanksgiving here one year. As the dinner guests departed, each was given a small package with pumpkin nut bread. The bedrooms are nice, but there is no parlor where you can sit. There is a bar, though."   —*Ora and Phil Beilock*

Open all year, except one week in spring, one in fall, and Christmas Eve and Christmas Day.
10 rooms, all with private bath.
Rates $39.50 single, $46.50 double.
Credit cards: MasterCard, Visa.
Bus service to Keene. Nearest airports: Keene, Manchester.
Innkeepers: Patricia and Glynn Wells.

_____*Hanover*

Hanover Inn
South Main and East Wheelock, at Dartmouth College
Hanover, New Hampshire 03755
Telephone (603) 643-4300

"Throughout my drive from New Haven, Connecticut, to Hanover, New Hampshire, one September, I was enthralled with the beauty of the rolling hills and farmland. As I entered the front door, I was absolutely amazed by the charm of old New England. The lady behind the desk was perhaps the most courteous and pleasant registration clerk I had ever encountered. Grabbing my few bags and getting onto the elevator, I couldn't help but compare this charm with the finest of small northern Italian pensiones or Bavarian Zimmerhausen which I had stayed in during the 1960s. I opened the door to my room and wow! There was the most elegant colonial room in which I had stayed in my entire life. The quilted bedspreads, the antique chests and dressers, the beautiful colonial wallpaper, the dormer windows, not a speck of dust anywhere. After unpacking, I found the sitting room adjacent to the main lobby an absolutely fantastic place to sit with the evening paper, unwind and relax. And, dinner was superb. What a joy it was to return to my room, look out the window to see the moonlit Dartmouth campus across the street, and hear the chimes of the clock echoing in the background." *—Dr. Gilbert L. Whiteman*

"The twin-bedded room was small but adequate. Furnished with reproduction Hitchcock furniture, it had a warm feeling. We could not help but notice that the pale-gold comforters folded at the foot of each bed were exactly the same color as the pattern in the wallpaper. The hallway leading to the elevator was a disappointment. On the strategically placed tables were arrangements of poorly made artificial flowers. They seemed incongruous and detracted from the overall picture. All was forgiven when we entered the elegantly appointed dining room. Every table was being used, but the tables were placed far enough apart so that conversation from other tables did not bother us at all." *—Kay Wilder*

Open all year.
100 rooms, all with private bath.
Rates $76–$106 single, $82–$114 double.
Credit cards: American Express, Diners Club, MasterCard, Visa.
Dining room.
French spoken.
Lebanon airport, 5 miles away. Vermont Transit bus and Amtrak train service to White River Junction, 5 miles away.
General Manager: Robert B. Merrow.

Henniker

Colby Hill Inn
The Oaks (Box 778)
Henniker, New Hampshire 03242
Telephone (603) 428-3281

"In 1821, in the town of Henniker, New Hampshire, Bartlett's Tavern was built for the purpose of tending to tired travelers. In 1976, the Glover family took over what is now known as the Colby Hill Inn; and nary a colonial could complain that the fine innkeeping tradition has not been fully upheld. A fine variety of well-prepared veal, fresh fish, steak, and other dishes is served in the relaxing setting of the charming dining room. Luckily, the tables are large enough to accommodate the extra servings of home-baked breads, pickled beets, and applesauce that somehow make their way to one's table. Vegetables grown in the backyard garden are used liberally.

"The best thing about the Colby Hill Inn is the attitude of the Glovers. Whenever I visit this rustic, white clapboard house, my every need is attended to with sincere concern. An ambience of comfort permeates every room. To me, this is what traveling to country inns is all about."   —*Vincent J. Kish*

"A fire in the stove, shelves full of books and magazines, and a jigsaw puzzle spread out on a table invite guests to enjoy the sitting room rather than hide away in their rooms. Innkeepers and guests alike are friendly and the conversation is easy. Upstairs the floors slope a bit, but that adds to the charm of the place.

"Located on the outskirts of the small town that is home to New England College, the Colby Hill Inn was once a working farm. The dining room is open to the public for dinner, and the food is good and bountiful.

"Every season offers activities such as swimming, bicycling, and tennis in summer; mountain climbing, antiquing, and foliage watching in autumn; skiing (both alpine and cross-country), ice fishing, and snowmobiling in winter; flycasting, horseback riding, and canoeing on the swollen streams in spring."   —*JLS*

Open all year.
12 rooms, 8 with private bath.
Rates $38–$45 single, $29–$32.50 per person double, including full
   breakfast.
Dining room and bar.
Credit cards: American Express, MasterCard, Visa.
Bus service to Henniker from Boston.
Innkeepers: The Glover family.

_____*Jackson*

Christmas Farm Inn
Jackson, New Hampshire 03846
Telephone (603) 383-4313

"As one proceeds north through Mount Washington Valley on Route 16, a side road leads through a quaint covered bridge into Jackson. Through the village and up a steep hill, you notice a large, well-kept white farmhouse. Here, high on the slope of one of the area's lesser mountains, with outstanding views of Mount Washington and the Moat Range, are the main farmhouse (really several buildings in one), an expanded Cape Cod cottage (Red House), a large barn, a sugarhouse, and a log cabin—the Christmas Farm Inn. Enter the main house and find typical old New England-style decor, functional and attractive. Off the hall and 'lobby' are two small living rooms, a spacious dining room, and a small lounge. Upstairs, bedrooms are obviously meant primarily for sleeping. It is very much like a visit to Grandma's, provided yours lived in the country. The other buildings offer newer and more spacious rooms (Red House), privacy (Sugar House), and family or group accommodations (Log Cabin).

"The real charm of an inn is the friendly warmth and hospitality it can offer. The owners of Christmas Farm Inn, Bill and Sydna Zeliff, seem more like old friends than innkeepers, and they have selected their staff carefully to ensure that this feeling prevails. Add to this a significant number of repeat guests, and the casual evenings in the living room before the fireplace or in the cozy lounge are indeed enjoyable. Children are welcome, of course, but they are expected to take noisier activities to the game room in the barn.

"Food has always been of prime importance at Christmas Farm; it is 'just plain good.' Although lunch is not served, a sandwich 'trail lunch' is available. Enjoy the homemade soup, salad bar, and the entrée, but save room for desserts. These are varied but always include the popular 'Christmas Farm Sundae' (New Hampshire maple syrup over vanilla ice cream decorated with nonpareils)."

—*Mr. and Mrs. Donald Chesebrough and family*

"I think you should emphasize that this is an excellent place for children; that would appeal to a lot of families. The food is good, with an emphasis on quantity—they keep pushing those blueberry muffins at you. They also make a good box lunch. The rooms are not all the last word in comfort, but that doesn't bother me. Life at Christmas Farm is very informal—'undressy'—and that might not appeal to people who want a more sophisticated place. This one is family oriented."   —*Patricia Lievow*

"It is Christmas here twelve months of the year. The accommodations are excellent, as is the food. Don't pass this one up, especially if you have never been in the White Mountains."

—*Ora and Phil Beilock; also recommended by Gayle Bolinger*

Open all year.
27 rooms, 22 with private bath.
Rates $42–$52 per person, breakfast and dinner included.
Credit cards: American Express, Diners Club, MasterCard, Visa.
Dining room and bar.
Concord Coach Lines to Jackson.
Innkeepers: Sydna and William H. Zeliff.

The Dana Place Inn
10 Pinkham Notch Road
Jackson, New Hampshire 03846
Telephone (603) 383-6822

"Just above the village of Jackson on Route 16 leading toward Mount Washington, lies Pinkham Notch and the Dana Place Inn. With the majesty of Mount Washington as a backdrop, the Dana Place seen from its apple orchards on the Ellis River Trail presents one of the prettiest views anywhere in the Northeast. We have been frequent visitors over the years. In winter our lives revolve around cross-country skiing, and there is no finer anywhere for our money than in Mount Washington Valley's Jackson Ski Touring Foundation and Appalachian Mountain Club networks. Our visits have not, however, been limited to snow season. The Dana Place is an ideal headquarters for hiking in the White Mountain National Forest; in the summer the inn offers tennis in the shadow of Mount Washington, a swim in the pool or, even better, in the natural pools of the Ellis River and Winneweta Falls, which flow nearby. The inn itself has comfortable, cozy rooms, an elegant dining room, personalized service from all the staff, and a special warmth created by Betty and Mal Jennings, the innkeepers.   —*Lee and Margaret Phillips*

"Breakfast is a hearty meal and dinners are truly outstanding. There are three dining areas, each with a charm of its own. An open fire lends warmth to the central area, while hanging baskets and glass walls provide interest in the others. There are gentle walks beside a lovely trout stream on the grounds and, for the more ambitious, a mountain to climb across the road and hiking trails as far as anyone cares to go. Within a few miles there are several streams for the trout fisherman, early summer being the most productive time for this activity."   —*Yetta C. Samford, Jr.*

Open mid-June to late October and mid-December to late March. Rooms available on weekends in May and early June. 14 rooms, 6 with private bath.
Rates $25–$35 per person, double occupancy.
Credit cards: American Express, MasterCard, Visa.
Dining room and bar.
Concord Trailways bus from Boston to Jackson. Vermont Transit from Portland, Maine, to North Conway. Guests met at North Conway. Nearest scheduled air service by Delta to Portland, Maine.
Innkeepers: Malcolm and Betty Jennings.

_____*Jaffrey*

Woodbound Inn
Post Office
Jaffrey, New Hampshire 03452
Telephone (603) 532-8341

"The Woodbound is a lovely old country inn nestled on the shore of Lake Contoocook at the base of Mount Monadnock—an inn for all seasons and for all ages. People return year after year to this wonderful place run by the Brummer family. They come as children and come back with their children and grandchildren. There are plenty of activities, both summer and winter, for all age-groups— tennis, golf, skiing, tobogganing, water-skiing, sailing, horseback riding, ping-pong, shuffleboard, and evening entertainments in the barn. Antique and gift shops abound in the area, and church suppers, flea markets, historical commemorations, and more take place regularly. So do hayrides, sleighrides, square dances, and cornhusking bees. Beach luncheons, suppers in the pines, and wonderful buffets keep energy levels high. A special treat is the winter cookout, with hot oyster stew and sugar on the snow beside the bar."

—Betty G. Mower

"This is a family-owned and -operated inn catering to family-oriented people. The rooms are comfortable, clean, attractively furnished, and well maintained. Pine-paneled lakeside cottages with fireplaces offer excellent accommodations (with a view) for family groups. Congeniality is the keynote of the Woodbound Inn."

—Constance H. Eng

Open all year.
50 rooms, 48 with private bath; 2 suites.
Rates $45—$65, full AP.
Credit cards: American Express, MasterCard, Visa.
Dining room.
Bus service to Jaffrey from Boston and Fitzwilliam. Nearest airport: Keene. The inn is 2 miles by road from the junction of Routes 202 and 119.
Innkeeper: Jed Brummer.

_____*Littleton*

Beal House Inn
247 Main Street
Littleton, New Hampshire 03561
Telephone (603) 444-2661

"While its white clapboard exterior is not prepossessing, its interior is delightful. The place is furnished with antiques, most of which are for sale. I suspect the building dates from the era of toilets out back, but now modern facilities are tucked into each room most ingeniously—no two alike. And no two rooms are the same in size, shape, or furnishings. If you wish to sleep in a glamorous canopy bed or opt for a nostalgic brass one, you can be accommodated. Or, if one of you snores and the other takes umbrage, you can choose a pair of connecting rooms.

"Breakfast in front of the roaring fire is a must. Oh, those tender, crisp waffles with all the genuine Vermont maple syrup you want, or scrambled eggs served under an antique glass hen. And don't miss the coin silver flatware, pewter serving dishes, and old red-and-white table linen. The town has the usual shops and country-type houses and is not inspiring, but its location in the center of the most beautiful and spectacular part of the White Mountains, as well as near some excellent eateries and antique shops, makes it a great place to stay or to jump off from."   —*John M. Belding*

"The inn is situated on the main street of Littleton, a town in the northern part of the state close to the Vermont border and very near to the scenic Connecticut River Valley. The mountain slopes of both Vermont and New Hampshire are nearby, and the air is said to be the purest in the country."   —*Dr. John A. Roque*

Open all year.
11 rooms, 10 with private bath; 2 suites.
Rates $25–$30 shared bath, $33–$50 private bath.
Credit cards: American Express, Carte Blanche, Diners Club, MasterCard, Visa.
Bus service 8 miles away.
Innkeepers: Brenda and Doug Clickenger.

Edencroft Manor
RFD 1, Route 135
Littleton, New Hampshire 03561
Telephone (603) 444-6776

"We are returning again to the U.S.A. and to Edencroft to see the proprietors, whom we now regard as friends. The inn is owned by two couples and run on a very friendly basis, while the standards are kept particularly high. The restaurant is probably the best we have eaten in in the U.S.A. Each dish is cooked individually when ordered. The New England clam chowder has to be tasted to be believed."   *—Janet Ruff*

"I have visited the inn during four of the five New England seasons (I skipped 'Mud'), and have found it to be one of the most friendly, relaxing, and hospitable places I have ever stayed at. I feel more that I am visiting friends than staying at a hotel (at least until I get the bill). The rooms are named for the primary color of the decor. Keys are optional. The cuisine is excellent and the prices moderate. Most recently, six friends and I booked several of their rooms for a week-end during leaf-peeping season. The group included several gour-mands, three moderate-to-good chefs, and several critical over-achievers. We ordered just about everything on the menu (not to mention the wine list and bar). The bottom line is that there are six new Edencroft Manor fans."   *—Bill Carlson*

"Bill Walsh is a very good chef, and Ellie Bliss makes fantastic desserts. The location of the inn is great, just beyond Franconia Notch, ideal for skiing, fall foliage, or spring and summer touring."
—Vincent LaPorte

Open all year except "Mud Season" (2 weeks in March).
6 rooms, 4 with private bath.
Rates $25–$45.
Credit cards: American Express, MasterCard, Visa.
Innkeepers: Bill and Laurie Walsh, Barny and Ellie Bliss.

_____*North Conway*

Eastern Slope Inn
Main Street
North Conway, New Hampshire 03860
Telephone (603) 356-6321 or toll-free (800) 258-4708

"Located in the White Mountains of New Hampshire is a delightful inn, standing stately, all dressed in white—the Eastern Slope Inn. Each of us has a romantic and/or historic vision of what the perfect inn should be, but does it exist? You bet it does. At the Eastern Slope, from the moment you enter your room a luxurious feeling surrounds you: from Daisy's Quaint Walnut Tavern where the best 'strong waters' we have ever sipped are poured, to the creative cookery served in Daisy's Dining Room (lunch is a treat on the terrace, weather permitting, in summer and fall); from the grounds with clay tennis courts and swimming pool, to the Mt. Cranmore Tennis/Racquetball Club with health club and sauna. And if this isn't enough, a winter wonderland of four major ski mountains is within minutes, as well as numerous cross-country ski trails. This is an inn for all seasons and an inn for all reasons."

—Mr. and Mrs. John Capuano

Open all year.
73 rooms, all with private bath.
Rates $25–$80. Optional MAP available.
Restaurant and pub.
No credit cards.
Innkeeper: Darrell Trapp.

White's Old Red Inn
Route 16 (Box 467)
North Conway, New Hampshire 03860
Telephone (603) 356-2642

"White's Old Red Inn has something special which separates it from the other pretty places in the area. It's not the awe-inspiring views of the mountains from the second floor of the 173-year-old inn. It's not the warmth and quiet comfort of the ten cottages. It's not the convenient location of the inn near the center of town. It is the Whites themselves, who give each traveler a welcome rather than just a place to stay.

"At the time of my last visit, Winnie was deeply involved in making quilts. Ask her about the dried flower arrangements in the rooms and you'll likely be treated to a tour of her award-winning flower and herb garden.

"North Conway, the Gateway to the White Mountains, is a four-seasons area and has attractions for skiers, hikers, leaf watchers, and tennis buffs; and there is more than enough to keep bargain hunters, antique collectors, and gourmets busy."   *—Vincent Kish*

Open all year.
7 rooms, 5 with private bath; 10 cottages, all with private bath.
Rates $30–$48 double occupancy, including continental breakfast.
Credit cards: MasterCard, Visa.
French spoken.
Innkeepers: Don and Winnie White.

Do you know a hotel in your state that we have overlooked? Write *now*.

_____ *Shelburne*

Philbrook Farm Inn
North Road
Shelburne, New Hampshire 03581
Telephone (603) 466-3831

"Sometime when your New England explorations lead you to U.S. Highway 2—which stretches all the way across northern Vermont, New Hampshire, and Maine—you will find as you pass along the White Mountains that you are surrounded by forests of white birch trees. A few miles east of Gorham these trees line the road and arch overhead, making a virtual birch bower. These are known widely as the Shelburne Birches, and you are now within a few miles of Philbrook Farm Inn. Watch carefully for North Road, turn left, and follow the inn signs over the Androscoggin River bridge. No adequate description of this century-old inn can be written within the limits of this space. The inn, always owned and operated by the Philbrook family, has a large, beautifully furnished parlor at its east end and an attractive, spacious dining room at the west end. After meals many guests seem to gravitate to a smaller sitting room in between, where the fireplace is rarely without a flame. Other guests will congregate on the front porch, where the view sweeps across fields, with cattle grazing, to the New Hampshire-size mountains of the Moriah Range.

"Between meals the inn serves as home base for a dozen or more half-day auto trips—north through Berlin to explore genuine backwoods country, east into nearby Maine, west into nearby Vermont, south through one of the White Mountain notches to shop in Jackson and the Conways. The Appalachian Trail runs within a few miles of the inn, and many guests spend between-meals hours hiking over well-marked paths."   —*Robert Dixon*

Open December 26 to March 31, May 1 to November 30.
19 rooms, 6 with private bath; 1 cottage.
Rates $30–$50, MAP; $225–$358 weekly, full AP.
No credit cards.
Transportation from Gorham bus stop on request. Trailways bus
    from Boston.
Innkeepers: Nancy Philbrook and Constance Leger.

All inkeepers appreciate reservations in advance; some require them.

_____ *Snowville*

Snowvillage Inn
Box AW
Snowville, New Hampshire 03849
Telephone (603) 447-2818

Patrick and Ginger Blymyer left full-time careers in Hollywood filmmaking a few years ago to run this mountain inn near Eaton Center in New Hampshire's White Mountains. The couple, with their daughters Tanya and Xochi, had visited the inn as travelers before they bought it.

"On our first trip, we arrived near midnight to find Ginger abed, so we rambled through this Swiss-style inn and found two brothers—one from Norway—engaged in the almost lost art of conversation. They searched for Ginger while we absorbed the charm of this newfound inn. Had we but realized it then, we could have rustled ourselves up a meal or a cup of tea, as the kitchen is always open to all. We slept well and awakened refreshed, vigorously inhaling the clear, cool mountain air. We drew back the curtains and the view of Mount Washington and the Presidential Range was breathtaking. For the next seven days we spent most of our time sitting on the veranda, taking in the majesty and quietude of the mountains—hazy in the morning, brilliant by day, and serene in the evening. It is the most beautiful view I've seen—and coming from Ireland, that's saying something!

"The cuisine is excellent. Ginger and Pat and the family are wonderful people. (We traded books. We acquired *A Path to Rome.* I don't know what Allen pawned off on her.)

"This year we went back again after long deliberations on where to spend our vacation. That's three out of four years. This time the flower gardens were exquisite—Ginger had won first prize for the best-kept garden on a large estate. The food was even better under chef Jean: lobster, veal piccata and veal cordon bleu, roast beef and Yorkshire pudding. Gracie the pig now lives in 'Gracie Mansion,' subsisting on gourmet leftovers. Peter and Cindy bunny had joined the family. When we left we took Sandra, Cindy's sister, home with us."
                                        —*Pauline O'Reilly Weakland*

Open all year.
14 rooms, all with private bath.
Rates $47.50–$55 per person, including breakfast and dinner.
Credit cards: American Express, MasterCard, Visa.
Dining room.
French and Spanish spoken.

Bus to Conway. Nearest airport: Portland, Maine. Guests are picked up free at bus; small charge from airport.
Innkeeper: Ginger Blymyer.

_____*Sunapee*

Dexter's Inn
Stagecoach Road (Box W)
Sunapee, New Hampshire 03782
Telephone (603) 763-5571

The main house was built in 1801 by Adam Reddington, a craftsman who earned his living making the bowls in which sailing ships carried their compasses. It was remodeled in the 1930s by Samuel Crowther, a financial adviser to President Hoover. The house became an inn in 1948.

"I have been a guest at Dexter's every summer and several autumns since 1972. The inn is small and intimate, the guests pleasant and considerate. The staff remains much the same year after year and warmly greet each guest by name. The innkeeper, Frank Simpson, a gentleman in every sense of the word, quietly goes about the business of making your stay at Dexter's a memorable one. Whatever your interests, Frank is always available to give suggestions for enjoyable side trips or daylong excursions. Shirley Simpson, Frank's wife, is a creative force behind the scenes—supervising the immaculate kitchen and bringing her special decorative touches to individualize each room.

"The surrounding area has much to offer; excellent gift and antique shops, an extremely well-stocked ski shop, and a woolen mill store are ten minutes away. An outstanding championship golf course, Eastman, at Grantham, is a mere fifteen minutes away. A fascinating side trip is to Ruggles Mine, an open-pit mica and feldspar mine on top of a mountain. Mineral picks may be rented there; all you need is a sturdy bag to carry away your finds. Hanover, home of Dartmouth College and Hopkins Center for the Arts, is but thirty minutes away from Dexter's."   —*Julia Steere Koech*

Open May through October.
17 rooms, all with private bath.
Rates $50–$67 single, $40–$54 per person double, including breakfast and dinner. Breakfast only May to mid-June.
No credit cards.
Dining room and bar.
10 minutes to Mount Sunapee ski area and Lake Sunapee.

Vermont Transit bus from Boston to Mount Sunapee or New London. From New York use Greyhound to Claremont. Guests met. Nearest airports: Lebanon and Manchester, 28 and 48 miles away. Innkeepers: Frank and Shirley Simpson.

_____ *Tamworth*

Tamworth Inn
Main Street (Box 184)
Tamworth, New Hampshire 03886
Telephone (603) 323-7721

"The Tamworth Inn has been the highlight of my two fall foliage trips to New England. The innkeepers, Kelly and Larry Hubbell, have a wonderful way of making you feel at home in their lovely inn. The rooms are decorated with antiques and country quilts. Dinners and breakfasts rival the finest meals I have ever had, and the service is excellent. A delightful place off the beaten path."

—Dodie Bump

Open all year except the first three weeks in November.
22 rooms, 10 with private bath.
Rates $38–$40 with shared bath, $48–$50 with private bath.
Credit cards: MasterCard, Visa.
Restaurant and pub.
Innkeepers: Larry and Kelly Hubbell.

American hotels and inns generally list rates by the room, assuming one person in a single, two in a double. Extra people in rooms normally incur extra charges. Where rates are quoted per person per day, at least one meal is probably included under a Modified American plan (MAP). A full American Plan (AP) would include three meals.

The 1661 Inn,
Block Island

Rhode Island

Block Island

1661 Inn and Hotel Manisses
Spring Street
Block Island, Rhode Island 02807
Telephone (401) 466-2421

"The 1661 reminds us of the Italian expression _È dolce far niente,_
meaning 'How sweet it is to do nothing'—in this case, just strolling
along the countryside or biking, enjoying the unexpectedly beautiful beaches or reading a book on the inn's old-fashioned porch. The
inn has the atmosphere of the small family-owned inns on Britain's
Scilly Isles. During the complimentary wine and cheese hour, guests
have the opportunity to chat with their hosts and get acquainted
with each other. We also like the intimacy of the Settler's Pub, just
off the antique-filled living room. We look forward to seeing the
paintings, especially the Winslow Homers from the collection of the
owners, Justin and Joan Abrams. The Abrams tend a two-acre vegetable garden across the road, where everything is organically grown.

"Since we first wrote about the 1661 Inn, a few more oceanfront
rooms have been added to the annex, a cottage next door that is
open year round with a bed-and-breakfast program. Guests at the

1661 can now dine either at the inn or at the Manisses, the old restored Victorian hotel diagonally across from the inn, which the Abrams have refurbished authentically. Its guest rooms will soon be completed. At the Manisses, there is a beautiful library cocktail lounge stocked with first editions of Victoriana. Both the inn and the Manisses have outdoor decks for cocktails and dining—something new for the inn."   —*Mr. and Mrs. J. T. Lemkowitz*

"The Abrams have made the 1661 the 'in' inn on the island of Block. We enjoy being on the island in October for the Audubon bird watching, when all the 'action' has left and there's a crisp fall chill and a zillion birds whistling in the bush. That's the real Block Island!"   —*Bernice and Sam Gourse*

"I fell in love with Block Island in 1957 and every year I go back to it, finding the familiar places and discovering some wonderful new things about the island: its history, geology, the mysteriously quiet places. All the lighthouses, the bird sanctuary—breeding place and dying place for gulls—the placid ponds and pounding surf, the tones and colors of the water according to the weather, the wail of the foghorns, the heavy morning mists, exciting storms, and lazy warm sunshine. Flying over, it looks like such a little island, yet when you are bicycling up some of the hills toward the bluffs, it seems endless."   —*Ding Gerry*

Open all year.
42 rooms, 29 with private bath.
Rates $65–$135, including breakfast.
Credit cards: American Express, MasterCard, Visa.
Restaurant and bar.
Block Island is reached by boat or plane. For ferry information write to Interstate Navigation, Box 482, New London, Connecticut 06320, or call (203) 442-7891 or (203) 442-9553. Flights link the island with Westerly, Rhode Island, and New London, Connecticut. For information on these and air taxi flights call Block Island State Airport, (401) 466-5959.
French, German, Portuguese, and Spanish spoken.
Innkeepers: Justin and Joan Abrams.

Spring House Hotel
Spring Street (P.O. Box 206)
Block Island, Rhode Island 02807
Telephone (401) 466-2633

"Many of the buildings on Block Island are of the late 1800s to early 1900s on the outside, but more modern inside. The beaches are among the best in the world and are known for their fine and, in many places, black sand. (The black sand is supposed to be good for arthritis.) The water is as clear as can be and the waves are generally not rough. There is also a beach for surfing. The Spring House sits on top of a hill only a short walk to the center of town. The hotel supplies bus service to the state beach where you can rent a bathhouse (or you can change at the hotel). The hotel grounds are spacious and beautifully kept and the views from the wide veranda (with its old-fashioned wooden rocking chairs) are magnificent. From one end of it you can see the Montauk, Long Island, light to your right and the Point Judith, Rhode Island, light to your left, and in front the coastal and Europe-bound ships.

"The inn is run by Douglas and Kandi Mott, a delightful couple. The rooms are plain and in some cases quite small—but then one does not go there to spend much time in a room. The public rooms are comfortably furnished, and there is a small bar. The dining room is very large and the food is excellent and plentiful. The staff, mostly college students, is courteous and friendly. Many of them first came to the island as children with their parents.

"Block Island is a fifteen-minute flight by small plane from Westerly, about an hour by ferry from New London, Connecticut. If you are planning to bring your car to the island, an advance reservation must be made. It is also advisable to make your return reservation at the same time."   —*Margaret Givens*

Open June 4 to September 10.
75 rooms, 35 with private bath.
Rates $32–$45 per person, including breakfast and dinner.
Credit card: American Express.
Dining room.
Ferry and air service to island.
Innkeepers: Mr. and Mrs. Douglas Mott.

Surf Hotel and Surfside
Block Island, Rhode Island 02807
Telephone (401) 466-2241

"If you're looking for an impeccable, totally informal, rambling Victorian beach hotel where there is overstuffed comfort with good breakfasts and dinners, where checkers, chess, and good books make up the evening's entertainment in a communal living room (and you don't mind a pair of Lhasa apsos living in a corner of the front desk), and there is a shining crescent beach out the back door, and you like old-fashioned wooden porches for watching the sunset and a communal refrigerator for storing beer, wine, and luncheon meats for picnics—if you can accept all this, combined with friendly owners who let you enjoy your vacation or weekend quietly and in peace, try the Surf Hotel (and don't miss the moosehead in the dining room). Next door is a bike rental shop; pedaling the length and breadth of the seven-by-three-mile island is the best way to discover the many coves of beaches that rest at the base of the majestic Mohegan Bluffs at the south end of the island. The Surf is a few steps from Block Island's tiny commercial street, and across the street from the excellent Block Island Library, which gives borrowing privileges to tourists."   —*Mark Bloom*

Open Memorial Day weekend to Columbus Day weekend.
47 rooms, 3 with private bath.
Rates $30–$85.
No credit cards.
French spoken.
Ferry and plane service to island.
Innkeepers: Beatrice and Ulric Cyr.

_____*Newport*

The Inn at Castle Hill
Ocean Drive
Newport, Rhode Island 02840
Telephone (401) 849-3800

"Our exposure to the inn dates back to World War II when, going into Newport to offload torpedoes, I admired its beauty from Narragansett Bay. It is named after the Castle Hill Light, which guards the eastern entrance of the bay. We were recalled to the Navy for the Korean War and liked the area so much that we spent every summer and fall vacation there. We saw the transition from a quiet hotel with no bar, operated at a low key as a sort of private club for its distinguished owner, Mr. J. T. O'Connell, to its present active state with guests from all over the world. They come to enjoy the natural beauty, private swimming coves, and the vantage points where you can observe all the sea traffic entering and leaving Narragansett Bay (from tankers to international sailing craft)."
                    —*Marshall and Miriam Monsell*

"Our favorite time to visit the inn is after the season in September, before the rush in May, and anytime in between. 'Our' room, overlooking the Atlantic Ocean and the bay, is furnished in mahogany and chintz and has a private bathroom large enough to accommodate four additional guests. Friendly foghorns lull us to sleep after a busy day of swimming, tennis, and buying antiques."

—*Mr. and Mrs. Martin M. Temkin*

"The inn is located right on the rocky coast on Ocean Drive, not far from many of Newport's stately mansions. Guests can relax on the outdoor terrace and watch the sailboats." —*JLS*

"The inn has excellent rooms and one of the best locations in Newport." —*Tim Mulligan;*
also recommended by Neil and Karen Silverstein

Open all year.
10 rooms in inn, 6 in Harbor House, 13 with private bath; 38 cottages.
Rates $40–$165, including continental breakfast.
Credit cards: MasterCard, Visa.
Dining room.
Train service to Kingston, ½ hour away. Buses to Newport, then taxi to Castle Hill.
Danish and French spoken.
Innkeeper: Paul McEnroe.

—————————————————————— *Wakefield*

Larchwood Inn
176 Main Street
Wakefield, Rhode Island 02879
Telephone (401) 783-5454

An inn with a Scottish accent that holds a "Bobbie Burns" night every year. It is close to the Pine Top and Yawgoo ski areas.

"One of the few remaining unspoiled old New England inns, the food, service, and comfortable rooms are a real and memorable pleasure. The grounds with their flowers, unusual shrubs, and trees supply charm and quiet." —*George Gidge*

Open all year.
12 rooms, 8 with private bath; 8 rooms in guesthouse.
Rates $40–$60.
Credit cards: American Express, Carte Blanche, Diners Club, MasterCard, Visa.

Restaurant and bar.
French and Spanish spoken.
Innkeeper: Francis J. Browning.

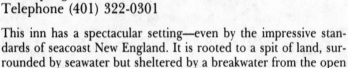

_____ *Weekapaug*

Weekapaug Inn
Weekapaug, Rhode Island 02891
Telephone (401) 322-0301

This inn has a spectacular setting—even by the impressive standards of seacoast New England. It is rooted to a spit of land, surrounded by seawater but sheltered by a breakwater from the open sea. It describes its setting as "noncommercial"—the emphasis is on nature.

"A fine and friendly place. They have excellent cuisine. The help are college and prep school young, and give good service."

—*Mrs. Gordon McCulloh*

"We have not missed a summer since 1943 when a group of sixteen friends from New Jersey arrived for a two-week stay. Mrs. Nicolson and I feel that Weekapaug must be unique among inns. We are waited on by the handpicked group of college students who consider themselves lucky to be chosen—everyone smiles at Weekapaug. Of course, the heart of the entire operation is Sydney and Bob Buffum, whom we have watched grow up from children. They can handle any emergency without excitement and with maximum efficiency, and come up smiling. The greeting from them when you arrive sets the spirit of the inn. Carrying out the rule of three generations of innkeepers, Bob buys nothing but the best, whether food, linen, or equipment; then West, the master chef, turns the raw food into superb meals. What do we do besides eat? At 9:30 every morning the men and women play boccie, tennis, golf, or shuffleboard, then down to the fine two-and-a-half-mile crescent beach."

—*H. Whitcomb Nicolson*

Open mid-June to after Labor Day.
62 rooms, 50 with private bath.
Rates $110–$150 per person, AP.
No credit cards.
Limousine from Westerly train station or Providence airport.
Innkeeper: Robert Buffum.

Turn to the back of this book for pages inviting *your* comments.

Westerly

Shelter Harbor Inn
Route 1
Westerly, Rhode Island 02891
Telephone (401) 322-8883

"An eighteenth-century farmhouse and barn have been restored to make this pleasant inn, which is not far from the ocean and beach on Route 1. The inn has a cozy library with stove and a pleasant restaurant with some tables and the bar in an enclosed sun porch, a nice place for luncheon, even on a rainy day." —*JLS*

Open all year.
22 rooms, all with private bath.
Rates $50–$60 in summer, $45–$55 the remainder of the year, including full breakfast.
Credit cards: American Express, MasterCard, Visa.
Innkeepers: Jim and Debbye Dey.

Would you be so kind as to share discoveries you may have of charming, well-run places to stay in Europe? Please write to *Europe's Wonderful Little Hotels and Inns,* c/o Congdon & Weed, 298 Fifth Avenue, New York, New York 10001. (By the way, a new and greatly expanded edition of this splendid guide is now available at your bookseller's.)

Saxtons River Inn,
Saxtons River

Vermont

Bethel

Greenhurst Inn
Bethel, Vermont 05032
Telephone (802) 234-9474

"The inn is a beautiful old Victorian home, completed about 1891, on the outskirts of Bethel (formerly a mill town) which has been undergoing a face-lift and looking better each year we have gone back. There are many lovely old homes being restored, some new shops and some of the old ones. If you're looking for crowds, head for Woodstock (beautiful but full of leaf-watchers in the fall, skiers in winter, and summer people in the summer). We drove through Woodstock (at a snail's pace because of the traffic) en route to lunch at the Bridgewater Mill, an old woolen mill now converted to shops with a lovely place for lunch (or dinner) called the Weaving Room. We had excellent homemade soup served in attractive Bennington pottery bowls, delicious homemade bread, and well-prepared sandwiches. The dessert menu sounded great but we were too full to sample it.

"My husband wanted to add that his reason for enjoying Greenhurst is that he really relaxes there away from a busy practice of psychiatry."
—*Helen E. Hanni*

Open all year.
9 rooms, 2 with private bath.
Rates $24–$44, including continental breakfast.
No credit cards.
Closest bus service to Rutland, 35 miles away. Amtrak to White
River Junction. Plane to Burlington.
Managers: Lyle and Barbara Wolf.

_____ *Bondville*

Bromley View Inn
Route 30 (Box 161)
Bondville, Vermont 05340
Telephone: (802) 297-1459

"Bromley View Inn is located just outside Manchester Center in
Southern Vermont. We have stayed at Bromley View several times
while skiing at Stratton and have never been disappointed. Breakfast is included in the price with the large breakfast window facing
Bromley Mountain. What an excellent view, especially in winter."
                              —*George and Helane Roukas*

Open all year.
12 rooms, all with private bath.
Rates $58 double, fall and winter, lower in summer, including full
breakfast.
Credit cards: American Express, MasterCard, Visa.
Innkeepers: Bick and Amy Atherton.

_____ *Brandon*

The Brandon Inn
On the Village Green
20 Park Street
Brandon, Vermont 05733
Telephone (802) 247-5766

"Since 1786, Brandon has had an inn for all seasons. In winter,
when the snow is postcard-pretty on the eaves of old houses, and
steepled churches chime the hours, ski-tired guests, back from
mountain slopes and Robert Frost's woods, gather before the ever-
burning wood fire to read or talk or sing to the accompaniment of
innkeeper Al Mitroff's guitar. In spring, new syrup on the chef's
secret-recipe French toast lures late risers to early breakfast. In
summer, there is Sunday music in the bandstand on the green and

concerts on the lawn behind the inn, where guests can listen in the shade of patriarchal trees. In fall, the fire is relit, and Al and Trudy Mitroff welcome weary leaf-peepers, returned from mountain gap and gorge, to their dining room, where Trudy's prizewinning arrangements of candles, leaves, and flowers, reflected in sparkling glass and silver, echo the brilliant changing foliage outdoors. Al offers the best of wines to suit his imaginative menus.

"Whatever the season, the inn is a timeless place. It is old Vermont, defying fad and fashion. There, townspeople and travelers enjoy together local events (such as concerts, an occasional lecture or art exhibit, and the annual flower show), returning again and again for anniversaries, family celebrations, and friendly reunions. Nearby, in addition to central Vermont's extraordinary natural beauty, there is always something interesting to see: a reenactment of the Battle of Hubbardton, a horse show, ski races, a collection of strangely carved stones that may tell a story of ancient inhabitants from across the sea, antique shops, a marble quarry, the view from the gondola to the top of Killington, the Shelburne Museum. We make the trip from Wisconsin to Brandon as often as we can; whenever we arrive, we are sure to meet others whose company we have enjoyed before."   —*Janet and Gareth Dunleavy*

Open all year.
38 rooms, 9 suites, 42 with private bath.
Rates $45–$55 per person, including breakfast and dinner.
Credit cards: American Express, Carte Blanche, Diners Club, MasterCard, Visa.
Dining room.
Czech spoken.
Bus to Brandon, or plane to Burlington or Rutland, then bus to Brandon.
Innkeeper: A. P. Mitroff.

Churchill House Inn
RD 3
Brandon, Vermont 05733
Telephone (802) 247-3300

"Churchill House Inn is a wonderful old farmhouse near Brandon, Vermont, fifteen miles south of Middlebury. It is filled with warm hospitality and cozy, comfortable rooms furnished with country antiques. The winter day starts with a hearty breakfast served not too early, then down to the ski shop where you are quickly outfitted for cross-country skiing on miles of beautiful trails passing by quiet brooks or frozen lakes. Late afternoons and early evenings can be spent sipping a glass of wine by the Victorian stove while reading or chatting with an enthusiastic group of skiers—doctors, teachers, lawyers, musicians—take your pick. Each candlelit dinner, served family style, around an old oaken oval table, is memorable. What a place for a true winter holiday! And they say spring and summer are even more wonderful for hiking and fishing in those Robert Frost Vermont woods."   —*Mr. and Mrs. W. Reid Thompson*

"The inn is our winter retreat. We escape from New York City— usually in late January because that's when ski touring is best—and drive north to where the snow is still clean and the air is cold, dry, and smelling of pine. The inn borders on state forest land, and this is part of what makes it special; Churchill's guests can fall out the back door, hitch up their skis, and be off into the woods. Ski touring, or cross-country skiing for the uninitiated, involves trudging through the forest on skinny skis for miles and miles, returning to the inn exhausted and hungry.

"The Churchill House Inn is an old farmhouse that has been renovated—but not too much. Necessities, such as hot water (for aching muscles) and steam heat (for sleeping comfortably through the night), are abundant, but the atmosphere remains. In the den, logs are ablaze much of the afternoon and evening, until the last skier is tucked away."   —*Suzanne and Mark Lamberg*

Open December 15 to April 1, May 15 to October 25.
8 rooms, 7 with private bath.
Rates $48–$60, MAP.
Credit cards: MasterCard, Visa.
Nearest airports: Burlington and Rutland.
Innkeepers: Roy and Lois Jackson.

_____*Chester*

Chester Inn
Main Street
Chester, Vermont 05143
Telephone (802) 875-2444

"The New England breakfast is included with your room. A very special lady comes in early every morning to bake the many kinds of good muffins. Innkeeper Tom Guido is the fine chef, Betsy Guido the hostess in the dining room. For early risers, the cleaning ladies will get a cup of coffee for the guy who can't wait till the dining room opens. The Guidos have two darling children and young guests are welcome; baby-sitters are available.

"Chester is an interesting, quiet village. There is the Flamstead Store, where silk-screened fabric, hats, skirts, totes, and other bags are specialties. The old stone houses on the edge of the village are of historic interest. You can get to lots of other interesting places from Chester; we enjoy golf at the Windham Country Club. There are interesting shops, several churches, and the market store. Ski areas, flea markets, shopping centers, mills, and a cheese factory are all nearby. Each day at 5 P.M. the Baptist church chimes play a hymn. At twilight, a short walk away, you can spot a deer."

—*Margaret and Ervin K. Wax*

Open all year, except for April and first two weeks in November.
31 rooms, all with private bath.
Rates $55–$65 double occupancy, including breakfast.
Credit cards: MasterCard, Visa.
Vermont Transit buses stop next door.
Innkeepers: Tom and Betsy Guido.

_____*Craftsbury Common*

The Inn on the Common
Main Street
Craftsbury Common, Vermont 05827
Telephone (802) 586-9619

"In a small town atop one of Vermont's green hills, the inn overlooks a patchwork of well-kept farmlands, cow barns, country roads, and woodlands, all interspersed with clearwater streams and ponds, and with Mount Mansfield in the background. The building is set back of lovely old maples and looks very much like the substantial white clapboard homestead it was before Michael and Penny Schmitt converted it to an inn a few years ago. In doing so they succeeded to a remarkable degree in preserving an informal country home atmosphere—with family portraits on the walls and overflowing bookcases—while at the same time weaving in an unusual assortment of amenities. Dinner in the evening—at which superior dishes are served with delicately flavored wines, family style, at a pair of tables set with silver and candles—is not only delicious, but also socially refreshing and stimulating. The same mixture of simple country atmosphere with the best attributes of modern urban American life is reflected in the individualized bedrooms. There are a flower garden, tennis court, and swimming pool in summer. In winter a large supply of cross-country ski equipment is available for guests' use." —*Nathan B. Talbot*

Open all year.
16 rooms, 12 with private bath.
Rates $50–$80 per person, including full breakfast and dinner with
    wine.
Credit cards: MasterCard, Visa.
Dining room and bar.
By air to Montpelier or Burlington; Amtrak trains to Montpelier.
Innkeepers: Penny and Michael Schmitt.

_____*Cuttingsville*

Shrewsbury Inn
Route 103
Cuttingsville, Vermont 05738
Telephone (802) 492-3355

"The inn, a 130-year-old building, sits by the side of the road just a short distance from the post office and 'downtown' Cuttingsville. The all-white building has a full porch, enclosed to keep out the Vermont winter. We were greeted at the door by innkeeper Lois Butler and her son and daughter.

"The restaurant is the only one in town. Although the inn serves only a few diners, there were four items on the menu. We sampled two, and both were excellent. While we were there a single guest arrived, and Lois invited him to eat with her family rather than sit alone at his own table. The warmth of the family is tops. (A friendly cat spent the night in our room.)

"When you consider that the building had been very run down when it was bought several years ago, the effect that has been achieved in creating turn-of-the-century atmosphere is absolutely remarkable." —*Leonard Kessler*

"A lovely, small, and friendly inn with large, beautifully decorated bedrooms. Downstairs is a very comfortable sitting room with fireplace, chessboards, and a good selection of books and magazines. There is a small bar (papered with wine labels) and a dining room decorated with medieval brass rubbings and a collection of china and glassware. Gil Dillion is the chef, and breakfast and dinner are delicious.

"Cuttingsville is about ten miles south of Rutland, close to Killington, Pico Peak, and Okemo for downhill skiing and also near several cross-country ski areas. The Shrewsbury Inn is highly recommended as a place to relax after a day on the slopes."

—*Jane H. Bachner*

Open all year, except November and mid-April to mid-May.
5 rooms with shared baths, 1 suite with private bath.
Rates $30–$40 per person, including full breakfast and dinner.
Credit cards: MasterCard, Visa.
Dining room and bar.
4 miles from Rutland airport. Buses from Boston to Rutland.
Innkeepers: Don and Lois Butler, Kerry and Laurie Dillon.

Dorset

Barrows House
Box 98
Dorset, Vermont 05251
Telephone (802) 867-4455

"Barrows House, a typical Vermont inn, is in the center of a typical Vermont village that is worth the visit in itself. The rooms are most comfortable and very clean, situated in the inn itself and in several other buildings on the grounds. Innkeeper Charlie Schubert, who looks after the place, and his wife, Marilyn, who tends to the guests, are most hospitable and make every effort to see to your comfort. There is a large swimming pool and two excellent tennis courts."

—*Charles L. Newberry;*
also recommended by Neil and Karen Silverstein

Open all year, except from November 1–20.
29 rooms and suites, 27 with private bath.
Rates $55–$88 single, $110–$138 double, including breakfast and dinner.
German spoken.
By air to Albany, New York, airport, or by bus to Manchester.
Innkeepers: Charles and Marilyn Schubert.

The Little Lodge at Dorset
Route 30
Dorset, Vermont 05251
Telephone (802) 867-4040

"A delightful small lodge in a beautiful little village. No meals are served, but there are good eating places nearby. There are spacious grounds for walking and a pond for fishing. A spot for relaxing, indoors or out."   *—Mrs. J. F. Schoff*

Open all year, except a brief period in April and November.
5 rooms, 3 with private bath.
Rates $40–$50.
Credit cards: American Express, for deposits only.
Innkeepers: Allan and Nancy Norris.

_____*Grafton*

The Old Tavern at Grafton
Main Street
Grafton, Vermont 05146
Telephone (802) 843-2231

"The Old Tavern is run by the Windham Foundation and includes not only the inn—beautifully restored and filled with antiques—but also houses in the village that can be rented. The accommodations are perfection, the food good. Tennis and swimming are available in summer and skiing in the winter."   *—Tim Mulligan*

"We first visited the Old Tavern in the summer of 1961 on the very enthusiastic recommendation of friends at Martha's Vineyard. We have returned two or three times a year since. Each season has an appeal all its own, but perhaps the most beautiful of all is the fall foliage season. We have watched the restoration of the original tavern of 1801 to its present structure, and it has lost none of its original charm. Excellent meals are served in a setting of Early America. The town carries one back to the 1800s and establishes that slow and peaceful pace of life. A walk of a quarter mile in any direction will lead to a quiet country road or into the woods where you are certain there is not a town in miles."   *—Jean E. Cutting*

Open all year, except April and Christmas Day.
35 rooms, all with private bath, plus 5 houses with 18 rooms; one 2-bedroom suite.
Rates $45–$80. Special rates for houses: $175–$275 per night complete. Suite: $100.
No credit cards.
3 dining rooms; 2 bars.
German spoken.
Train and bus to Bellows Falls, 15 miles away.
Innkeeper: Lois Copping.

_____*Lower Waterford*

Rabbit Hill Inn
Lower Waterford, Vermont 05848
Telephone (802) 748-5168

"The Connecticut River flows placidly here between Vermont and New Hampshire. Right on the edge of the river valley, looking over the river toward the New Hampshire mountains known as the Presidential Range, is the village of Lower Waterford, called the 'white village' locally. Back in the 1800s someone purchased the village and painted all the houses white with green shutters. Though properties have changed hands over the years, the color scheme has become unwritten law. The focal point of the village is Rabbit Hill Inn (there is a Rabbit Hill behind the inn), a rambling 1830 Greek Revival structure whose front is dominated by four Doric columns that originally, as four huge New Hampshire pine trees, were hauled by a team of oxen across the frozen Connecticut River. Don't let the impressive front with its pillars and three levels of verandas intimidate you. Inside are large sun-filled rooms, fireplaces (in the bedrooms, too!), overstuffed chairs, soft beds, wide pine floors, two antique grandfather clocks and, of course, the staff.

"On our first visit, we felt guilty at not doing anything. But in a village of fewer than a dozen buildings, including the church, inn, and library (operated on the honor system: no librarian), what is wrong with just going for walks or sitting on the veranda watching the mountains change colors, and listening to the birds?"

—Dennis and Barbara Cavendish

"A pleasant room, good beds, restful view, and delicious food. The country-style ribs in teriyaki sauce were the best we've ever tasted. For breakfast, we had fresh strawberry pancakes.

"Best of all, one of the guests turned out to be an excellent pianist, and we sang as we haven't sung in years!"

—Michael and Mary Jane Durishin

Open early May to November 1, December 15 to early April.
20 rooms, all with private bath.
Rates $31–$70 double occupancy.
Credit cards: MasterCard, Visa.
Dining room and bar.
French spoken.
Vermont Transit bus to St. Johnsbury. Boston bus will stop at inn.
   Nearest airports: Montpelier and Burlington.
Innkeepers: Eric and Beryl Charlton.

_____*Ludlow*

Echo Lake Inn
Box 154
Ludlow, Vermont 05149
Telephone (802) 228-8602

"My wife and I enjoyed our recent overnight at Echo Lake Inn. Being able to stop with Mr. and Mrs. Mark Brown at their wonderful inn on our vacation trip to Vermont was a rare privilege. I was grateful for their kindness to us. I was a church organist and choirmaster for many years, and the lovely grand piano in the lobby said a lot to me."   —*Rev. Dr. N. Paul Francis Arline*

"What a wonderful way to find out I could live without TV and a newspaper and to be able to put my feet up and relax. The rooms were so comfortable and the food was delicious, but most important we got to meet new, nice people. I loved Echo Lake and their fireplaces at the end of September on a cool afternoon."
                                            —*Monica Dolan*

Open all year.
20 rooms and 5 family units, 4 with private bath.
Rates $15–$39, depending on room, season, and meal plan.
Credit cards: American Express, MasterCard, Visa.
2 dining rooms; bar.
Innkeepers: Mark H. and Jo Brown.

_____*Manchester Village*

The 1811 House
On the Green
Manchester Village, Vermont 05254
Telephone (802) 362-1811

The 1811 House has been in and out of innkeeping since 1774. Its name comes from the date the Munson family raised the roof for major redecorating. The inn is set on five and a half acres of formal gardens that were planted by Mary Lincoln Isham (the granddaughter of Abraham Lincoln), who owned the house for thirty-three years and used it as a private residence. In 1939 the house became an inn again. It now has a library, formal parlor, dining room, small pub, and twelve fireplaces, three of them in guest rooms.

"Jack and Mary Hirst, the new innkeepers, are restoring the 1811 House to its original style, which primarily involves removing the

Victorian embellishment acquired over this century. We stayed in the spacious Martha room (to be renamed), beautifully decorated with four-poster bed and fireplace overlooking the quiet square of Manchester Village. Breakfast is served each morning from 8 to 9 o'clock (request Jack's eggs Benedict, the sauce is superb). They have a "help yourself—keep your own tab" policy at the bar, which is more like a taproom with seating around a fireplace and equestrian prints on the walls. Jack tallies up the tabs at the end of your stay.

"While we were there, my husband sprained his back playing golf, and both Jack and Mary couldn't have been more concerned for his welfare. They rousted the neighborhood chiropractor out on Sunday, made the prescribed ice pack, and offered to have dinner catered in!"
—*Barbara Van Doren*

Open all year.
10 rooms, all with private bath.
Rates $60–$90, including breakfast. No children under 12.
No credit cards.
Bar.
Bus service to Manchester; air service to Albany, New York, or Hartford, Connecticut. Private planes can land at Bennington or Rutland.
Innkeepers: Jack and Mary Hirst.

The Reluctant Panther
Manchester Village, Vermont 05254
Telephone (802) 362-2568

"Our hosts at the Reluctant Panther were warm and congenial and our dinner there that evening was excellent, but we were very disappointed with our room. Shag carpeting covered our floor and ran up to the ceiling. It was cheap-looking."
—*Brent Pallas*

Open Memorial Day to October 31, December 11 to April 15.
7 rooms, all with private bath.
Rates $27–$45.
Credit card: American Express.
Vermont Transit buses to Manchester.
Innkeepers: Ed and Loretta Friihauf.

Turn to the back of this book for pages inviting *your* comments.

_____*Mendon*

Red Clover Inn at Woodward Farm
Woodward Road
Mendon, Vermont 05701
Telephone (802) 775-2290

"If you are looking for a quiet place to get away or a base from which to hike or ski, we recommend the Red Clover Inn. It is a charming former country estate sitting high in the hills just east of Rutland, in the shadow of Pico Peak. We discovered the inn by chance and were taken with the quiet and the mountains.

"The Red Clover Inn is a family affair, owned and operated by Dennis and Bonnie Tallagnon. Dennis is the chef and Bonnie is the hostess. The menu includes honey bran bread, gourmet entrées, homemade soups, and desserts like fresh rhubarb crisp. Breakfast means homemade jam and French toast of homemade bread.

"In the lounge or dining room you are greeted with great warmth by Bonnie and Dennis, who are instantly friends. Their sons assist in the dining room, where the waitresses make you feel at home. You can stay in the inn or in a nearby building, the Plum Tree House, which has been converted to large rooms with private baths and private entrances. The inn is near the shops of Woodstock and Rutland. Altogether a great place to get away from the job and the kids, but still in easy reach of shopping and entertainment."

—*Bruce and Barbara Conroe*

Open mid-June to mid-October, Thanksgiving to Easter.
14 rooms, 8 with private bath; 2-room suite.
Rates $35–$40 per person, double occupancy, including breakfast and dinner.
Credit cards: American Express, Carte Blanche, Diners Club, MasterCard, Visa.
Restaurant and bar.
French and German spoken.
Buses or planes to Rutland; guests met.
Innkeepers: Bonnie and Dennis Tallagnon.

_____*Newfane*

The Four Columns Inn
230 West Street
Newfane, Vermont 05345
Telephone (802) 365-7713

"After driving through the beautiful green and white village of Newfane, you reach the lovely Four Columns Inn and park in the spacious driveway. We have entered the inn at mealtimes, with the dining room filled, and not heard a sound. Indeed 'our' room is directly over the dining room and we have never been able to tell if it was crowded or empty below. From the windows of our room, we look out on the magnificent Windham County Courthouse, the Grange building, and a lovely, spired church, surrounding a tree-lined village green. The inn's rooms are large and airy, and the decorations are mostly Early American with some lovely prints. The rooms are spotless; the bathrooms sparkle."

—*Marian and John Herman*

Open end of May through October, and all Tuesdays.
10 rooms, all with private bath; one suite; one 2-room cottage.
Rates $55–$75, including continental breakfast.
Credit cards: MasterCard, Visa.
Restaurant and bar.
French spoken.
Within 10 miles of bus.
Innkeepers: Sandra and Jacques Ailembert.

Old Newfane Inn
On the Common (Box 101)
Newfane, Vermont 05345
Telephone (802) 365-4427

"The food is superlative, the service impeccable, yet the inn remains entirely 'country' in feeling despite a largely French (or at least continental) menu. The proprietors, Mr. and Mrs. Eric Weindl, are European. The service in the dining room was in the hands of American women who knew precisely what they were doing and did it very well. Our room (number 23) was comfortable, immaculate, and quiet. I must say, however, that a few guests whose rooms were not at the back of the house found that some kitchen and dining room noise filtered upward. Our only ungratified wish was for an open fire in the spacious, attractive guest-sitting room during the beautiful but chilly October weather of our visit.

"Newfane itself is a tiny, attractive village where there is, thank God, nothing whatever to do. We brought a bag of books, hearty appetites, and warm sweaters, and spent a blissful week. If fanfare and hoopla are your goals, stay out of Newfane and this charming

inn. If peace, quiet, exquisite landscape, and the best food imagin-
able give you pleasure, go there."   —*Dr. and Mrs. Francis Silver*

Open May to late October, December to March.
10 rooms, 9 with private bath.
Rates $65–$85.
No credit cards.
Dining room.
French and German spoken.
Greyhound buses and Amtrak trains to Brattleboro, where taxi ser-
   vice is available.
Innkeepers: Eric and Gundy Weindl.

_____*Proctorsville*

Golden Stage Inn
Depot Street (P.O. Box 218)
Proctorsville, Vermont 05153
Telephone (802) 226-7744

"What can you say about an inn that has a fascinating 200-year
history (which includes being a stop on the 'Underground Railroad'), is located in a quiet, picturesque setting, serves outstanding
food, and is run by a pair of innkeepers who are exceedingly entertaining? Not nearly enough.

   "Guests can enjoy the Golden Stage without ever leaving for any
of the many nearby activities. The bedrooms are pleasantly decorated, and have the firmest, most comfortable mattresses I have ever
slept on. The two-level porches provide fresh air and captivating
views of the nearby mountains. The library offers peaceful reading.
The living room is for inspired conversation with newly made
friends. It was here that I found myself in what must have looked
like a scene by Norman Rockwell."   —*Vincent J. Kish*

Open all year.
10 rooms, 2 with private bath.
Rates: Summer—$58 per room, including breakfast; other seasons
   —$45–$48 per person, including breakfast and dinner.
Credit cards: American Express, MasterCard, Visa.
Restaurant.
Vermont Transit bus from New York or Boston will stop at inn on
   signal. Guests met at Amtrak train in Bellows Falls with advance
   notice; nominal charge. Guests met for no charge at Springfield
   airport (service from Boston by Precision Airlines).
Innkeepers: Tim and Shannon Datig.

_____ *Saxtons River*

Saxtons River Inn
Main Street
Saxtons River, Vermont 05154
Telephone (802) 869-2110

"The inn sits squarely in the center of a small town lying in the shallow valley west of Bellows Falls on the road to Grafton. The town is relatively secluded, architecturally charming, and virtually unspoiled. Being happily at some remove from the nearest ski area, the town has avoided the excesses of American Tyrolean-style architecture and associated commercial banalities that invariably plague such resorts. Rockingham, a twenty-minute drive to the north, boasts a magnificent eighteenth-century meetinghouse that stands in solitary grandeur on a hilltop overlooking a sloping, grassy cemetery, some of whose slate gravestones bear wondrous primitive designs.

"The inn was renovated in 1973 by the Campbell family. They wisely chose to retain the character of the building. Each bedroom is decorated in individual style with taste and panache and a rare attention to detail. A house across the street has additional bedrooms. The bar and dining room are filled with plants and morning sunlight. The food is interesting without being pretentious. The menu is comfortingly brief, though frequently changed, and is accompanied by a modest wine list. Special mention should be made of the homemade soups and the marvelous gateaux."

—*David Arnold*

Open April 1 through New Year's weekend.
21 rooms, 11 with private bath.
Rates $27.50–$55 double, including continental breakfast.
No credit cards.
Dining room and bar.
Some French spoken.
Amtrak trains, Greyhound and Vermont Transit buses to Bellows Falls, 5 miles away. Air service to Dillant Hopkins Airport in Keene, New Hampshire, 30 minutes away.
Innkeeper: Averill Campbell Larsen.

Do you know a hotel in your state that we have overlooked? Write *now.*

South Londonderry

Londonderry Inn
Route 100 (Box 301 LH)
South Londonderry, Vermont 05155
Telephone (802) 824-5226

"On a hillside overlooking the West River and the town of South Londonderry is the magnificent Londonderry Inn. The inn has a large, clean spring-fed pool, horseback riding, and fishing nearby. It is close to major ski slopes and many small towns to interest history and antique buffs. The spacious dining room is tastefully furnished and serves good food. A fine wine list and delicious desserts are available. We had lunch on the flagstone patio with a breathtaking view of Magic Mountain. Once a month in summer there is a seafood cookout with lobsters, clams, and such. Each Sunday there is a buffet brunch in the dining room."

—*James Beattie*

Open all year, except April and November.
25 rooms, 20 with private bath.
Rates $18–$54.50 single, $22–$54.50 double, depending on season and room, all including buffet breakfast.
No credit cards.
Dining room and bar.
Innkeepers: Jim and Jean Cavanagh.

South Woodstock

The Kedron Valley Inn and Stables
Route 106 (Box 145)
South Woodstock, Vermont 05071
Telephone (802) 457-1473

"The oldest part of this country inn was built in 1822. It has been added to and modernized through the years. There are six fireplaces, a Franklin stove, two parlor stoves—they all work—plus hidden modern features that add to the comfort. Paul and Barbara Kendall are the owners and innkeepers, and they pay attention to making their guests comfortable. They have a wonderful chef, who uses real whipped cream in large quantities. Fine fish comes in from Boston.

"The inn is five miles from a good golf course. There are stables with thirty horses, and good riding trails all around. The inn has a pond for swimming and a nice porch with rocking chairs. There are winter sleighrides—and a real country store across the street. Pleasant walking trails wind through the countryside. The little village of South Woodstock has old Vermont houses and is full of charm."

—*H. Thomas Hallowell, Jr.*

"Traveling by myself, I was happiest in inns where guests seemed to mingle. This was not so true of the Kedron Valley Inn and Stables. It was larger than the other inns I chose and, while it was comfortable and pleasant, I felt more alone. Also, I'm not a smorgasbord fan, and wasn't that impressed with the meals. (Breakfast was better.) But I do remember how the host took time out to visit with me on the front veranda, where we discussed inns and travel. I liked my room, with its cozy location in the main house."

—*Camilla Tanner*

"I felt Camilla Tanner's opinion didn't do the Kedron Valley Inn justice. We chose it over the Woodstock Inn, which we thought was overpriced and too commercial. At Kedron Valley, we were given a choice of rooms, and decided on the 'honeymoon' room, which was spacious and beautifully appointed, with a lovely four-poster bed. Our dining experience was very good. My husband enjoyed the trail ride he took. We would return for another stay."

—*Valerie Thorner*

Open all year, except one month in spring.
31 rooms, all with private bath.
Rates $28–$75.
Credit cards: MasterCard, Visa.
Dining room and tavern.
Innkeepers: The Kendalls.

Stowe

Andersen Lodge
Route 108 (Box 1450)
Stowe, Vermont 05672
Telephone (802) 253-7336

"Andersen Lodge on the mountain road in Stowe was purchased from the Andersens some years ago by a charming Tyrolean couple, Trude and Dietmar Heiss. The profits from the past have enabled the couple to expand the place and add a heated swimming pool. Rooms are cozy and *gemütlich,* but it is the food that is the inn's chief attraction. While Trude tends to the business of booking, running, and cleaning the inn, Dietmar practices his New York-polished skills as a four-star chef. Aside from the Topnotch up the mountain road, there are few restaurants in the area to match Dietmar's accomplishments. Schnitzels and roasts are served piping hot, graced with exquisite sauces; pastries and breads are home-baked."

—Michael W. Glueck

"A delightful place. Food is outstanding."

—Harold and Ruth Maxton

Open June to October, December to April.
17 rooms, 16 with private bath.
Rates $28–$40, MAP.
Credit cards: American Express, MasterCard, Visa.
Restaurant.
French and German spoken.
Guests met at Stowe bus station or Amtrak station in Waterbury.
Airport at Burlington, 45 minutes away.
Innkeepers: Dietmar and Trude Heiss.

_____*Stratton Mountain*

Birkenhaus
Stratton Mountain, Vermont 05155
Telephone (802) 297-2000

"Austrian atmosphere, Austrian cuisine, and personal attention unexcelled anywhere. Entertainment by the Stratton Mountain Boys is superb, and all in all one of the best motels in the east. The John Newcomb Tennis School, the golf course, and all of the amenities that Stratton Mountain has to offer are delightful."

—Mary and Dave Brown

Open December to mid-April, June to October.
20 rooms, 3 chalet apartments, all with private bath.
Rates $35–$45, including breakfast; $55–$75 per person, double occupancy, MAP.
Credit cards: American Express, MasterCard, Visa.
Restaurant.
French and German spoken.
Innkeepers: Emo and Annedore Henrich.

All inkeepers appreciate reservations in advance; some require them.

_____ *Warren*

The Sugarbush Inn
Warren, Vermont 05674
Telephone (802) 583-2301

"During a delicious home-style late dinner in the main dining room of the Sugarbush Inn, my husband and I agreed that if we were to own an inn, we'd want it to be just like the Sugarbush. There just doesn't seem to be a thing wrong with this slightly rambling, white clapboard structure situated both high and deep in Vermont's spectacular Green Mountains. In the winter this is prime ski country and the inn is totally prepared to handle cold, tired snowfolk. There are fireplaces sizzling and popping here and there to warm up around and plenty of windows from which to observe the goings-on if one is an armchair skier. In the summer, the inn has a truly picturesque outdoor pool where lunch and drinks are served every day, and an indoor heated pool (all glass-enclosed so you don't lose sight of those incredible mountains) to soothe any aching muscles that might be the result of the use of the inn's sixteen perfectly maintained tennis courts. There is an outdoor garden, surrounded by tall hedges, for lunching, afternoon drinks, or just relaxing and reading. The main dining room includes an enclosed plant-filled sun porch off the main sitting room.

"Downstairs is a less formal but equally charming restaurant, the Onion Patch, which delights everybody with its open hearth and busy staff preparing delicious steaks and burgers for all to see and smell. Upstairs is a moderate-size sitting area–bar with the inn's only television set, as well as a piano. There is a library with easy chairs, books, backgammon tables, and picture windows for more mountain viewing. The inn is immaculately clean and although it is quite large, you have the feeling of being in a cozy, all-familiar house."

—*Rikki Stapleton*

Open all year.
47 rooms, 50 condominium units, all with private bath.
Rates $70–$95 rooms, $98–$240 condominiums.
Credit cards: American Express, MasterCard, Visa.
Dining room.
Manager: Jane Moynihan.

Rates quoted were the latest available. But they may not reflect unexpected increases or local and state taxes. Be sure to verify when you book.

_____ *West Dover*

The Inn at Sawmill Farm
Crosstown Road (Route 100, Mt. Snow Valley)
West Dover, Vermont 05356
Telephone (802) 464-8131

"We discovered the inn by asking a famous French chef where he went on his days off. We were not disappointed. Sawmill Farm is the creation of a multitalented family. In a previous life innkeeper Rod Williams was an architect—he still keeps his hand in—and his wife, Ione, was an interior decorator. They took an old farmhouse and its outbuildings and created a hostelry of unique character. Each of the rooms is different. A tremendous old brick fireplace dominates a large sitting room, magnificent in its proportions yet rustic in its appointments. A lordly chime clock, such as once dominated the old Wanamaker's in New York, adds a rich sonorous note to the tranquillity. We have left till last Brill Williams, son of Ione and Rod, who has made of the kitchen a bastion of dedicated gastronomy. He, no doubt, learned a great deal from his mother, a fine cook in her own right, but he has gone on in his professional training to become an accomplished *chef de cuisine.*"   —*Dr. Bernard Berkowitz*

"If you never again wish to see plastic 'glasses,' paper tapes across a topless john, a cardboard cone advertising the location of the coffee shop, a foamex ice bucket, or those infuriating clothes hangers that fight back—and win—then Sawmill is for you. Step instead into a world of scented candles, brick fireplaces, beautiful antiques, and beds that are sybaritic. Bathroom mirrors are framed in gold, walls are done in contemporary florals. The springhouse suite has a kitchen and dressing room done in handsome print. No phones, no ice machine, no noise. In the spring peepers sing from the pond, in winter the dry crunch of powder snow—these are the only sounds that will assault your ears, other than the Sunday bells that toll from the church across the hill.

"If luxury is simply the removal of the mundane and ordinary, then this inn is its quintessence. Serenity with service is the keynote at Sawmill. Food is superbly and individually prepared and served in a candlelit setting of plants, equally attractive in winter and summer. Tea with cookies is served by the living room fire in winter, a welcome treat at the end of a day of skiing, walking, or just enjoying the beauty of this idyllic setting. The inn's popularity has grown by leaps and bounds, necessitating planning ahead to be accommodated—but it's worth the wait!"   —*Miriam H. Finucane*

Open all year.
12 rooms, 10 fireplace cottages, all with private bath.
Rates $130–$170 double, MAP.
No credit cards.
Restaurant and bar.
French and Spanish spoken.
Innkeeper: Rodney C. Williams.

Snow Den Inn
Route 100 (Box 615)
West Dover, Vermont 05356
Telephone (802) 464-9355

"Situated on gently curving Route 100, in sight of Haystack and Snow mountains, the exterior of Snow Den Inn is typically New England. Inside, however, is where the excellence of this establishment comes to the fore. A cozy, warm, and comfortable family room, the dining room a delight, and the bedrooms each decorated in distinctive style. Innkeepers Jean and Milt Cummings are really friendly and very knowledgeable of the surrounding area, so are a big help to their guests for whatever activity is desired. Milt's meals are the highlight and would hold their own anywhere. Wonderful place."
—*J. D. Garrison*

"Our accommodations were absolutely charming. Each room was decorated with matching wallpaper, drapes, and upholstery. We spent five days there and had a chance to enjoy their whole menu. The food and hospitality were superb."
—*Kaye Fuller*

Open all year.
9 rooms, 7 with private bath.
Rates $25–$35 per person.
Credit cards: MasterCard, Visa.
Dining room.
Innkeepers: Milt and Jean Cummings.

Weston

The Inn at Weston
Route 100 (Box 56 AW)
Weston, Vermont 05161
Telephone (802) 824-5804

"There are so many things that make this inn a special place. Two of the most important ones are the innkeepers, Stu and Sue Douglas. Another is the fantastic food. Stu prepares a breakfast that is so hearty one should really skip lunch. The pancakes are especially delicious, a house recipe served with Vermont maple syrup. Sue is in charge of dinners. Her specialties are soups and salads; in summer all the salads are made of vegetables fresh from the garden. The breads and desserts are all homemade. Vegetarian dishes are available on request.

"The area is a haven for people like us who feel the need to flee the city periodically to recharge their batteries. There are many ski areas for both cross-country and downhill enthusiasts. During the spring, summer, and fall there are hiking, fishing, canoeing, and biking. The quiet country roads are great for joggers, too."
—*Pamela Myers and Ruth Dickey*

"The Inn at Weston is a very cozy, warm, and friendly place. The food, especially the breakfast, is delicious. The town of Weston and its outskirts offer a wonderful and pretty vacation spot, with great bicycling, beautiful views, lovely shops. We are planning to return soon since we enjoyed our first visit so much."
—*Carol Cherhoniak*

Open mid-May to November 1, December 15 to April 15.
13 rooms, 7 with private bath.
Rates $36–$46 per person, including breakfast and dinner.
No credit cards.
Restaurant and bar.
French spoken.
Bus service to Manchester, within half-hour drive.
Innkeepers: Stuart and Sue Douglas.

_____ *Wilmington*

Nutmeg Inn
Route 9 (Box 818)
Wilmington, Vermont 05363
Telephone (802) 464-3351

"Coddled by the foothills of the Green Mountains, a stone's throw from the shopper's delight of Wilmington, the inn is centrally located for the summer Marlboro Music Festival, for winter skiing, and for the fall foliage season. No place in the world can compare with southern Vermont for foliage, and perhaps no place is more spectacular in the fall. Add the Bach Festival at Marlboro every

Columbus Day weekend, and you have an unbeatable combination.

"The area is also a skier's fantasy fulfilled, with six ski areas in easy reach. Cross-country skiing has been developed; there are a variety of very good and highly scenic cross-country trails originating from very close to the inn itself. Wilmington is chock-full of wonderful craft shops, many of which feature first-class New England textiles, ceramics, woodworking, and more esoteric originals.

"The Nutmeg Inn is suffused with the gentle warmth of its proprietors, Joan and Rich Combes, a transplanted Long Island couple who thrive on and share the tranquillity of southern Vermont. The rooms are modest, comfortable, and immaculately kept. The service is always willing, friendly, and efficient but never intrusive. The atmosphere is very informal and, most pleasant to us, homelike, with none of the pretentiousness of some of the older inns. That includes the reasonable prices. The Combes know the area intimately and are marvelous help in setting up a day's activities. During the off-season, the Combes serve only breakfast, but a full and satisfying one; the area abounds in truly fine restaurants."

—*Alison and Jerome Rogoff*

"A very comfortable inn and an enjoyable visit."

—*Gayle Bolinger; also recommended by Karen and Neil Silverstein*

Open Memorial Day to end of October, December 26 to mid-April.
9 rooms, 4 with private bath.
Rates $42–$58 double, including breakfast, in summer and fall;
$36–$48 per person, with breakfast and dinner, in winter.
No credit cards.
Nearest airports: Keene, New Hampshire, and Albany, New York.
Bus service to Wilmington. Train to Brattleboro or Albany, New York.
Innkeepers: Joan and Richard Combes.

Where are the good little hotels in Boston? Philadelphia? Omaha? Dallas? If you have found one, don't keep it a secret. Write *now*.

Part Two

Mid-Atlantic

Delaware

Rehoboth Beach

Delaware, next to smallest of the fifty states (only Rhode Island is smaller), is nonetheless one of the richest in history. Its old towns and cities go back well into the seventeenth century. Fought over by the Swedes, Dutch, and English, Delaware managed to establish its political independence long before the Revolution; after the war it was the first state to enter the new Union. Though much of Delaware, lying in the shadow of the Philadelphia metropolitan area and astride the busy northeast corridor connecting Washington to New York and Boston, is densely developed, a surprising amount of farmland and quiet seacoast remains. There are carefully maintained historical buildings in a number of colonial-period towns, among them New Castle, Lewes, Odessa, and Dover, the state's capital and the site of an excellent historical museum. Best known of the state's coastal resorts is Rehoboth Beach. The town, surrounded by sea, bay, and state parks, was once known for its quiet sophistication and attracted many summer visitors and residents from the Washington area. Over the last decade or so, Rehoboth Beach has grown rapidly; its year-round population of about 3,000 swells to 50,000 or 60,000 in the summer months. With the crowds have come motels, fast-food outlets, and shops. But it is still possible to get away from the worst of the new and be accommodated in the old manner here.

The Corner Cupboard
50 Park Avenue
Rehoboth Beach, Delaware 19971
Telephone (302) 227-8553

"On a beautiful spring day, driving through the residential area of Rehoboth Beach, I turned onto an unpaved sandy road with tall trees scattered down the center and found the Corner Cupboard nestled among the pines. The inn is only a block and a half from the beach, and within walking distance of most of Rehoboth's other attractions.

"The inn's front door leads right into the living room, with its rare and wonderful mixture of antiques and Orientals. The big brick fireplace always has a fire on a cool night, and innkeeper and guests gather there to talk. (In the summer, they meet on the brick patio.) The rooms I liked best were upstairs off the main hall, which had some antique pieces. Additional rooms next door and in the cottages across the patio were more simply furnished.

"Elizabeth Gundry Hooper, the innkeeper, is terrific. She bought the inn in 1974 from her aunt and uncle, who had turned this private home into an inn during the Depression so they could afford to have their friends stay at the beach in the summer. This helps to explain the delightful residential location: the Corner Cupboard was 'grandfathered in' to Rehoboth's first zoning code. Elizabeth, who worked at the inn as a teenager and later gained expertise through years in the hotel business, said that before the Bay Bridge was built, most people came to stay for a month. While this is no longer true, a friendly get-together atmosphere still prevails, with many people meeting from summer to summer.

"The dining room wasn't open while I was there, so I missed the clam bisque, crab imperial, or prime ribs by candlelight on the large screened porch. But I did get a delightful breakfast in the solarium-like breakfast/sitting room. In the summer, this room opens up and you can eat inside or on the patio under the trees, surrounded by Elizabeth's plants."
—*Catherine A. Crawford*

Open all year; restaurant open Memorial Day through September. 16 rooms, 9 with private bath.

Rates $75–$115 single, $95–$135 double, including dinner and breakfast in summer. Lower rates October to Memorial Day.
Credit cards: American Express, MasterCard, Visa.
Bus service to Rehoboth Beach from Washington, Baltimore, and Philadelphia. Nearest airport at Salisbury, Maryland, an hour away. Guests can be met by arrangement.
No bar.
Innkeeper: Elizabeth Gundry Hooper.

The Pleasant Inn
31 Olive Avenue
Rehoboth Beach, Delaware 19971
Telephone (302) 227-7311

"Pleasant Inn stands on a rise of ground looking down Olive Avenue to the broad Atlantic only a block away. Its wide, tree-shaded porches are a delight. This large Victorian four-square house with its distinctive widow's walk on top is venerable, but kept scrupulously up-to-date and comfortable within. The atmosphere is much like that of the old New England inns. Every guest becomes a friend."   —*The Rev. Richard S. Bailey*

Open all year.
10 rooms, 2 apartments, 1 carriage house, all with private bath.
Rates $50 double, $60 for 3 people, $70 for 4. Apartments and carriage house $100 a night, $350 a week, maximum 4 people; linens $25 a week.
No meals included, though there is a coffee bar for guests' use at breakfast. Inn is within walking distance of restaurants.
Credit cards: MasterCard, Visa.
Innkeeper: Peck Pleasanton.

_____ *Wilmington*

Hotel du Pont
Rodney Square
P.O. Box 991
Wilmington, Delaware 19899
Telephone (302) 656-8121 or toll-free (800) 323-7500

For all their age, Delaware's cities have regrettably failed to save the oldest hotels and taverns that could give a traveler a taste of the state's history. But Wilmington, Delaware's largest city, does have an early twentieth-century hotel of some distinction. The Hotel du Pont, built in 1913 and named for Delaware's leading family, reflects in its ornamentation both the opulent tastes and the optimism of the day: there are walls of marble and polished wood, examples of sgraffito etchings in plaster done by thirty Italian artists over a period of two years, and staircases, pilasters, and ceilings of interest at every turn. Apart from being a haven for business and professional people visiting Wilmington, the hotel is also an appropriate base from which to roam the Brandywine Valley, the setting for several museums—including the Winterthur collection of early American furniture and decorative arts, the Hagley Museum of industrial history and the Brandywine River Museum, born of Howard Pyle's School of Illustrators and now housing the works of three generations of Wyeths—and Longwood Gardens, with both indoor and outdoor displays of horticulture unrivaled in the Northeast; some would say anywhere.

"On the outside it looks like an office building, which it is in part. But inside the hotel, there is an air of spaciousness, elegance, and hospitality. The high-ceilinged lobby, recently restored, is designed as a place for people to meet. The dining areas range from the formal Green Room, with tall windows looking out on the city's central square, through the more intimate Christina Room, to the Brandywine Room, reminiscent of a gentlemen's club. Unique to the Hotel du Pont are the paintings in its public rooms, originals by N. C. Wyeth, his son Andrew, and his grandsons Jamie and A. N., as well as by other members of the Brandywine School. Most of the Wyeth family pieces are in the Christina Room, while the balance of the hotel's collection of several hundred works of art, most of them by distinguished area artists, is displayed throughout the building. The Gold Ballroom, richly decorated as its name implies, is the setting for special functions. Also in the building is the Playhouse, a 1,250-seat theater."   —*Dorothy Walker Greer*

Open all year.
280 rooms, all with private bath.
Rates $80–$125 single, $95–$125 double, $200–$285 suites.
Credit cards: American Express, Diners Club, MasterCard, Visa.
18 languages spoken, including French, German, Italian, Japanese, and Spanish.
Hotel runs shuttle service to Amtrak station for small fare. 30 minutes to Philadelphia International Airport by limousine.
General Manager: Ferdinand Weiland.

District of Columbia

Washington, D.C.

For all its cold glass and marble—or maybe because of it—Washington, D.C., is a city where there are a number of alternatives to the many in-town motor inns or chain hotels. There has been for some years a roster of classic hotels that belied the city's former reputation as a hick town among world capitals. Add to those an increasing number of smaller inns created from one or more of the city's rich supply of grand nineteenth- and early twentieth-century houses, and a sprinking of new establishments marked by the size, service, and elegance of another age of hotel-keeping.

The Canterbury Hotel
1733 N Street N.W.
Washington, D.C. 20036
Telephone (202) 393-3000

The block of N Street between Connecticut Avenue and 17th Street in northwest Washington has a handful of small hotels—as well as the Iron Gate restaurant, unexceptionally Middle Eastern but with a popular outdoor garden dining area for the warmer months. The location is good, within walking distance of Dupont Circle—the closest Washington gets to what used to be a Greenwich Village atmosphere—as well as the downtown office and shopping center, the White House, and other federal buildings. Among the places to stay, the newest is the Canterbury. It is undistinguished in external appearance—a converted apartment building—but guests seem to like it.

"Though this small hotel has been 'decored' to the eaves (it must hold the record for the number of linear feet of gilded picture framing), it's been done quite well, and the overall effect is pleasing. The small lobby, with its pink-marble fireplace, is welcoming, and the adjacent bar (one free drink per guest per evening) is ideal for a civilized rendezvous. Manager Lanny Lewis has inspired her staff, and the service is just right. She has each staff member and his or her family sample a dinner in the cozy, attractive Chaucer Room— so they can see how the service and food seem to the clientele. Maybe that's why both are so good. (She should give them breakfast too; the pastry tends to be cold and doughy.) The Canterbury will disappoint no one and charm many."   —*Tom Congdon*

"This small hotel is in a gorgeous neighborhood. It has an excellent restaurant, Chaucer's, in the basement."   —*Judith A. Barr;*
                              also recommended by Jeanne Jacores.

Open all year.
99 suites, all with private bath.
Rates $118–$160, including continental breakfast. Special rates for
   weekends and long stays.
Credit cards: American Express, Carte Blanche, Diners Club, MasterCard, Visa.
French, Hindi, and Spanish spoken.
2 blocks from Dupont Circle Metro station.
General Manager: Lanny Lewis.

The Jefferson Hotel
1200 16th Street N.W.
Washington, D.C. 20036
Telephone (202) 347-4707

The Jefferson may be the perfect city hotel. It is small. It is quiet. And it is located downtown—or what passes for "downtown" in Washington. The service may sometimes come perilously close to pretentious; and the kitchen and dining room staff get thrown off by anything approaching a full house. But the setting always seems to compensate. There is perhaps no more civilized place than one of the Jefferon's small dining rooms for a modest-scale version of the ubiquitous Washington breakfast. The hotel's motto: ". . . delightfully anachronistic."

"It was nice staying in a hotel that had nothing synthetic about it, but felt very human."   —*Laura Reinking*

Open all year.
104 rooms, 30 suites, 5-bedroom Presidential apartments, all with
   private bath.
Rates $110–$135 single, $125–$145 double, $175–$800 suites.
Credit cards: American Express, Diners Club, MasterCard, Visa.
Many foreign languages spoken.
Manager: Paul J. Limbert.

The Kalorama Guest House
1854 Mintwood Place
Washington, D.C. 20009
Telephone (202) 667-6369

"Except for its number and a small plaque, the Kalorama is just another town house on the quiet streets of the handsome Kalorama neighborhood. There is no doorman, no reception desk, and no bellhops—all arrangements should be made in advance. But do not let the absence of staff lead one to believe there is an absence of service. Somehow, between being a drama major and a part-time waiter, innkeeper Jim Mench manages to keep the house spotless, well stocked and with a continental breakfast ready in the morning. If the maps and brochures stacked in the foyer are not information enough to get the visitor oriented, Jim will also help guests find their way.

"Though it took nine months to restore the house, overcoming the toll that several years of neglect had taken on the rooms, the interior gives the impression that a dedicated innkeeper has been maintaining the house in immaculate condition for half a century. The atmosphere is placid and a little intriguing, somewhat like the old British hotels that appear in Agatha Christie mysteries. The woodwork is slightly worn, the floors roll, and the stairs creak. In the halls, bathrooms, and guest rooms there are plants and fragrant bouquets in every corner. The bedroom dressers have fragrant flower petals tucked at the back of the drawers.

"This guesthouse is not for the demanding visitor who needs constant attention for numerous small chores. I enjoyed it as much for the tranquillity as for the privacy and freedom. The front door is always locked; guests get keys. The house, on a safe and quiet street, is near two business areas with enough restaurants and stores to meet anyone's tastes. Buses are nearby on Connecticut Avenue, Calvert or Columbia Road. For the fastest and easiest trip to other parts of town, the Metro stop at Woodley Road is the best bet."

—*Jonathan Crossette*

Open all year.
6 rooms, all with sinks, sharing baths.
Rates $30–$35 single, $35–$40 double, including continental breakfast.
Credit cards: American Express, MasterCard, Visa.
Innkeeper: James Mench.

The Ritz-Carlton Washington, D.C.
2100 Massachusetts Avenue N.W.
Washington, D.C. 20008
Telephone (202) 293-2100

Those who know Washington will remember this as the Fairfax Hotel. It changed its name late in 1982. The hotel's Jockey Club is a fashionable—and very expensive—place to eat.

"A plush, well-run, formerly very private hotel, which is now one of the most luxurious hostelries we have. Don't miss the hunt paintings which surround one at lunch or dinner in the Jockey Club."

—*George Herzog*

Open all year.
163 rooms, 18 suites, all with private bath.
Rates $110–$165 single, $130–$185 double, $275–$550 suites.
Credit cards: American Express, Carte Blanche, Diners Club, MasterCard, Visa.
French, German, and Spanish spoken.
General Manager: Paul E. Seligson.

The Tabard Inn
1739 N Street N.W.
Washington, D.C. 20036
Telephone (202) 785-1277

In letters to this book over the last five years, the Tabard has never ceased to be a subject of controversy. There are complaints about peeling paint and slapdash housecleaning, about scatty service in the dining room and occasionally about cold and/or overpriced food. After four or five visits there, a traveler comes to realize that the rooms are wildly different from one another in size and furnishings. But for some reason, those of us who know it go back again and again for the Tabard's special atmosphere. Its staff is young and friendly—a veritable United Nations of faces—and its dinner guests an unusual blend of establishment and anti-establishment Washington. The Tabard has an inviting lounge with overstuffed furniture and a blazing fire whenever there is half an excuse for one, and a pleasant dining area made even more attractive by colorful Haitian art. The kitchen can be a little experimental, but it can send out exquisite concoctions; and all the food is fresh.

"The inn is a nineteenth-century town house, or rather three of them side by side. The rooms are furnished with comfortable hand-me-downs (one of them even has a piano!) and you get the feeling that if a piece of furniture breaks it would be unthinkable to replace it with anything new. The bookshelves in the rooms are furnished with collections of books and magazines left behind by previous guests. The sunny dining room overlooks a garden, where overnight guests are served what they call a continental breakfast, but it can be in reality an American breakfast, with eggs and fruit added to the traditional croissant. The Tabard has the air of a country inn, yet it's a short walk from the White House, not far from the Metro, and is surrounded by Hiltons and Holiday Inns."

—*Bill Harris*

Open all year.
40 rooms, 26 with private bath; 1 penthouse with kitchen and sundeck.
Rates $35–$75 single, $50–$100 double, including continental breakfast.
Credit cards: MasterCard, Visa.
Several foreign languages spoken.
Innkeepers: Fritzi and Edward Cohen.

Maryland

Annapolis

Gibson's Lodgings
110 Prince George Street
Annapolis, Maryland 21401
Telephone (301) 268-5555
Guest phone (301) 268-2523

Gibson's Lodgings combines two homes—one eighteenth and one nineteenth century. The properties, in what was once the notorious Hell's Point district of Annapolis, trace their history to an even earlier time: part of the area was assigned in 1684 to the First Naval Officer of the Port of Annapolis. Ask the present owners to tell you about the houses' wildly varied histories: both rose garden and junkyard have flourished here.

"This was really a find; we were just a half-block from the dock. We were pleased with our large room, although we did have to share a bath. All the rooms were filled with wonderful old furniture, and hundreds of pictures hung on the walls throughout. There was a very nice breakfast in the dining room." —_Ann M. McSwain_

Open all year.
14 rooms, 7 baths.
Rates $38 single, $42 double, including continental breakfast.
No credit cards.
In the Annapolis Historic District, 2 blocks from the United States
    Naval Academy.
Limousine available from Baltimore-Washington International Air-
    port.
Innkeeper: R. Cary Gibson.

Maryland Inn
Church Circle
Annapolis, Maryland 21401
Telephone (301) 263-2641

"This is a fine old inn, with ivy growing on the walls, large rooms,
and a wonderful staff. We stayed in Room 400, and our beds were
turned down in the evening and mints left on our pillows. A newspaper was at our door in the morning. Parking was a problem, with
only a pay lot ($3 a day) down the street. But the inn and the town
of Annapolis were so nice, and the Naval Academy was within walking distance.   —*Mark L. Goodman*

Open all year.
44 rooms, all with private bath.
Rates $45–$75 rooms, $85–$100 suites.
Credit cards: American Express, MasterCard, Visa.
Restaurants and bar.
Innkeeper: Peg Bednarsky.

Buckeystown

The Inn at Buckeystown
3521 Buckeystown Pike
Buckeystown, Maryland 21717
Telephone (301) 874-5755

When the author Barbara Michaels was researching her latest book,
Here I Stay, a thriller set in a country inn, she discovered some small
hotels she especially liked.

"The Inn at Buckeystown is one of a dozen magnificent Victorian houses that line the streets of this small Maryland town. Guest and reception rooms are furnished with antiques, and the innkeepers, Marty Martinez and Daniel Pelz, serve breakfast and dinner. On weekdays the latter meal consists of simple, hearty country food, served family style. On weekends the menu includes gourmet delicacies, also home cooked. The house and grounds are beautiful, the town is charming, and the area is full of antique shops, historic sites, and splendid scenery."   —*Barbara Michaels*

Open all year
7 double rooms with shared baths.
Rates $105 double on weekends, $75 weekdays, including full breakfast and dinner with wine.
Credit cards: MasterCard, Visa.
No public restaurant.
Innkeepers: M. G. Martinez and D. R. Pelz.

_____*Easton*

Tidewater Inn
Dover and Harrison Streets
Easton, Maryland 21601
Telephone (301) 822-1300

"The Tidewater is in the heart of some of the best hunting and fishing territory on the East Coast. I return to it time and time again, knowing that I will be graciously and competently taken care of. The inn's longtime employees go out of their way to make you feel relaxed and comfortable. The bedrooms are spacious and cheerful, many decorated in colonial style. The dining room is equally well run. First-time visitors are almost always bowled over by the vast array of fresh fish available; there is also some of the best game in the country. You don't have to fish or hunt to enjoy the Tidewater, but it helps if you like dogs. Dogs are most welcome at this inn, and should you be accompanied by a good-looking black Labrador, he will get more compliments than you!"   —*Wedgebury Jayes*

Open all year.
120 rooms, all with private bath.
Rates from $52, double occupancy, on weekends; lower on week-nights, when single rooms are available. Suites from $120.
Credit cards: American Express, Carte Blanche, Diners Club, MasterCard, Visa.

Restaurant and bar.
Innkeeper: Anton J. Hoevenaars.

_____ *Frederick*

Spring Bank Farm Inn
7945 Worman's Mill Road
Frederick, Maryland 21701
Telephone (301) 694-0440

"Beverly and Ray Compton are turning this imposing 1880s mansion into a fascinating inn. Spring Bank Farm is on the route presidents take to Camp David, and guests often see the limousine or helicopter pass the house. More important, perhaps, is the fact that the house is a splendid example of Victoriana—and that the amiable owners are eager to share their discoveries with guests interested in restoration. Some of the rooms have painted ceilings; all are furnished with period pieces. Innkeeper Beverly Compton serves breakfast at your door at the hour you designate."

—*Barbara Michaels*

Open all year.
5 rooms, 1 with private bath.
Rates $35–$60, including breakfast.
No credit cards.
No smoking permitted.
Innkeepers: Beverly and Ray Compton.

_____ *New Market*

Strawberry Inn
17 Main Street (Box 237)
New Market, Maryland 21774
Telephone (301) 865-3318

New Market is a town whose reputation was made in the eighteenth and nineteenth centuries by its inns—at least eight hotels and taverns once lined its Main Street. This was a stopover between Baltimore and Frederick, Maryland, and local historians record that Conestoga wagons frequently creaked through town on their way west into the new country beyond. New Market's inns were supported by a flourishing collection of stables, blacksmiths, wheelwrights, and even a nail shop. Today they are gone, and the town lives on as an antiques and crafts center. All of New Market is registered as a historic district by the State of Maryland.

"We found friendly people and a quaint town. Both the inn and New Market were charming. Jane and Ed Rossig have furnished their inn nicely. The high point of our stay was the excellent continental breakfast delivered to our door so that we could enjoy a luxurious breakfast in bed."   —Bill and Jill Neugent

"This one's a gem. Only a few rooms. It was started as a second career by the Rossigs. It is only an hour and a half from Washington, near a lovely Maryland state park."   —Judith C. Heffner

Open all year.
5 rooms, all with private bath.
Rates $55–$60, including continental breakfast served in the room.
No credit cards.
Innkeeper: Jane Rossig.

_____*Oxford*

The Robert Morris Inn
Morris Street (P.O. Box 70)
Oxford, Maryland 21654
Telephone (301) 226-5111

"We came upon it as most people must have been coming upon it for centuries: along the tree-shaded main street leading to the ferry slip. There it stands, at the edge of the water, full of dignity and age. A couple of days at this inn go far in recreating the comfortable and graceful colonial style for which the Eastern Shore is so well remembered. The inn was built as a home early in the eighteenth century by ship's carpenters using hand-hewn beams, pegged wooden paneling, and ship's nails. In 1730 an English trading company bought it as a residence for Robert Morris, its representative in the area. Morris died in 1750 after being struck by wadding from a ship's gun being fired in his honor. His son, Robert Morris, Jr., became a partner in a Philadelphia mercantile firm. A well-to-do man, he used his entire savings to help finance the Continental Army in the Revolutionary War.

"Murals in the inn's dining room were made of wallpaper samples carried by manufacturers' salesmen 135 years ago; the tavern's slate floor is from Vermont, and artworks throughout the building come from local painters and craftspeople. The inn still has old stairs to climb, floors that aren't quite straight, and windows not quite symmetrical—and the shared bathrooms are as idiosyncratic in design as those in a comparable British inn. Our room had a trundle bed and a view from a small gabled window of the little ferry docking, then making its way back across the Chesapeake inlet called the Tred Avon River. Oxford is a waterside town made for walking— as is St. Michaels, another memorable village not far away."

—B.C.; also recommended by Nancy Nelson

"The inn is a gem, but the food is very ordinary."

—Judith C. Heffner

"We thought both the food and our room were excellent. We had a great time."   *—Mark L. Goodman*

Open all year, except one week at Christmas.
36 rooms, 22 with private bath.
Rates $31–$90.
Credit cards: American Express, MasterCard, Visa.
Innkeepers: Ken and Wendy Gibson.

_____*Royal Oak*

The Pasadena
Royal Oak, Maryland 21662
Telephone (301) 745-5053

"Royal Oak is about an hour and a half's drive from Washington or an hour's sail from the eastern part of Chesapeake Bay. If you're fortunate enough to be traveling by boat, you can pull up right at the Pasadena's dock on the Miles River. If you're not, you can always use one of the inn's canoes, rowboats, or sailboats when you get there. If you don't have a bike, the Pasadena can lend you one of those, too. Royal Oak is a post office and two antique stores, and a very pleasant bicycle ride from St. Michaels and Easton. The area is known for its natural beauty, its fishing, and its geese.

"The Pasadena is known for many things. This beautiful 250-year-old plantation house has 135 acres of land, some of which is devoted to growing fresh corn and asparagus for the guests' supper. The inn is reputed to have a friendly ghost, Fred, who shuts the windows when it rains. The Stuttgart-based Swaben International uses the house for a conference center and cultural retreat "to promote better world understanding," so you may well sit down to eat with a group of artists, dancers, or musicians. This also means that you get great beer here, since the repeat international guests (mostly Germans) bring a supply.

"The Pasadena also has Mickey McCrae, the warm and energetic innkeeper who seems willing to accommodate his guests any way he can. We chatted while he was building an archway on the lawn for a wedding, ordering food, and training a young helper in carpentry. Mickey seems to love improving the inn and creating good times for guests: a hayride one night, a barbecue or crab feast another.

"The food at the inn is served family style, and can best be described as good basic country. I ate with a group of watercolorists in from a day's painting. We had honey-baked chicken and broiled fresh fish. When I missed breakfast taking a morning walk, the cook fixed me up 'a little something'—scrambled eggs, creamed chipped beef, bacon, and toast with marmalade—to tide me over."

—*Catherine A. Crawford*

Open mid-March to mid-December.

44 rooms, 20 in the main house, 24 across the street in cottages, some with shared baths.

Rates $30 single, $56 double, including dinner and breakfast. Special off-season, weekly, weekend, and group rates available.

Credit cards: MasterCard, Visa.

Bar.

Innkeeper: Mickey McCrea.

_____*Smith Island*

Mrs. Kitching's
Smith Island
Ewell, Maryland 21824
Telephone (301) 425-3321

"Never did I realize so far away was so close at hand. Smith Island, settled in 1657, is about one and a half square miles of land and accessible only by boat. The 750 Smith Islanders are largely descendants of the original Cornish settlers, and they speak with an accent that some say harks back to Elizabethan times. The rhythm of island life is set by two factors: when the crab and oyster boats come and go, and when the mail boat leaves or returns from the mainland. Adults rise well before dawn for breakfast, with the men going off in their boats and the women going back to rest for their job later in the day of cleaning and packaging the day's catch to put on the next day's mail boat. The island has a few old cars for carting things around, but generally everyone walks.

"I arrived on Captain Jason's 4:30 mail boat, filled with Smith Islanders returning home after shopping and hospital visits. They were loaded down with everything from groceries to one complete bedroom set. When we arrived, the captain made sure I got a ride to Mrs. Kitching's, an unassuming white frame house that is comfortable and homey throughout. Dinner was served family style at the dining room table for me and an Australian family of five who were two and a half years into sailing around the world. Starting with that increasing rarity, homemade soup, we were then deluged with crabcakes, broiled fresh fish caught by Mr. Kitching, vegetables, ham, corn pudding, rolls, and coconut custard pie. We enjoyed a bottle of Mexican wine the Australians had brought along.

"After dinner, I thumbed through Mrs. K's new recipe book and we chatted of various things, such as the time the family went to Washington to take part in the Smithsonian's American Folk Life Festival, and when Margaret Trudeau arrived for dinner with a mysterious man. I even learned at long last how to clean crabs. Now I ask you, what more could you want from a twenty-four-hour trip?"

—*Catherine A. Crawford*

Open May 1 to October 1, but may be closed at times.
5 rooms with shared bath.
Rate $35 per person, including dinner and breakfast.
No credit cards.
The Island Belle makes one or two trips a day from Chrisfield,
    Maryland. Call (301) 425-2351 for information.
Innkeeper: Frances Kitching.

Would you be so kind as to share discoveries you may have of charming, well-run places to stay in Europe? Please write to *Europe's Wonderful Little Hotels and Inns,* c/o Congdon & Weed, 298 Fifth Avenue, New York, New York 10001. (By the way, a new and greatly expanded edition of this splendid guide is now available at your bookseller's.)

*The Chalfonte Hotel,
Cape May*

New Jersey

Beach Haven

St. Rita Hotel
127 Engleside Avenue
Beach Haven, New Jersey 08008
Telephone (609) 492-9192; 492-1704

"The St. Rita was built over a hundred years ago in typically ornate Victorian style. Its first innkeeper named it for her favorite saint and rented rooms only to clergymen. The front porch is now furnished in wicker rockers and lounges, with pillows covered in traditional flowered cretonne. Pots of geraniums hang from the gingerbread trim. The inside retains the same feeling of years ago; there is a typical parlor with bow window seats, cushions, flowers, and comfort. There are three floors of bedrooms, old-fashioned baths with modern plumbing—plus views of the sun rising over the ocean and setting over the bay."
—*Ella Tagg*

Open all year.
23 rooms, 6 with private bath, 2 with half-bath; two 2-room suites;
    3 apartments.
Rates $30 double–$75 suite, depending on room and season.

Weekly rates for apartments range from $225 in April or October to $375 in August.
Credit cards: MasterCard, Visa.
The St. Rita is half a block from the beach, and within walking distance of several restaurants and a summer playhouse.
Inn will meet buses to Beach Haven or planes to Atlantic City airport on advance notice.
Innkeepers: Harold and Marie Coates.

_____ *Bernardsville*

Bernards Inn
Route 202
Bernardsville, New Jersey 07924
Telephone (201) 766-0002

"During the early 1900s, a summer colony arose here in the Somerset Hills, with mansions owned by rich New Yorkers, many of them financiers. The Bernards Inn, built in 1886, handled the weekend house-party overflow. In a 1906 reconstruction, the inn incorporated a staircase, mantels, mirrors, and hand-carved columns from New York City's Plaza Hotel. In the 1930s and 1940s, the inn was a popular stopover on the way to Princeton from New York.

"I was impressed by its wide stairways and halls, plus the high ceilings that provide a spacious, airy, and cool atmosphere. There is a quiet dignity about this inn; you do not encounter any hustle and bustle, and the thickness of the old walls prevents hearing other guests. The large bedrooms are furnished traditionally and most are paneled. The baths are not motel modern, but are very large and comfortable anyway.

"No meals are included in the room rate, which for this area is very reasonable, but there are dining facilities, also open to the public. The Catch Penny Pub downstairs serves lunch and dinner. (The Welsh rarebit at $4 is superb.) Lunch is also served upstairs on the front porch. The menu there is different, featuring sandwiches such as chicken or lobster salad ($2.75) on home-baked croissants. Breakfast is served there, too—from 7.a.m. on weekdays and from 9 on weekends. It features omelets plus fruit croissants topped with sour cream.

"There is no elevator service. Since the staircases are quite long, this might prove a disadvantage to some. Incidentally, reservations here are a must."
—*Marion Smith*

Open all year.
30 rooms, all with private bath.
Rates $38–$52. Weekly rates and group rates available.
Credit cards: American Express, MasterCard, Visa.
Innkeeper: Beverly Cramer.

_____*Cape May*

Cape May, well away from New Jersey's urban sprawl, is an American classic. Despite a period of slump and neglect earlier in this century, when Americans took to their cars and to the utilitarian motels that sprang up along the Jersey shore, enough of this Victorian seaside resort had been preserved by the town's history-conscious people to save the character of old Cape May. Now a new generation of young innkeepers who love the place are devoting themselves to its maintenance and restoration. Cape May is a National Historic Landmark.

_____

The Abbey
Columbia Avenue and Gurney Street
Cape May, New Jersey 08204
Telephone (609) 884-4506

In 1869 a wealthy Pennsylvanian named John B. McCreary built himself an opulent summer home overlooking the Atlantic Ocean. The house was a Gothic-style building with a 60-foot tower, arched windows, and shaded verandas. The house, in Cape May's historic district, is now the Abbey, a small hotel furnished in Victoriana—down to an old chain-pull "water closet" in one of the baths and ceiling fans in some of the rooms.

"I have seen each unique bedroom, and vacationed in several of them. Most recently my room was the Natchez, with a half-canopy bed and beautiful arched windows. Although the house itself—painted in a four-color Victorian scheme outside—appears very elegant and formal, the owners take special care that the atmosphere is relaxed and friendly. Food at breakfast, served family style, is abundant and delicious."   —*Eleanor A. Redmond*

"During the summer, breakfast is served on the porch. Conversations, skillfully guided by innkeepers Jay and Marianne Schatz, include discussions of local restaurant fare and activities and generally friendly banter. By the second or third day, guests often start going to dinner together and looking forward to the 6 P.M. gathering on the porch for wine and a chat. The Abbey has a loyal following of guests who come back year after year. Readers of this book will want to be among them."   —*Michelle Rapkin*

Open March 31 through Thanksgiving.
7 rooms, 4 with private bath.
Rates $50–$75 double.
Off-street parking.
Commuter airlines serve Cape May County airport. There are buses from major cities; summer train service connects Cape May to Camden and Philadelphia.
Innkeepers: Jay and Marianne Schatz.

The Barnard-Good House
238 Perry Street
Cape May, New Jersey 08204
Telephone (609) 884-5381

"Built in 1869, in the elegant style of the Victorian era, the Barnard-Good House retains the spirit created by craftsmen years ago. Each guest room combines charming antiques and modern comforts. Fluffy comforters, thick towels, and lace curtains are in abundance. Nan and Tom Hawkins are the delightful, hospitable owners. Nan's continental breakfast table of homemade goodies is surpassed only by Tom's pleasure in making his guests comfortable."
    —*George and Helen Mushinsky; also recommended by Rosalie and Sal Cassati*

"The house is about three blocks from the seafront, a pleasant short walk to the beach. You pass the quaint district of restored shops and pubs. Not to be overlooked are Tom's building and decorating talents; we have seen the Victorian restoration take place."
    —*Nev and Carol Jackson*

"For the price of your charmingly appointed room, you also get free use of the bicycles and the sunny porch, and free beach badges."
    —*Deborah Stillwell*

Open April 1 through November.
5 rooms, 1 with private bath.
Rates $55–$75.
No credit cards.

Guests met at Cape May airport.
Innkeepers: Nan and Tom Hawkins.

The Brass Bed
719 Columbia Avenue
Cape May, New Jersey 08204
Telephone (609) 884-8075

"The gaslit, treelined street leads to a large front porch with wicker chairs and rockers. We spent quiet evenings there, enjoying the cool sea breezes and conversation. The front parlor has an upright Victorian piano with sheet music for sing-alongs. Rooms are bright and comfortable, furnished with, of course, brass beds. Each room is named for a great Victorian hotel and there are pictures of them in their appropriate places. Breakfast is served in the beautiful dining room. We liked the atmosphere: no phones, no TV; just old-fashioned peace and quiet."   —*U. Alice Ziplies and Ruth von Castel*

Open all year.
8 rooms, 2 with private bath.
Rates $30–$50 shared bath, $40–$60 private bath, including breakfast.
No credit cards.
No restaurant or bar.
Innkeepers: John and Donna Dunwoody.

The Chalfonte Hotel
301 Howard Street
Cape May, New Jersey 08204
Telephone (609) 884-8409

The Chalfonte is one of Cape May's originals: it has been in business as a hotel for more than 100 years, much of that time owned by only one family. The hotel's cooking is Southern style, and people come from great distances for that alone. Each night a single dish is featured—batter-fried chicken, herbed roast leg of lamb, deviled crab à la Chalfonte, and Virginia country ham are among the house specialties. Guests get a Virginia country breakfast each morning, with fresh fish and spoonbread for the hearty. Many people have written to this book about the Chalfonte. Below are a few sample raves.

"The Chalfonte is unique in the same way that the Algonquin in New York is unique, or that Rosa Lewis's Cavendish Hotel on Jermyn Street in London was unique. All three hostelries bore the stamp of their original owners, whose discrimination and charm have magically survived the deterioration of good manners in our lifetime. One still looks forward to a gay and amusing holiday when planning a visit to the Chalfonte."   —*Marion S. Wescott*

"There is a Brigadoon quality here. Guests who return after many years find everything the same. The same cooks turn out the same great meals. Management changes only gradually; waitresses, bellboys, night watchmen, and desk clerks become guests—or vice-versa.

"The Chalfonte is good for parents and children. Children under six are encouraged to eat in the children's dining room, where they can have fun and be looked after while their parents have cocktails and dinner. Older children who want to eat earlier can go there, too."   —*Merrinell Sullivan*

"This is the place to go in Cape May for good food and service."
                    —*Mark L. Goodman*

"A fine place for Southern cooking."   —*George Herzog*

Open Memorial Day weekend to mid-September; weekends until mid-October.
103 rooms, 11 with private bath; several family suites and cottages.
Rates $39–$53 single, $69–$88 double, $96–$98 with bath, MAP. Weekly and family rates.
Credit cards: MasterCard, Visa.
Bar and restaurant open to the public.
French spoken.
Bus service from New York and Philadelphia; train from Philadelphia; commuter airlines from Philadelphia and New York.
Innkeepers: Judy Bartella and Anne LeDuc.

Gingerbread House
28 Gurney Street
Cape May, New Jersey 08204
Telephone (609) 884-0211

"It is a perfect Victorian house, imaginatively and tastefully furnished with Victorian pieces as well as with the photos and handmade mirrors of owner Fred Echevarria, who, it turns out, is a talented photographer and craftsman. The common first-floor sitting room is lively, warm, and cozy, and the front porch with its comfortable collection of wicker furniture is a place you could rock for hours with your Sunday paper or mystery novel. The front yard is beautifully gardened in the Cape May style—hydrangeas, petunias, salvia, verbena."   —*Judy and John Heffner*

"The Gingerbread House is conveniently located on quiet Gurney Street, a short walk to the beach and in the heart of the historic area. The Echevarrias were very helpful in guiding guests to enjoyable restaurants and in providing all the other little pieces of information that make a visit to a new spot so much nicer."   —*Brooke DeCamp Myers*

"Even in February, when the beach is cold and gray, the Gingerbread House has a warm fire and a hearty welcome."
                              —*Mr. and Mrs. Smith B. Coleman III*

Open all year.
6 rooms, 3 with private bath.
Rates $38–$72 double, according to season, including breakfast.
No credit cards.
Train, bus, and air connections.
Innkeepers: Joan and Fred Echevarria.

The Mainstay Inn
635 Columbia Avenue
Cape May, New Jersey 08204
Telephone (609) 884-8690

In Cape May's age of glory, more than a century ago, a couple of wealthy gamblers built a club for their friends, where they engaged in what has been described as "gentlemanly amusements." History is evasive on what the town thought of the activities, but there is no doubt that the building was an attention-getter, with its superb construction and expensive interior furnishings. The present innkeepers describe the effect as "ostentatious Victorian splendor"— and they have been faithful to that sense of style.

"The Mainstay is the gem of the town. One can observe people strolling by, stopping to stare at the beautiful old inn: you can tell that they wish they were staying there too. Inside, the house is full of beautiful antiques. Guests may sit in the parlor, play cards or checkers, or read the books about old Cape May—there was even a time when men and women had separate hours to go to the beach. A crowning touch is the cupola, a spot to retreat with a good book. But on a lazy summer afternoon you may find that you're napping or just enjoying the four-sided view of the town and the sea. It's also nice when the moon is full.

"The Carrolls have added the Cottage next door, an equally old, revitalized Cape May home. I stayed in the Lily Langtry room, high on the top floor with a view of the ocean. The room, done in pink and white, with brass bed and wicker rockers, is surely one Lily would have loved. I did."   —*Jessie C. Daniels*

Open April through October.
10 rooms, 2 suites, 7 with private bath.
Rates $50–$75, including breakfast and afternoon tea.
No credit cards.
Innkeepers: Tom and Sue Carroll.

The Queen Victoria
102 Ocean Street
Cape May, New Jersey 08204
Telephone (609) 884-8702

"Each room has a handmade quilt on the comfortable bed, attractive wallpaper and furnishings, and good reading material at hand. No detail has been overlooked. A good reading light, turned-down bed, a bit of Love (a piece of homemade candy) on my pillow each evening, the fabulous country breakfasts with fresh fruit and juices, a delectable casserole (homemade granola), the loan of an inn bicycle to ride about this Victorian community—all these added up to a marvelous place to spend a pampered vacation."

—*Frances Facey*

"A sumptuous breakfast and a companionable tea help you meet the owners and other guests. The furniture is period, but unassuming. The quilts are a generous and homey touch. The Queen would have given her seal of approval."   —*Mary Ann Jung*

"Were it served at noon, the breakfast could easily be called a brunch."   —*Henry J. Magaziner*

Open all year.

12 rooms, 4 with private bath.

Rates $40–$90, depending on room, including full breakfast and afternoon tea.

Credit card: American Express.

French spoken.

Bus from New York or Philadelphia stops at inn; guests met on request at Cape May County airport.

Innkeepers: Dane and Joan Wells.

_____ *Lambertville*

Lambertville House
32 Bridge Street
Lambertville, New Jersey 08530
Telephone (609) 397-0202

" 'In the wayside inn,' wrote Harriet Martineau, the Englishwoman who reported in 1837 on Jacksonian America, 'the disagreeable practice of rocking in the chair is seen in its excess. In the inn parlour are three or four rocking-chairs in which sit ladies who are vibrating in different directions, and at various velocities, so as to try the head of a stranger almost as severely as the tobacco chewer his stomach. How this lazy and ungraceful indulgence ever became general, I cannot imagine, but the nation seems so wedded to it, that I see little chance of its being forsaken.'

"Over the years, Americans have remained faithful to the rocking chair, and it is the Europeans who have come to adopt it as a restful and admirable piece of furniture. One of the first things a visitor notices at the Lambertville House is the bright red rockers all along the grillwork-decorated porch. Together with flower-filled window boxes, they add the right touch to a hotel that is smart and always busy. Lambertville is just across the Delaware River from the more popular town of New Hope, Pennsylvania, and used to have none of the latter's charm. But Lambertville is changing, and there are those who prefer it and its small restaurants to the hustle of New Hope.

"Opened as a stagecoach stop in 1812, the hotel, on Lambertville's traffic-choked main street, has little atmosphere left of earlier times. Somewhere along the line it decided to go for modern comforts in its public rooms, with a quiet, cool old English-style bar. On the wall is a photograph of the flood of 1955, a catastrophe about which the residents of the Delaware Valley constantly talk. Upstairs, there are thirty-two rooms, some of which are small but attractive inasmuch as they have slightly sloping floors and four-poster beds or beds with iron frames.

"The management is proud of the history of this hotel. The register has signatures such as 'Andrew Johnson, President U.S.A.,' and 'U.S. Grant, Lieut. Gen., U.S.A. 1866.' Edward VII of Britain stayed here before he became king. But this, compared with many inns on the Pennsylvania side of the river, still feels more like a working hotel—mainly a center for the commercial life of the town."

—*David Wigg*

Open all year.
32 rooms, 5 with private bath.
Rates $30–$50, including continental breakfast.
Credit cards: American Express, MasterCard, Visa.
Frequent buses from Trenton and Manhattan.
Innkeeper: D. Susan Darrah.

_____*Milford*

Chestnut Hill on the Delaware
63 Church Street
Milford, New Jersey 08848
Telephone (201) 995-9761

"Unremarkable little Milford—part mill town, part country village—is getting a new personality. The small settlement at one end of a bridge across the Delaware (facing equally unremarkable Upper Black Eddy, Pennsylvania, on the other side) has begun to feel the effects of spreading 'artsification' in this serenely beautiful part of the Delaware River Valley. Milford, which once was distinguished by a small supermarket, laundromat, and trackside eating establishment known as Ma-De's (where the quality of both the welcome and the service appeared to be directly proportional to the length of time your ancestors had inhabited the valley), now has a fine little Oyster House restaurant, a crafts center in a restored gristmill, a gift shop that also sells the finest imported cheeses and other delicacies—and an elegant bed-and-breakfast inn.

"This last improvement came to pass because a couple of years ago, Linda and Rob Castagna were traveling in Britain—enjoying bed-and-breakfast style living—when they heard that Rob was about to be transferred by AT&T from Detroit to a new job in New Jersey. For Linda, that meant giving up working in the medical field and caring in her home for young people with problems. Back in the states and house-hunting, with the memory of their bed-and-breakfast vacation fresh and the need for the energetic Linda to find something to do in her new life, the Castagnas happened on a mid-nineteenth-century home in Milford not far from Rob's new job, and immediately saw its potential as a family inn. Within a few months the little town and its new family clicked, and Rob, Linda, and their son Michael were in business and enjoying it thoroughly.

"Chestnut Hill was a house in mint condition when the Castagnas bought it; they are only the third family to own it in over a century. Linda, who is also an artist with a good eye for design, has made a point of not disturbing the graceful riverfront home for the sake of modernization. Guests here will feel more part of a family than customers at an inn. There is one bathroom—with its 1901 tiles and shoulder-high tub—to share on the second floor, and another newer model on the third, and breakfast is served, by Linda, at the family dining table. Recreation may extend no further than rocking on the front porch, watching the river below. Or in a matter of minutes, guests can drive into historic Bucks County across the bridge, where there is a wide choice of dining and sightseeing, and several places to rent a raft or canoe."   —B.C.

Open all year.
5 rooms with shared baths.
Rates $50–$65, including full country breakfast.
No credit cards.
No smoking permitted.
Innkeepers: Linda, Rob, and Michael Castagna.

_____*Spring Lake*

Colonial Ocean House
102 Sussex Avenue
Spring Lake, New Jersey 07762
Telephone (201) 449-9090; winter (201) 449-3552

Spring Lake (or Spring Lake Beach, as it is called locally) is a small and spacious community where trees, grass, and flowers reach almost to the oceanside. This 1878 building—originally called the Ocean House, but known as the Colonial Hotel while under the ownership of the Taylor family from 1925 to 1979—is now owned by a family named Mitchell, who have at least partly restored its Victorian name. The hotel is only a few minutes' walk from the beach and equally near Spring Lake, for those who like their water without waves.

"My wife and I spent a Memorial Day weekend there. It was a handsome building with clean and simple rooms and attractive and interested managers—a nice kind of personal attention without that hovering quality of a fourth-rate place. Tell people to go there."

—*Leonard E. Opdyke*

Open Memorial Day to the weekend after Labor Day.
50 rooms, 15 with private bath.
Rates $20–$60, including continental breakfast.
Credit cards: MasterCard, Visa.
Innkeepers: Charles and Virginia Mitchell; Managers: Bill and Jill Mitchell.

The Normandy Inn
21 Tuttle Avenue
Spring Lake, New Jersey 07762
Telephone (201) 449-7172

"Spring Lake is a gem of a village, hard by the Atlantic, filled with striking Victorian homes and maintained by a community seemingly fanatic about neatness, cleanliness, and hospitality. You wonder: do they sweep the beaches at night? A long boardwalk runs the length of the town, and then some. Since our recent weekend there happened to be a mild one, we spent hours on the boards.

"Just back from the beach and boardwalk stands the Normandy, a sparkling example of nineteenth-century graciousness, built in 1888 and moved to its present location in the early 1900s. The inn is filled with antique furniture, clocks, and all the little touches suggesting that a great deal of love—and intelligence—have gone into this home. Rooms are spacious, handsomely decorated, and interesting: no two are alike.

"My wife and I are fans of hearty breakfasts. The Normandy proved to be the ideal place to exercise that particular passion."

—*George P. Berger*

Open all year.
16 rooms, one 2-room apartment, all with private bath.
Rates $50–$70 double, June 24–September 7; $37–$45 off-season, all including full breakfast.
No credit cards.
Innkeepers: Michael and Susan Ingino.

Greenville Arms,
Greenville

New York

Auburn

Springside Inn
41 West Lake Road
Post Office Box 520
Auburn, New York 13021
Telephone (315) 252-7247

Travelers to Auburn, in the Finger Lakes area, have been served by
this inn since 1919. The present innkeepers are the second generation of the family that has owned the hotel since 1941. Springside
began life in 1851 as a boarding school for boys founded by a Dutch
Reformed pastor, the Reverend Samuel Robbins Brown. His aim
was to provide an educational environment that would "avoid the
evils necessarily attendant upon large and promiscuous assem-
blages of the young." In 1867 the building became a private residence, and the legend is that it was a station on the Underground
Railroad for runaway slaves during the Civil War. In addition to
being a year-round hotel now, Springside also has a summer theater, begun in 1970; the opening show was *The Fantasticks.* Broadway
musicals and comedies, performed by professionals, play five nights
a week, Wednesday to Sunday, in July and August.

"Close by Owasco Lake, the inn is comfortable and competently run. It is obviously well appreciated in the region for its fine food, judging by the many dinner guests. There are pleasant drives and walks around the lake, or you can shop in the nearby towns of Auburn and Syracuse." —*Peter and Barbara Liehr*

"The baritone warming up in the next room for his role in *South Pacific* gave us a real pickup after a long day on the road. So did the friendly innkeeper, Bill Dove, with whom we had a nice conversation at the bar. The prime rib was especially good and the shrimp and sauce served before dinner an unexpected treat. It's a bustling place because of the dinner theater, but they manage to keep a separate dining room for weary travelers."

—*Mary Jane and Michael Durishin*

Open all year.
8 rooms, 4 with private bath.
Rates $28–$30 single, $40–$45 double, including continental breakfast. Two-night Weekend Fling for two people, including Friday and Saturday dinner and Sunday brunch: about $150. The inn also caters to Executive Thinking Sessions.
Credit cards: MasterCard, Visa.
Bus service to Auburn.
Innkeepers: Bill and Barbara Dove.

Bemus Point–Lake Chautauqua

Hotel Lenhart
Bemus Point, New York 14712
Telephone (716) 386-2715

"On Lake Chautauqua, the Lenhart is a comfortable hotel that has been in the same family of innkeepers since 1881. The large porch facing the lake is a favorite gathering place for guests. The sunsets are beautiful! There is a small bar, and opportunities for boating, fishing, golfing, and tennis are close at hand. There are interesting little shops around the general area. Jamestown is at one end of the lake and Mayville at the other. We have been going to the lake, and the Lenhart, for many years." —*Margaret Bernaky*

Open Memorial Day weekend until mid-September.
50 rooms, 35 with private bath.
Rates from $20 single, $30 double, room only, in June and September; from $25 single, $50–$65 double or twin, with dinner and full breakfast in July and August. Parlor suites available in season at $40–$75.

No credit cards.
Cocktail lounge and restaurant.
5 miles to Chautauqua Institution.
Guests met free at airport or Greyhound bus in Jamestown.
Innkeepers: John L. and George A. Johnston.

_____*Canaan*

The Inn at Shaker Mill Farm
Canaan, New York 12029
Telephone (518) 794-9345

Ingram Paperny figures among a small group of innkeepers nation-wide whom many accept as doyens of their profession. Judging from the reports of his guests, he runs a place whose casual atmosphere and sparse Shaker furnishings conceal a precisely managed hotel. Visitors are encouraged to ask for special treatment: the inn will cook for vegetarians, for example. Shaker Mill takes pride in its international following. With its multilingual staff, it has become a favorite among people from the United Nations, where Paperny, the son of a Russian doctor, once worked. Canaan, in the foothills of the Berkshires, is a short drive from Lenox, Massachusetts, and the Tanglewood summer concerts of the Boston Symphony.

"When we arrive at the Mill, peace descends. The New York City week falls away like an outmoded skin. There is a calm beauty in everything, from the simple but well-equipped bedrooms and the great circular fireplace round which one takes tea or a predinner drink, to the glory of the meadows and woods and the gentle sounds of Bach or Purcell. There is a lot of lovely walking here, in places where no highways ever have been. Food is sinfully good. One often has to choose between imaginative hors d'oeuvres—served around the fireplace before dinner—and dinner itself, because there are just too many good things to eat. In winter the marvelous trails and roads become cross-country ski trails. There are also a number of first-rate commercial slopes very close by. A natural pond for swimming in summer and early fall is on the grounds.

"Other inns may have more sumptuous facilities or larger grounds, but what makes this one unique is the personality of its owner-host, Ingram Paperny. It was he who transformed the precious shell of an old Shaker mill into a living space of both function and old-fashioned comfort. He combines craftsmanship with sophisticated taste, and intellectual curiosity (he holds a graduate degree in political science) with interest in people and warm affection for his guests, who often become his long-term friends. This

is one of the reasons that a steady core of often unusual people regularly return to the inn. They know that, in an ambience of social ease, they will meet old friends and perhaps make some new ones."
—*Dr. Ernest and Evelyn Angel*

"The setting and the building itself are charming, the innkeeper gracious. But future guests should know that the accommodations seemed rather spartan for the high cost. Do not expect a comfortable old country place—it's more like a sophisticated college dorm. There is a brook which does indeed babble, and is delightful."
—*Dr. Jeanne M. Safer*

Open all year.
20 rooms, 19 with private bath; 2 suites.
Rates $35 per person, including breakfast; $65–$75 per person, AP.
No credit cards.
French, German, Italian, and Spanish spoken.
Bus service to Pittsfield, Massachusetts; train service to Hudson, New York. Guests can be met.
Innkeeper: Ingram Paperny.

_____*Castile*

Glen Iris Inn
Letchworth State Park
Castile, New York 14427
Telephone (716) 493-2622

Letchworth State Park, about thirty-five miles south of Rochester, includes 14,350 acres of land along the Genesee River. As the river races through the park, it drops over three major waterfalls and continues to whittle away at the dramatic cliff faces of its gorges. The park has the normal complement of outdoor facilities, including campsites. There is a museum devoted to the history of the Seneca Indians and the region's tumultuous years of struggle over the land. There is also the Glen Iris Inn, once the home of State Senator William Pryor Letchworth, who granted the park's first 1,000 acres to the state in 1907. "God wrought for us this scene beyond compare," an inscription at the park's Inspiration Point says, "but one man's loving hand protected it and gave it to his fellow men to share."

"The Glen Iris Inn is as delightful as its name suggests. Nestled in a glen in a utopian setting above a waterfall second in size in the East only to Niagara, it is a restful haven for vacationers. The inn has been preserved in its Victorian style. Dining and sleeping wings have been added and although rooms are generally small (no phones, radios, or TVs) they are comfortable. Several larger suites are available, one complete with parquet floors, Victorian furnishings, and a balcony overlooking the falls. One can comfortably lounge in the Senator's library on the third floor, but with seventeen miles of gorgeous parkland in which to hike and observe nature, or swim and fish, one doesn't stay inside too much.

"The food served by Peter and Cora Pizzutelli, the innkeepers, is truly Lucullan. Their large dining rooms are known far and wide by hungry nondieters. It is always a problem to decide what treat to devour—the seafood is outstanding, the roast beef superb, and the veal white and succulent. Wines and liquors are available. The staff is friendly and efficient.

"I have been going to Letchworth Park since the early 1930s (as a camper then) and for the past dozen years to the inn. I think I'd move in if they'd let me!"   *—Lola Rothmann*

"It should be noted that the autumn season is the most magnificent time in which to see the Glen Iris, when the trees are resplendent. You must book several months in advance for any of the suites, and dinner reservations for the weekends must be made several days in advance, since travelers come from as far as Rochester and Buffalo simply for the fine food."   *—James and Patricia Vazzana*

Open Easter through October.
18 rooms, 3 suites, all with private bath.
Rates $31–$36 standard rooms, $41–$50 suites.
Credit cards: American Express, MasterCard, Visa.
Public dining room, with bar for hotel and dinner guests.
Located in Letchworth State Park near Portageville—Routes 19A and 436.
Innkeepers: Peter, Cora, and Paula Pizzutelli.

_____ *Cazenovia*

Lincklaen House
71 Albany Street (Box 36)
Cazenovia, New York 13035
Telephone (315) 655-3461

"Cazenovia Lake is one of the loveliest of the many lakes in central New York. At the southern tip of the lake is Cazenovia, a village with personality—part resort, part college town, part rural community. And in the heart of the village is the Lincklaen House, built as a hotel in 1835 and still admirably fulfilling that function. The name comes from John Lincklaen, a land agent for the Holland Land Company, who bought the land in the 1790s and founded Cazenovia. All sleeping rooms are on the second and third floors, so the lack of an elevator and the probable absence of any bellhops are not too discouraging. There are small rooms, large rooms—in fact if there are any two just alike, I haven't found them. The elderly plumbing has asthmatic wheezes, but it works; the rooms are clean and the beds are comfortable. There is no chrome and plastic uniformity; these rooms have individuality.

"The real charm of this hostelry is twofold: the friendly, willing service of the staff, and the comfortable, attractive public rooms. In the graciously furnished main dining room, high-ceilinged and with a huge fireplace, excellent food is served for lunch and dinner. The adjoining Terrace Room, bright and cheerful, has a fine breakfast menu. The fenced-in outdoor patio with its greenery is an ideal spot for reading, playing cards, or just plain loafing on a summer afternoon; it is surpassed, however, by the comfort and charm of the East Room, with its own large fireplace, during winter evenings. The old-fashioned tavern, tucked into an out-of-the-way corner, is a popular but rarely crowded watering spot. Innkeeper Helen Tobin and her associates have well maintained the spirit of the old hotel: Lincklaen House itself seems to say, 'Welcome, traveler. Enter, relax, and rest. I'll take care of you.'" *—Roger B. Cobb;*
also recommended by Jeanne and Bob Glass

"We spent one night at Lincklaen House, which had plenty of atmosphere and a good dining room. But our bedroom was cramped, not really large enough for two adults, and rather overpriced, especially without air conditioning. There was also a quibble about using American Express, and we had to insist before the card was accepted." *—Gilbert Ross*

Open all year.
25 rooms, 23 with private bath; 4 suites; 2 bed-sitting rooms.
Rates $40–$60 single, $40–$65 double, $70–$90 suites.
Credit cards: American Express, MasterCard, Visa.
Public restaurant and bar.
French spoken.
Daily bus to Cazenovia; guests met. Planes to Hancock Airport, Syracuse; trains to East Syracuse, where taxi service is available.
Innkeeper: Helen Tobin.

Where are the good little hotels in Boston? Philadelphia? Omaha? Dallas? If you have found one, don't keep it a secret. Write *now*.

_____*Chautauqua*

The Chautauqua Institution
Box 1095
Chautauqua, New York 14722
Telephone (716) 357-6200

"The Chautauqua Institution, on the western edge of New York State, near Ohio and Pennsylvania, is considered by many to be a package of all that is best in America. The institution, more than a hundred years old, is set on 700 acres, beautifully positioned along Lake Chautauqua. It includes hotels and inns, churches and religious houses, theaters, interesting wood-frame homes built at the turn of the century, tennis courts, and an eighteen-hole golf course. The purpose of the institution is 'to promote the intellectual, social, physical, moral and religious welfare of the people.' To this end, it holds meetings, seminars, and concerts, provides recreation and instruction, maintains libraries and museums, offers reading and study clubs, and publishes books.

"During its nine- or ten-week season from the end of June to the end of August, a nominal gate fee is charged to guests, and this entitles them to attend nightly events in the amphitheater, a spacious open-air wooden structure. Automobiles are permitted only for the loading and unloading of baggage and supplies, and are then parked in well-protected areas outside the gates.

"Distinguished celebrities have appeared in Chautauqua's century-long history, including famous composers and musicians, authors, diplomats, scholars, legislators, presidents, and foreign heads of state. Chautauqua has its own symphony orchestra, choral groups, and a company of performing artists who present concerts, plays, and operas. Each week of the summer season has a theme—national- or international-affairs week, for example.

"Accommodations are ample and reasonable in the 168-room Athenaeum Hotel, smaller hotels and inns, or private cottages and homes. The Athenaeum, my favorite, is the largest wood-frame hotel in the United States, and has beautiful Victorian-era porches and other details. Home-cooked food is available at a number of hotels, cafeterias, or sometimes in individual homes.

"Whether it be for two days, two weeks or two months, the time spent at Chautauqua will be a spiritual, refreshing, rewarding experience."
—*Byron H. Luers*

Open late June to late August.
Several hundred rooms in hotels and cottages. For a complete list, write for the Chautauqua Information Book.

Rates $15–$70 for rooms. Rates with meals and weekly rates available. All guests also pay a gate fee ranging from $8.50 to $14 for
adults, depending on day and time of entry; reduced rates for
young people 13–17; children 12 and under free.
No credit cards accepted for most accommodations.
No alcoholic beverages served in hotels.

_____ *Chestertown*

The Balsam House
Friends Lake
Chestertown, New York 12817
Telephone (518) 494-2828

John Butler Yeats, the Irish landscape painter who spent the later
years of his life near this small town, once wrote of the area:

> "Let me walk your gentle hills,
> traverse your peaceful valleys.
> Let me rest by your quiet shores . . .
> let me call this gentle land home."

The innkeepers of the Balsam House on the shores of the lake Yeats
loved use his words to introduce guests to their newly refurbished
inn, with its backdrop of Gore Mountain. The area, relaxing in the
summer months, is an active center in winter for skiing, skating,
tobogganing, and ice-fishing.

"The Balsam House has only recently reopened. We have watched
the restoration of this old hotel—the date 1891 is inscribed on one
beam—to its beautiful new look. We feel that it now rates a place
in your book."   —*Warren and Jackie Sholes*

Open all year.
20 rooms, 1 suite, all with private bath.
Rates $49–$54 per person, with dinner and breakfast.
Credit card: American Express.
Public bar and restaurant.
Inn will provide or arrange for winter sports equipment.
French spoken.
Innkeeper: John Preece.

Turn to the back of this book for pages inviting *your* comments.

_____ *Clarence*

Asa Ransom House
10529 Main Street
Clarence, New York 14031
Telephone (716) 759-2315

Clarence, first opened to settlement by Europeans in 1799 when a plot of land went for $2 an acre, is the oldest town in Erie County. Asa Ransom was the first settler to take up the offer of the Holland Land Company, and he built a two-story log cabin that had begun to take in travelers by the turn of the nineteenth century. The core of the present Asa Ransom House dates to about 1853. The dining rooms were added in 1975.

"How nice it is to find an Asa Ransom House in the midst of the motels in the Buffalo area. From arrival to departure the hospitality extended by innkeepers Bob and Judy Lenz is unmatched. There are two dining rooms, the larger of which is reserved for nonsmokers. Hurray! The menu always has some unusual items to offer. The food is superbly prepared, using fresh ingredients and as few additives as possible, and service is excellent. A continental breakfast is included in the price of the room, and what a masterpiece it is. The restaurant is not open to the public for breakfast, so one can fairly well set one's own time to eat. Bob serves freshly baked bread or pastry, several kinds of fruits and juices, a quiche, and of course coffee, tea, or what have you. Not to be missed is the Clarence Community Park just a block or two up the street. This is a delightful area of trees, large grassy areas, a lagoon complete with ducks, geese, and boys fishing, two tennis courts, flowers—a real treasure. The flowers in large masses are phenomenal."

—*Charles L. Newberry*

"Upstairs there are four rooms in the inn, each prettier than the other—furnished with beautiful antiques and decorated with unbelievable charm and good taste. On our first visit we chose to stay in the Gold Room with its iron and brass beds, a beautiful old writing desk, comfortable chairs, and a spacious, ultramodern, immaculate bathroom. A knock at the door soon after our arrival brought a bowl of fruit with the innkeepers' best wishes. Dinner in the evening was country cooking at its finest, with the touch of a master chef in the kitchen. There were homemade soups, fresh vegetables, crisp green salads with just the right dressings, home-baked breads, a choice of entrées to suit any taste, and always a daily specialty. A nice touch, we thought, was the offer of the innkeeper to serve small portions to guests with smaller appetites—at a reduced price.

"We have since returned for a week's stay and found everything better than the first time. It's a great place for a mini-vacation to Niagara Falls, the Finger Lakes, Rochester, the Genesee Folk Museum, and of course Buffalo. We still give the Lenzes four stars for superb accommodations, warm hospitality, and excellent food. We have never been to a better inn."   —*Martha and Carl Anderson*

"We love the fresh flowers from the garden and the dry arrangements placed here and there. We have often seen the owners scoot out to the herb garden to select something special to adorn our plates."   —*Mr. and Mrs. Clarence A. Britell*

Open all year, except January.
4 rooms, all with private bath.
Rates $40 single, $55–$60 double, including full country breakfast.
No credit cards.
French and German spoken.
11 miles from Amtrak, 9 miles from airport.
Innkeepers: Bob and Judy Lenz.

_____*Clinton*

Clinton House
21 West Park Row
Clinton, New York 13323
Telephone (315) 853-5555

The inn was once a home built in 1820 for the Williams family. In 1870 Judge Othniel S. Williams, a local dignitary, had the house remodeled. By 1942 the house had become Ade's Restaurant. Three years later a group of Hamilton College alumni and local residents bought the building and reopened it as the Alexander Hamilton Inn.

"Clinton House, the former Alexander Hamilton Inn, has five large, airy, light bedrooms, a pleasant bar and sitting room–lounge downstairs. Food is excellent and reservations are needed for dinner. The inn is located at one end of the village green and evokes a tranquil country-village feeling. Parents of Hamilton College students like to stay here, as do alumni when they return to the Hill. This part of New York state is bucolic, with many historical spots close by. In twenty minutes you can be in the foothills of the Adirondack Mountains—a region of lovely valleys, rivers, and hills."
—*Mr. and Mrs. G. H. Dalton*

Open all year.
5 rooms, all with private bath.
Rates $35–$40.

Credit cards: American Express, MasterCard, Visa.
Innkeeper: Robert J. Hazelton.

_____ *Cooperstown*

Otesaga Hotel and Cooper Inn
P.O. Box 311
Cooperstown, New York 13326
Telephone (607) 547-9931, 547-2229, for hotel; 547-2567, 547-2249, for inn

This establishment, with its refreshing lakeside setting, has several parts: a large hotel with extensive and varied recreational facilities, a twenty-room inn, a carriage house, and a cottage. Guests in all buildings are invited to use all the facilities of the resort complex.

"The view from a rocking chair on the veranda of the grand old Otesaga Hotel stretches on the left from the golf course and on the right from the swimmers' pier over the green hills across Lake Otsego. There are days when a guest might imagine that he was on Lake Como in Italy rather than upstate New York.

"There is an outdoor café with tables under umbrellas for lunch and, for dinner, a formal dining room with a violinist, pianist, bassist, and drummer playing songs your children may not remember. The dress is formal enough at dinner to match the decor and service, with 90 percent of the men wearing neckties and all of them wearing jackets. After 6 P.M. even the children are in dressy clothes, and it all melds into a picture of gentility and courtesy. After dinner there is sometimes a band concert on the lawn or other entertainment for those not interested in cards, chess, Scrabble, or the nightclub. Upstairs, the corridors between the guest rooms are as wide as some hotel rooms. There are views of the lake or the town from the high-ceilinged rooms, and some of the bathrooms are large enough for a party.

"There are swimming, sailing, and fishing on the lake, and Cooperstown has museums with first-class collections of folk art and exhibits of all kinds from early rural America. It also has the Baseball Hall of Fame."   —*William P. Luce;*
also recommended by Karen and Neal Silverstein

Open May through October.
125 rooms in hotel, all with private bath; 20 rooms in Cooper Inn,
    Carriage House, and Jordan Cottage, 15 with private bath.
Rates $50–$80 per person in hotel, with dinner and breakfast; $20–

$60 per person in inn, carriage house, or cottage, with continental breakfast, from beginning of July to Labor Day. Golf packages available.

Credit cards: American Express, MasterCard, Visa.

Trailways bus to Cooperstown. Catskill Airways to Oneonta.

Manager: John Watt.

_____*East Hampton*

The Maidstone Arms
207 Main Street
East Hampton, New York 11937
Telephone (516) 324-5006

The area known to New Yorkers as "the Hamptons" has become the region's most fashionable summering spot, attracting the literary, the trendsetting and, of course, the rich who don't need any other qualification. The Hamptons have splendid summer homes, good beaches, and shops to support the most expensive Manhattan tastes. The parties are legendary. But behind all the frenetic and costly seasonal activity are several old and attractive towns, surrounded by pleasant (and mostly flat) bicycling and walking country.

"Going out to this resort town off-season has its advantages. It is uncrowded and unhurried. Most shops are open. The Maidstone, a hotel since 1870, is a venerable place (part of it was built in 1660). It is in East Hampton's historic district, within fifteen minutes' walk of beaches. Rooms have a beachlike simplicity with rattan furniture all around. The dining room and bar are Victorian in decor. The food was excellent. We had duck, salad, Black Forest cake, and an excellent and reasonable California '79 Gamay Beaujolais. Continental breakfast on Sunday was fresh-squeezed juice, coffee, and croissants.   —*Mary and Joel Stein*

Open all year, except January and February.

16 rooms, all with private bath; 2 cottages.

Rates $70–$110, including continental breakfast.

Credit cards: American Express, MasterCard, Visa.

Public bar and restaurant.

East Hampton is on the Long Island Rail Road. Hampton Jitney bus service from Manhattan. Connections available to airports.

Innkeepers: Rita and Gary Rieswig.

If you would like to amend, update, or disagree with any entry, write *now*.

_Elka Park

The Redcoat's Return
Dale Lane, Platte Cove
Elka Park, New York 12427
Telephone (518) 589-6379; 589-9858

This was once Willie and Sadie Dale's summer boardinghouse where, before World War I, a guest got a room and full board for $25 a week. Willie and Sadie called their establishment, built on the Dale family's homestead land, the Grenoble. It flourished until after World War II, when tourist homes and summer boardinghouses went out of fashion. Thomas and Margaret Wright took over the property in 1972, winterized it, and refashioned it in the style of an English country inn.

"In the heart of New York's Catskill Mountains, England's flag flies beneath the Stars and Stripes at this charming inn atop Mount Platte Clove near Tannersville. The colorful carved signboard on the lawn tips the guest to both the creativity and sense of humor of the innkeepers. On one side of the sign is a Redcoat; on the other, an English barmaid. Of course, they are profiles of Tom and Peg Wright, the innkeepers. After sipping arrival tea, guests are warmly welcomed to individually decorated quarters. Thirteen upstairs bedrooms, many with private baths, are papered, curtained, and quilted, offering a spot to read, write, or rest. Inviting corners throughout the inn beckon guests to settle with a book. Besides several fine paintings and a set of Hogarth prints on the sitting room walls, the Wrights own a magnificent book collection that lines an entire wall of the elegant dining room. All the food is prepared by Tom, whose culinary credentials include London's Dorchester Hotel and the Cunard Line.

"Guests may hike one of the several fine trails nearby: Jimmy Dolan's Notch, Indian Head, and Devil's Kitchen Leanto each offer breathtaking views of the Hudson Valley. Other guests choose to golf, swim, ride, or play tennis. The artists' community of Woodstock, at the mountain's base, offers streets lined with galleries and pottery and craft shops."   —*Liz Einstein*

"It has marvelous down comforters, a lovely bar with a fireplace, and wonderful food. A romantic and magical place, just two hours from New York City"   —*Alan H. Bomser*

"Guests will find glasses and a small welcoming bottle of sherry in their rooms. One of the Wrights' dogs or cats may come to escort you back to the inn as you return from a walk to a wonderful meal or a drink of mulled wine in the cozy bar."   —*Peggy Middendorf*

Open all year, except April 1 to May 30 and November 1 to November 15.
14 rooms, 7 with private bath.
Rates $60–$70 double, including full breakfast.
Credit cards: American Express, MasterCard, Visa.
Trailways bus service to Tannersville.
Innkeepers: Peg and Tom Wright.

Geneva

Geneva on the Lake
1001 Lochland Road
Geneva, New York 14456
Telephone (315) 789-7190

"This Palladian villa, copied from one in Florence, is under new and excellent management. All architectural details have been kept. The apartments have been redone in exquisite, expensive taste. The lake setting is gorgeous, and all apartments have views of extensive lawns and water. It really is a lovely place to hide and relax in a pastoral setting."   —*Judith Trowbridge*

Open all year
29 suites, all with private bath.
$88–$165 a night per couple, including continental breakfast and Sunday buffet dinner. Wine and cheese party for guests on Friday evening.
Credit cards: American Express, MasterCard, Visa.
No public bar or restaurant.
Innkeepers: Dennis and Petie DiMuzio.

The Inn at Belhurst Castle
Lochland Road (P.O. Box 609)
Geneva, New York 14456
Telephone (315) 781-0201

On the shores of Seneca Lake, near New York State wine country, the Inn at Belhurst Castle was built as a home of red Medina stone in the late 1880s. Most of the building materials used in this turreted romantic fantasy were imported. The owners have maintained the feeling of the old home with paintings, figurines of antique porcelain, and stained-glass windows.

"A beautiful, atmospheric old castle that we found by accident, just down the road from Geneva on the Lake, where we had been staying. The rooms were expensive, but magnificently furnished. The food was good, but not sensational. Service was excellent."

—Judith Trowbridge

Open all year, except January.
5 rooms, 1 suite, all with private bath.
Rates May 1 to October 31: $75 double, $125 suite; November 1 to April 30: $50 double, $80 suite, including continental breakfast or Sunday brunch.
Credit cards: American Express, Diners Club, MasterCard, Visa.
French and Italian spoken.
Innkeeper: Robert J. Golden.

Greenville

Greenville Arms
Greenville, New York 12083
Telephone (518) 966-5219

The inn, in the foothills of the Catskill Mountains, was built in the 1890s as a home for William Vanderbilt. The inn's guest rooms are in two buildings: the home and the original carriage house.

"Greenville is ideally located: a pleasant back-road drive to Albany and its many attractions, or to Saratoga for the August racing season. There are many, many delightful day trips. Greenville is at its best in the summer. A short drive or walk in any direction brings you in touch with the natural wonders of the northern Catskills. Fall and spring offer the splendors of the changing seasons, and winter is lively: there are many ski runs nearby.

"The best thing about Greenville is the Greenville Arms. There is always a sense of quiet and rest. The rooms and especially the dining rooms are furnished in lovely, timeworn Early American antiques, enhanced by paintings of mostly local scenes by well-known local artists. Fireplaces with old burnished-copper accessories enhance the public rooms. The grounds are surprisingly spacious and beautifully landscaped, with a swimming pool ringed by majestic pine trees." *—Mr. and Mrs. George Arancio;*
also recommended by Karen and Neal Silverstein

Open April through November.
20 rooms, 14 with private bath.
Rates $37–$50 per person, including breakfast and dinner. Weekly rates from $185 per person.

No credit cards.
No bar, but guests are invited to bring their own beverages.
Shortline or Mountain View buses from New York City to the inn's
    door. Train service to Hudson, New York.
Innkeepers: Barbara and Laura Stevens.

_____ *Hamilton*

Colgate Inn
On the Green
Hamilton, New York 13346
Telephone (315) 824-2300

"The inn is at one end of a park at the one business corner in
Hamilton, a village with gracious old houses and stately trees. One
of the joys of the town is a stroll past these houses, and one of its
surprises is the way the village residents greet strangers with a
friendly 'Good Evening.' The Colgate University campus, one of the
most beautiful in the Northeast, is on a hill at the edge of town. A
lake with swans and walks with willows make the campus seem a
well-tended park. Most winters the snow is deep and clean. The
countryside is beautiful, with rolling hills.

"The Tavern, where generations of Colgate University under-
graduates learned to drink beer, has disappeared from the first floor
of the Colgate Inn, and that's good news for travelers. The old
tavern has been renovated and is now a dining room, unconducive
to cries of chug-a-lug and choruses of old college drinking songs.
There is a roomy cocktail lounge, and the guest rooms have been
painted, refurnished, and air conditioned.

"In the spring and fall the inn is usually booked to capacity, and
on football weekends the whole town is crowded. But in summer
and winter rooms are not usually hard to come by."
    —*William P. Luce; also recommended by Karen and Neal Silverstein*

Open all year.
46 rooms, all with private bath.
Rates $38–$60.
Credit cards: MasterCard, Visa.
Public bar and restaurant.
Nearest airport: Syracuse.
Manager: John Van Amburgh.

Do you know a hotel in your state that we have overlooked? Write
now.

_____*Hillsdale*

L'Hostellerie Bressane
Hillsdale, New York 12529
Telephone (518) 325-3412

The Hostellerie Bressane figures among a limited number of inns with truly outstanding cuisine. Since 1973, the owner and chef, Jean Morel, has conducted cooking schools here, while continuing to gather stars for his dining room from the most demanding and discriminating food writers. Expect to pay Manhattan or Paris prices for the pleasure of dining here, however. The inn itself is a good example of eighteenth-century Dutch colonial architecture, built of home-made brick.

"Those unfamiliar with the bucolic environs of Columbia County might locate Chef and Madame Morel's inn by its proximity to Tanglewood. For me, the finest orchestration in the area is to be found in the dining room, not the Shed. My preference is for a leisurely meal with chicken liver soufflé, pea soup with sorrel, and poached salmon in champagne sauce. For the selection of wine, I yield to my wife. Such a meal makes the entire evening for us. I have observed, however, that Madame Morel and the staff pace the meal appropriately for those who feel the need for Tanglewood or the Berkshire ski slopes. What is a recommendation without a comparison? In a frame of reference encompassing Lyons and New York City, Jean Morel excels. Choose your own standards and make your own comparisons."
                                        —*Dr. James T. Corkins;*
                    also recommended by Wolfgang and Karin Kutter

Open all year, except March and either February or April.
6 rooms, 2 with private bath.
Rates $45–$75, including breakfast.
Four-day cooking course, including accommodation, breakfast, and
    lunch $432–$530.
No credit cards.
Public bar and restaurant.
French spoken.
Buses to Hillsdale, trains to Hudson.
Innkeepers: Jean and Madeleine Morel.

_____

Swiss Hütte
Hillsdale, New York 12529
Telephone (518) 325-3333

Swiss Hütte has several kinds of accommodation: four rooms in the main inn, one cottage, and fourteen motel-style rooms. The complex, with spring-fed ponds and flower gardens, is in a rolling wooded area good for both summer walks and winter sports.

"An extremely comfortable place in the Catamount ski area just over the New York State line from the Berkshires. The public rooms —a rustic lounge, large bar, and a dining room—are all done in simple ski-lodge fashion. Tom Breen is the chef, and the food is remarkably fine. The cuisine is French, with a large, varied menu. Wines can run from simple nameless carafe reds and whites (probably California) to good French vintages. There is a large swimming pool, and a most attractive swimming pond, with a profusion of flowers everywhere. The gardener must be a key man on the staff. The whole place, and it is not large, faces Catamount, which is thickly wooded, with trails peeping through. A year-round place. Four stars without question."   —*Mort Stone*

Open all year, except April.
21 rooms, all with private bath; one 2-bedroom suite with 2 baths and living room.
Rates $45–$70 per person, including 2 meals.
Credit cards: MasterCard, Visa.
Public bar and restaurant.
French and German spoken.
Bus service to Hillsdale.
Innkeepers: Thomas and Linda Breen.

_____*New Paltz*

Mohonk Mountain House
Lake Mohonk
New Paltz, New York 12561
Telephone (914) 255-1000

"In the world of hotels, where the description "unique" is thrown around frequently and carelessly, there is one place that restores purity of meaning to the word. Anyone who has ever been there could be brought back blindfolded to almost any corner of its quirky magnificence and would say in instant recognition: Mohonk! One hundred whimsical gazebos perched in precarious and unexpected spots, miles of fussy railing on hundreds of creaky little porches, sensibly shod guests hiking into the sunrise under the command of a formidable Swede or dozing over immensely serious books on rocking-chaired verandas, summer-camp meals served lickety-split in a barn-size dining hall—images of Mohonk don't easily get confused with images of other places.

"Albert and Alfred Smiley, straitlaced but savvy twin brothers, found a little tavern on Lake Mohonk in 1869, and quickly decided there was scope for a resort hotel in this laurel-covered landscape. From 1870 until 1902, their hotel grew from 40 to 300 rooms, its present size. The Smiley family still owns Mohonk, now surrounded by 2,000 acres of hills, fields, and lawns. There is a nine-hole golf course, horseback riding, tennis and platform tennis, and a small lakeside beach. There are also organized outdoor activities, house rules—and no bar. (No one, however, asks where you are going with the ice bucket.) Somehow, guests can create their own amusements here, and lose themselves in the maze of the place. The privacy of Mohonk, rather than its size, is what you remember."

—B.C.

"Mohonk is an ideal retreat for nonswinging New Yorkers. It is less than two hours from Manhattan by car or bus. It's a huge, rambling place with fireplaces in most of the rooms, which are furnished with oak dressers and rocking chairs and are simple and comfortable. Each has its own porch. The public rooms are spacious and inviting, with grand pianos, Victorian sofas and stuffed chairs, huge fireplaces, and gently worn carpets. There's a surrey for summer jaunts and sleighriding when there is snow. Evening activities are old-fashioned, with occasional movies, slow dancing, or variety shows. There are weeks or weekends of special events such as astronomy, nature, chamber music, or jogging. Drinks are now served with meals in the dining room for those who ask. Food is country American, with generous portions and excellent soups, breads, and desserts."

—Patricia Berens;
also recommended by Karen and Neal Silverstein

Open all year.
300 rooms, 250 with private bath.
Rates a day, depending on room and season, AP. Midweek packages and ski-tour plans available.
Credit cards: American Express, MasterCard, Visa.
Adirondack Trailways buses from New York City to New Paltz. Amtrak train to Poughkeepsie from Grand Central. For a small fee and by prior arrangement, guests are met at train or bus.
Manager: Frank A. Hamilton.

All inkeepers appreciate reservations in advance; some require them.

New York City

_____

The Algonquin
59 West 44th Street
New York, New York 10036
Telephone (212) 840-6800

"The Algonquin's reputation blossomed in the 1920s when its Round Table became a sort of clubhouse for New York's reigning literary wits—Dorothy Parker, Robert Benchley, George S. Kaufman—many of whom worked for *The New Yorker* across the street. In 1977 the magazine threw a seventy-fifth birthday party for the hotel and a few writers were on hand, but lately the clientele has become more theatrical—Laurence Olivier, Yves Montand, Jeanne Moreau. (We were once audience to a matchless Peter Ustinov pantomime as he sucked in his considerable girth to allow ladies-first off the elevator. Ustinov is a favorite with the staff, reportedly dealing with all the bellhops and waiters in their various mother tongues.)

"Europeans love the Algonquin for the personal service and the musty dowdiness, reminiscent of so many continental hotels. In fact, much of the Algonquin's antiquity is facade. A few years back, owner Ben Bodne and his son-in-law/manager Andrew Anspach spent over a million dollars fixing it up—they just didn't tell anyone. Wing chairs from the lobby-lounge (a beehive of a cocktail party every evening from five to seven) were secretly smuggled out for reupholstering, and the carpets were replaced in the dead of night to avoid worrying the regulars about renovations. The cranky elevator is, in fact, rather new. It's just that Mr. Bodne likes operators, hates pushbuttons. About the only changes anyone noticed were the redecorating of the Rose Room (by Oliver Smith, who designed *My Fair Lady*) and the introduction of Cardgards—an electronic door-opening system far more secure than keys with room numbers and mail-back tags.

"The Algonquin works hard at being an unchanging home for its clients. It took us four visits to notice that we always had, not just the same floor location, but the same room every time. The reservation desk keeps files. Other guests' cards note 'two single beds pushed together' or 'thermos of milk and bowl for cat.' Food in the Oak Room and the Rose Room remains maddeningly inconsistent, just like home."   —*Mechtild Hoppenrath and Charles Oberdorf*

"The Algonquin has an upstairs/downstairs problem. Upstairs, the rooms can be pretty tacky. But the downstairs parlor, with its bustle of assorted types all enjoying the heck out of having a drink at the

Algonquin, their eyes darting this way and that for a glimpse of someone who might be someone, is one of the most intensely cosmopolitan spaces in the nation—not to be missed."

—*Tom Congdon*

Open all year.
185 rooms, all with private bath.
Rates $90–$94 single, $95–$100 double; suites from $176.
Credit cards: American Express, Carte Blanche, Diners Club, MasterCard, Visa.
French, German, Spanish, and Swedish spoken.
Manager: Andrew A. Anspach.

American Stanhope
995 Fifth Avenue, at 81st Street
New York, New York 10028
Telephone (212) 288-5800

"The hotel has one of the nicest locations in the city: across from the Metropolitan Museum of Art and Central Park, close to the Madison Avenue galleries, and within walking distance of New York's best residential and shopping neighborhoods. The size of the American Stanhope's public rooms—dining room, bar, and small tearoom—give it the feeling of an inn rather than a city hotel. The building, designed in 1926 by Rosario Candela, has recently been restored and refurbished. The hotel, formerly as the old Stanhope and now under its new name, always attracts celebrity guests. Among its present roster of names are Peter O'Toole, Dick Cavett, Lee Marvin, and Paul McCartney."

—*B.C.*

Open all year.
274 rooms, including 51 suites, all with private bath.
Rates $150–$400. Weekend package, including continental breakfast: $196 for two nights.
Credit cards: American Express, Carte Blanche, Diners Club, MasterCard, Visa.
French and Spanish spoken.
Manager: Singh Oberoi.

Rates quoted were the latest available. But they may not reflect unexpected increases or local and state taxes. Be sure to verify when you book.

Berkshire Place
21 East 52nd Street
New York, New York 10022
Telephone (212) 753-5800 or toll-free (800) 228-2121

The original Berkshire Hotel was built in 1926 to the designs of Warren and Wetmore, one of New York's best architectural firms of the interwar period. Then, as now, the hotel's location, ambience, and service attracted the well known: Salvador Dali painted here, Rodgers and Hammerstein worked on *Oklahoma!*, and Ethel Merman and Alfred Hitchcock came to stay when in town. In the late 1970s the Dunfey hotel chain bought and renovated the hotel, renaming it the Berkshire Place. The renovation was by most accounts very successful. Paul Goldberger, the architecture critic of *The New York Times* and the author of a book on New York buildings, describes it as a "handsome hotel," redone without losing the qualities of the original.

"The Berkshire Place was my biggest discovery in New York in years. No other hotel in that city offers all four of the following: A-1 location; great service; completely refurnished, spotlessly clean rooms; and, the scarcest commodity in New York—gracious, accommodating employees. There is nothing quite like it in Manhattan."
—*Robert J. Ringer*

Open all year.
450 rooms, 22 suites, all with private bath. Penthouse with 2 bedrooms, dining room, living room, study, 3 baths, Jacuzzi, kitchen, bar, and wraparound terrace with panoramic view of the city.
Rates $150–$200, suites $200–$1,500. Special penthouse weekend, $2,500, includes use of limousine to and from airport, private helicopter tour of the city, one dinner cooked by chef in penthouse kitchen and another at Windows on the World restaurant atop the World Trade Center.
All major credit cards.
Concierge staff speaks 10 languages.
General Manager: Volker Ulrich.

Where are the good little hotels in Boston? Philadelphia? Omaha? Dallas? If you have found one, don't keep it a secret. Write *now*.

Elysee Hotel
60 East 54th Street
New York, New York 10022
Telephone (212) 753-1066

"The Monkey Bar is a familiar stopping-in place for many New Yorkers. But if you were to ask the same folk about the Elysee Hotel, you would probably draw a blank from many of them. The Monkey Bar is the bar-lounge and breakfast room of the Elysee, the small East Side hotel that has been and is home to many of the great and near-great personalities visiting New York. (Tennessee Williams was staying here at the time of his death.) This is an excellent small hotel, extremely well managed. The lobby is unimposing. You will not be greeted by hordes of bellmen. There is a quietness that is remarkable for a New York hotel. You will be quickly registered, however, and shown to your room. My preference is one of the hotel's small suites—a small, beautifully appointed sitting room, a bedroom with two three-quarter-size beds (I can't stand conventional twin beds), and a good bathroom. On the occasion when a small suite was not available, I have been given a small room, which has always been comfortable.

"The Elysee is within walking distance of East Side shops and restaurants, and not too far from theaters and other points of interest on the West Side. The hotel has a steady following—make reservations well in advance."   —*Michael Stevens*

Open all year.
110 rooms and suites, all with private bath.
Rates $85–$125 single, $95–$135 double, $175–$225 suites.
Credit cards: American Express, Carte Blanche, Diners Club, MasterCard, Visa.
French, German, Italian, and Spanish spoken.
Managing Director: Leon Quain.

The Empire Hotel
44 West 63rd Street
New York, New York 10023
Telephone (212) 265-7400

"We got to New York quite often and we usually stay at the Empire Hotel, across from Lincoln Center. It is that rarity, a reasonably priced, clean, well-run New York hotel in the central area. It has a small coffee shop which serves enormous breakfasts. The area has a number of small, elegant restaurants and is within walking distance of the midtown sights."   —*Enid Robbie*

Open all year
520 rooms, all with private bath.
Rates $55–$70 single, $65–$80 double.
Credit cards: American Express, Carte Blanche, Diners Club, MasterCard, Visa.
General Manager: Joseph Filoseta.

Hotel San Carlos
150 East 50th Street
New York, New York 10022
Telephone (212) 755-1800

"From those 'I Love New York' ads on TV, I found the San Carlos. It was unimpressive from the outside, but very nice inside. The staff was friendly and seemed genuinely interested in your well-being— a situation unheard of on previous visits to New York. With the price of our room, we received a bottle of champagne on arrival, and a *New York Times* at our door when we awoke on Sunday. Our spacious, quiet, and comfortable room had a small safe to keep our valuables. The hotel is near the United Nations. We felt safe walking around. This is a real find for people who don't want to or can't afford to spend $100 a night or more."   —*Mark L. Goodman*

Open all year.
200 rooms, including some suites with kitchens, all with private bath.
Rates $79–$150.
Credit cards: American Express, Carte Blanche, Diners Club, MasterCard, Visa.
Japanese restaurant in hotel.
Executive Manager: Herb Goldstein.

The Sheraton Russell
45 Park Avenue
New York, New York 10016
Telephone (212) 685-7676 or toll-free (800) 325-3535

This small hotel is in the Murray Hill section of New York, where Park Avenue is somewhat less residential than it is farther uptown. But the neighborhood is an interesting one, and many of New York's attractions are within walking distance or a short bus or subway ride away. The atmosphere of the Sheraton Russell is serene: there is even a quiet library.

"This was first brought to our attention by an article in *New York* magazine, and we have made it our annual anniversary night-out special place ever since. The rooms are delightful. Our favorite overlooks Park Avenue, and is furnished with blue carpets, color-coordinated drapes, and a fireplace. The dining room is Victorian, with wallpaper and china in the same patterns. This might sound a bit much but its effect is delightful. The staff is friendly, helpful, and not overbearing."   —*Stephanie Jatlow*

Open all year
175 rooms, all with private bath.
Rates $110–$140 single, $130–$160 double, $195–$275 suites.
Credit cards: American Express, Carte Blanche, Diners Club, MasterCard, Visa.
General Manager: Jetta S. Brenner.

_____*Portageville*

Genesee Falls Inn
Main and Hamilton Streets (P.O. Box 396)
Portageville, New York 14536
Telephone (716) 493-2484

"We arrived late, and were made welcome—the dining room was opened to give us a meal. The dining and sitting areas of the inn are filled with interesting objects and pictures. The bedrooms are large, clean, and air conditioned, if rather basic. But the price was reasonable, and we were comfortable."   —*Gilbert Ross*

Open all year, except December and January.
7 inn rooms, 5 with private bath; 5 motel units.
Rates $16.50–$30.
No credit cards.
Innkeeper: Ed Brosche.

Turn to the back of this book for pages inviting *your* comments.

_____*Skaneateles*

The Sherwood Inn
26 West Genesee Street
Skaneateles, New York 13152
Telephone (315) 685-3405

There is an entertaining legend about how Sherwood Inn got its name. Isaac Sherwood built the first tavern on this spot, in 1807. But by 1840, when it was leased to a Colonel Alford Lamb, it had long lost the Sherwood name. It was known for the next century by a succession of names: Lamb's Hotel, Houndayaga House, Packwood House, and finally Kan-Ya-To Inn. It might still be called that today if innkeeper Chester Coats, preparing in 1945 to welcome General Jonathan Mayhew Wainright, the hero of Bataan and Corregidor, had not overheard someone call his inn "that nice little Japanese place." Mr. Coats thought it prudent to quickly change the name, and the long-departed Mr. Sherwood won the honor.

"This is a lovely old, beautifully restored country inn, with most of its rooms overlooking Skaneateles Lake in the Finger Lakes region. The large living room, filled with deep, comfortable chairs, invites guests to linger and rest awhile. The cocktail lounge with its dark, warm wood beckons folks to tarry over drinks. The several dining rooms (one filled with lush exotic plants) serve delicious soups, salads, main courses, and desserts fit for a king.

"A drive in almost any direction brings entertainment, be it a tour of a winery or glass-making factories or peaceful country with farms, lakes, and hordes of Canada geese."   —*Betty G. Mower*

Open all year; restaurant closed Christmas Day.
15 rooms, all with private bath.
Rates $35–$60, including continental breakfast.
Credit cards: American Express, Carte Blanche, Diners Club, MasterCard, Visa.
Bus service to Skaneateles.
Manager: Richard Hubbard.

_____*Speculator*

Zeiser's
Speculator, New York 12164
Telephone (518) 548-7021

It would be hard to top a recommendation like that of John D. MacDonald, and so it stands. One contributor, however, while seconding this famous author's comments, had only one problem: he found his room unsatisfactory because of a broken door lock and a less-than-sparkling shower. He was enthusiastic over the food, however, recommending the house poppy-seed dressing.

"I really believe you should include Zeiser's in Speculator, New York. It is owned by John and Genevieve Zeiser (and Ludwig, the cat). The operation is housed in what used to be the annex of the Sturges House, which was built in 1858 by David Sturges, back when the crossroads near the hotel was called Newton's Corners. The Zeisers have been in business for twenty-three years. There is an attractive bar, lunch areas—including a long screened porch in season—and a handsome formal dining room, with lighting, napery, silverware, and table settings beyond reproach. Every part of the operation is spotlessly clean.

"There is no American Plan. You are expected to find your breakfast elsewhere in the village. There is no room service for drinks or food. The food is excellent, tending toward the German. The wine cellar is heavy on good Moselles. Mr. Z, a tidy and formal man, reigns at the bar. His no-nonsense attitude has given the bar the flavor of a good, small private club. Service is swift and courteous, and one would go a long way to find a better dry martini—or more civilized conversation at the bar. Mr. Z is a host!

"Speculator, incidentally, is in Hamilton County, which is in the middle of Adirondack State Park Preserve and is the most sparsely settled county in New York State. It is reputed to have more black bears than people. The crossroads a couple of hundred feet from Zeiser's is the intersection of Route 8, which begins way down at Deposit, New York, on the Pennsylvania border and ends at Hague, New York, on the northwest shore of Lake George, and Route 30 which begins, or ends, down at Harvard and Shinhopple, New York, near the Pennsylvania border, and ends, or begins, at Trout River on the Quebec border.

"Lest this sound too obscure, let me say that Zeiser's is 42 miles from Gloversville, 61 from Utica, 75 from Schenectady, 90 from Albany, 94 from Troy, and 109 from Syracuse. The most handsome way of driving up to Speculator is to exit the New York State Thruway at Exit 29, Canajoharie, and drive north on route 10 to Route 8, and turn right on Route 8 to Speculator, twelve miles farther. The last seventeen miles of Route 10, before it intersects Route 8, are known locally as the Arietta Road. When it was repaved a few years ago, the Park Authority did not consent to the usual straightening. So there are sixty-five curves in those hilly miles, beautifully graded, a feast in autumn, but special at any time of year. Speculator is lakes and camping in the summer, hunting in the fall, skiing in the winter."

—*John D. MacDonald*

Open all year.
6 rooms, all with private bath.
Rate $35 double.
Credit card: American Express.
German spoken.
Innkeeper: John M. Zeiser.

_____*Stony Brook*

Three Village Inn
Dock Road
Stony Brook, New York 11790
Telephone (516) 751-0555

Whether or not by chance, the Three Village Inn is a favorite of British visitors to the United States. Two Englishmen have written enthusiastically about the place.

"I rank the Three Village Inn as one of the most pleasurable hotels I have stayed in in more than twenty countries. The quality and the quantity of the food, the friendly and willing service and very comfortable accommodations—including queen-size beds and television in the rooms—make the inn a welcome haven and an exceptional value.

"The local Stony Brook community works hard to conserve both beautiful old buildings and wildlife—watch for duck- and rabbit-crossing signs! The inn is in the center of trees and greenswards, squirrels and birds in profusion. Yet a few hundred yards away are an attractive marina and safe swimming beaches. Apart from the swimming there is also good fishing.

"The inn's dinners are an excellent value. There is a wide choice of seafood, juicy steaks, home-baked pies, and dishes of the day. There is an imaginative dessert menu and an excellent, well-presented Roquefort cheese. Unfortunately the wine list does not do full justice to the fare: it is adequate but lacks imagination, and the house wines are not always well served.

"To eat both dinner and the formal lunch would be an almost impossible task. Consequently, the bar snack of rich creamy clam chowder (the best I have eaten) and a good hamburger, accompanied by a really cold beer, is more than sufficient between the hearty breakfast and the splendid dinner.

"The quality of the Three Village Inn and the green beauty of Suffolk County proved a perfect antidote to the concrete and cacophony of New York."
                                                        —*Peter Webster*

"The best, most memorable stay we had on our trip was at the Three Village Inn. It was a lovely setting, with clean and pleasant rooms, a good dining room and plenty of atmosphere."

—*Gilbert Ross*

Open all year.
24 rooms, all with private bath.
Rates $45–$55 single, $55–$70 double.
Credit Cards: American Express, MasterCard, Visa.
French, German, and Spanish spoken.
Long Island Rail Road service to Stony Brook.
Innkeepers: Nelson, Monda, and Whitney Roberts.

Details of special features offered by an inn or hotel vary according to information supplied by the hotels themselves. The absence here of a recreational amenity, a bar, or a restaurant doesn't necessarily mean one of these doesn't exist. Ask the innkeeper when booking your room.

Century Inn,
Scenery Hill

Pennsylvania

Allentown

Coachaus
107–111 North Eighth Street
Allentown, Pennsylvania 18102
Telephone (215) 821-4854

"Finally in central Allentown, a once-nondescript city undergoing restoration and revitalization, there exists an alternative to the sterile atmosphere of the chain hotel. Coachaus, only half a block away from one of the restoration districts, has been splendidly and carefully restored from two adjoining buildings. It is a bed-and-breakfast sure to appeal to the discerning traveler. The beautiful decor in each room reflects the meticulous planning of the innkeeper, Barbara Kocher. Coachaus creates an inviting warmth.

"Within walking distance of Coachaus are a few of the best restaurants in Allentown, to which Barbara will direct you. Considering the apparent success thus far, Coachaus would seem to herald the long-awaited return to smaller and more intimate city lodgings in this area that has been for so long dominated by motels."

—*Jonathan Crossette*

173

Open all year, except Christmas and New Year's Day.

8 rooms, 1 suite, 6 apartments, all with private bath.

Rates $42–$48 single, $52–$58 suite, $62–$68 apartment, including breakfast on weekdays and on weekends by arrangement; $195–$285 weekly. Corporate rates available. Weekend package including champagne, fruit, flowers, and brunch $69 per couple for 1 night, $99 per couple for 2 nights.

Credit cards: American Express, MasterCard, Visa.

Central bus station 2 blocks away; airport 5 miles by taxi. Car rentals available at inn.

Innkeeper: Barbara Kocher.

Bethlehem

Hotel Bethlehem
437 Main Street
Bethlehem, Pennsylvania 18018
Telephone (215) 867-3711

"Bethlehem was one of many old American cities that let its history be swamped by its more recent industrial development—though here even industry is history, since the city began to boom before the turn of the nineteenth century. Recently, however, the people of Bethlehem have made some important and, for a visitor, welcome decisions. An area of eighteenth-century industrial development has been reconstructed. The old town center has not been torn down, but preserved or restored. Don't expect a charming colonial atmosphere, however. The feeling is more turn-of-the-century workaday, but that has an interest of its own, since so many Main Streets of that Industrial Revolution period have been effectively obliterated. Scattered throughout the area are also some exceptionally fine buildings of an earlier period, dating to the era of Moravian settlement that began in 1741.

"Bethlehem, known as the Christmas City, takes on a holiday atmosphere in that season. Visitors come from far away to see the Moravian Nativity tableaux, and the city is filled with traditional music. In the spring, a Bach festival is the city's major event. Bethlehem is the home of Moravian College, as well as Lehigh University and, of course, Bethlehem Steel.

"Right in the center of the old town is the Hotel Bethlehem, a premotel fixture of the city that has been refurbished to serve both businesspeople and tourists. Some of its rooms are truly fine: the Continental dining room has maintained its elegance; the Pioneer Room bar and restaurant has a collection of well-known murals from early Pennsylvania history and some other interesting Americana. But throughout the place, the decor—apparently intended to create cheerfulness—has introduced cacophony instead. Harsh colors, badly mixed patterns and styles, and a general feeling of overdecoration hide the building's inherent grace. Our room, for example, had lovely real-wood period furniture, but also motel draperies that clashed with well-chosen wallpaper, and terrible artwork on two of the walls. While the management had concealed the television set in a cabinet, the small refrigerator with its coffee maker and plastic cups was left in full view. The lobby, in hideous bright green, was without a single bench or chair in which to sit while waiting for a car to take us to a meeting. The staff was wonderful, however—nothing but smiles from waitresses who were about ready to go home just as we arrived for a late supper—and the service touches were superior: a choice of three or four kinds of soap in the bathroom and more towels than we could use in several days. With a little more attention to the decoration, this would be an outstanding hotel. Even as it is, it is probably the best place by far to stay in Bethlehem."   —B.C.

Open all year.
130 rooms and suites, all with private bath.
Rates $54–$70 single, $64–$80 double, suites vary in price.
Credit cards: American Express, Carte Blanche, Diners Club, MasterCard, Visa.
Bar and restaurants.
German and Spanish spoken.
6 blocks to intercity bus station; courtesy car to Allentown-Bethlehem-Easton airport.
Innkeeper: Elizabeth Emslander.

_____Buck Hill Falls

Buck Hill Inn
Box D-3
Buck Hill Falls, Pennsylvania 18323
Telephone (717) 595-7441 or toll free from New York
(800) 233-8113

"I first explored this old Pocono Mountain resort by the backstairs when, as a college student, I got a summer job there as a waitress more than twenty years ago. Buck Hill was then still its old Quaker self, a haven of quiet gentility set in 6,000 acres of woods and hills. Quaker equality meant that we, the help, were free to roam (almost) the whole wonderful place, from the quiet Sunday meeting room, to the tennis courts, to the nightly lectures and travelogues. I went back recently for a visit. "That Quaker stuff's all gone now," said the woman at the bar (a bar, at Buck Hill!). And so it is, along with the funky old reception desk and the hushed dining room—oh, how we once burnished silver and polished service plates. Instead there was a reception area of incredible hideousness and a buffet line of noisy conventioneers.

"But in the wide, dark lobbies upstairs, the old furniture was still there; a pianist was fingering the piano keys in the meeting room, and on the porch elderly regulars sat peacefully in chairs, looking at the equally peaceful hills. What's an inn like this to do? Once one of a handful of grand resorts in Pennsylvania's Pocono Mountains, frequented by the rich, the intellectual, the refined, it now lives on in a new world, and it has to hang there any way it can, I guess. At sunset it is still a marvelous pile of stone set on the green hills. Those of us who knew it then, wish it well."   —B.C.

Open all year.
250 rooms and suites, all with private bath.
Rates $79–$140 per person, including 2 meals.
Credit cards: American Express, MasterCard, Visa.
Public restaurants and bars.
Ask for the inn's free, comprehensive travel guide on how to reach Buck Hill. Limousines will pick up guests at the Mount Pocono bus depot.
Managers: Astrid and Jacob Keuler.

_____ *Canadensis*

The Overlook Inn
Dutch Hill Road
Canadensis, Pennsylvania 18325
Telephone (717) 595-7519

Canadensis is in the heart of the Pocono Mountains; the Overlook occupies one of the area's wooded ridges. Originally a farmhouse, with a carriage house and other outbuildings, the Overlook began to take in summer boarders at the turn of the century. It remains a small inn in an area of much bigger resort hotels and lodges.

"A really charming inn. Joe the chef tries *New York Times* recipes now and then. Innkeeper Lolly Tupper (these innkeepers always seem to have friendly names) ends each day, be it at 1, 2, 3 A.M., with "It's so nice to have you with us." In cold weather, the fire is lit at 11 A.M.

and stays lit till dawn sometimes. The staff is marvelous. We got stuck in the snow when we went there, and the experience has inspired my husband, Allen, to write a book about a family getting stranded and going through the forest to 'Treeple'-land. It's à la C. S. Lewis."   —*Pauline O'Reilly-Weakland*

Open all year.
20 rooms, all with private bath.
Rate $49 a day per person, including breakfast and dinner.
Credit cards: American Express, MasterCard, Visa.
Public restaurant; bar for house and dinner guests only.
Trailways bus service to Mount Pocono from New York; local taxis available.
Innkeepers: Bob and Lolly Tupper; Manager: Derald Evans.

_____*Erwinna*

Evermay on-the-Delaware
River Road
Erwinna, Pennsylvania 18920
Telephone (215) 294-9100

"Few places in the overbuilt, overpaved development area that passes for the Middle Atlantic states could be so overlooked and free of ruin as the riverside stretch of central and upper Bucks County that straddles the winding two-lane River Road—Route 32 —from New Hope north to Easton. Along the River Road with the Delaware River and canal running beside it, hotels and taverns have been in existence since fifty years or more before the American Revolution. The first of them marked ferry points across the wide river; they were later joined by newer hotels that followed the building of the nineteenth-century canal, or that brought summer tourism to the valley after the Civil War. These hotels served bargemen, farmers bringing grain to the mills, tourists and travelers on their way between cities linked by the waterways or reached by one of the river's ferries.

"Evermay was one of those genteel old country hotels overlooking the river that reached a peak of elegance (and business) between the Civil War and the Depression. After World War II, vacationing Americans abandoned many of these inns for places that seemed more exciting farther afield. While many of the neighboring bargemen's taverns remained open as local bars, a number of the resort inns were sold to private owners and became homes or summer houses. Now that the area is being rediscovered by travelers looking for quiet relaxation in unspoiled country, several of these inns are being restored.

"Evermay, one such restoration, is the second Bucks County inn to be opened by Ron Strouse and Fred Cresson. Their Sign of the Sorrel Horse near Lake Nockamixon and Quakertown is already widely known in the area for its outstanding cuisine. Over the last few years, the Strouse-Cresson team has refinished Evermay's handsome exterior and restored its library-parlour, conservatory, and guest rooms. They have also resurrected some old traditions: tea in the afternoon and sherry in the parlor each evening. Because of the culinary reputation of the owners, this restoration adds more than a nice place to sleep in a relaxing rural area: it provides a place to go just for the food."

—B.C.

Open all year.
16 rooms and suites in main house and carriage house, all with private bath.
Rates $48–$65, including breakfast and afternoon tea.
Credit cards: MasterCard, Visa.
The inn serves a five-course, one-sitting-only dinner at 7:30 on Friday, Saturday, and Sunday evenings. Reservations are necessary.
Innkeepers: Ronald L. Strouse and Frederick L. Cresson.

Golden Pheasant Inn
River Road
Erwinna, Pennsylvania 18920
Telephone (215) 294-9595

"The Golden Pheasant is a somewhat strange but interesting place, really two inns in one. We would almost certainly not have given it a second glance if we had not already made a reservation. With some trepidation, we pulled up to a building looking run-down and depressing, more like a small warehouse wedged between the Delaware River and the Delaware Canal. Once inside, however, we were charmed. There was a Victorian bar with dining area and a larger plant-filled dining room on the first floor, with sleeping rooms upstairs.

"The dining room's reputation for excellent food—standard American, classic French, exotic foreign dishes—draws diners from all over Pennsylvania, New Jersey, and New York. We were there in the fall and found the menu offering fresh game, including rabbit, quail and, of course, pheasant. The game was excellent, as were the liver with mustard sauce and the Sanjuk, an Asian dish of skewered beef with hot peanut sauce. Each entrée came with small servings of three or four vegetables, imaginatively prepared. The service was as good as the food.

"The second part of the inn, the Federal-style 1834 Isaac Stover Mill Mansion, which they call the Annex, is a mile or so upriver. There, our third-floor room was carefully furnished for both decorative appeal and comfort. We shared the bathroom with the three other rooms on that floor. We spent a pleasant evening before the fire in the parlor talking with several other couples with whom we shared the house. The following morning the housekeeper had coffee waiting for us in the big, homey kitchen. A nice send-off to a relaxing stay."   —JLS

"Our accommodations in the Annex smelled more musty than historic. The rooms were neatly decorated but disturbingly dirty. The furniture and floors needed dusting, as did the common bathroom. The continental breakfast consisted of soggy Danish and a quart carton of orange juice in an ice bucket. The coffee maker was broken: we found a dead fly in the water reservoir. The only highlight was dinner in the greenhouse in the main building. The cuisine was good (not excellent), with the usual New Hope overpricing. And the bar was gay. Many of the patrons were from New York, and to them perhaps this inn looked like a bargain compared with New York prices. But to native Pennsylvanians, inns such as this are overrated disappointments."   —Mr. and Mrs. Lawrence Liberti

Open all year, except January.
14 rooms, none with private bath.
Rate $45, including continental breakfast.
Credit cards: American Express, MasterCard, Visa.
Innkeepers: Reid Perry and Ralph Schneider.

_____*Holicong*

Barley Sheaf Farm
Route 202 (Box 66)
Holicong, Pennsylvania 18928
Telephone (215) 794-5104

"In 1936, George S. Kaufman bought a beautiful Bucks County spread known as Barley Sheaf Farm. While no evidence exists that the cosmopolitan Kaufman ever knew one end of a sheep from the other, it's well documented that Barley Sheaf Farm became a favorite gathering place for many of the brightest stars of the New York/Hollywood performing arts world. Several Kaufman biographies tell us that weekenders included Harpo Marx, Lillian Hellman, John P. Marquand, Alexander Woollcott, S. J. Perelman, Moss Hart, and a host of others.

"Most of the key characters in that glamorous scenario are gone. But Barley Sheaf Farm is alive and well, thank you, through the efforts of its present owners, Don and Ann Mills. They bought the spread in the early seventies as a private residence for themselves and their three growing children. A couple of years ago, however, the Mills family toured the country inns of England, and brought home with them the idea of turning Barley Sheaf into a bed-and-breakfast farm.

"We discovered the farm the day after Don Mills hung out a roadside sign. A quick and captivating tour of the house and grounds resulted in our names being among the first in the reservation book, a volume which has since become dog-eared with use. And no wonder! The lovely main section of the farmhouse—a nineteenth-century enlargement of an eighteenth-century structure—contains six charmingly decorated, antique-accented bedrooms, three with private baths. Our favorite served during the Kaufman era as the author's master bedroom, and features an ornate working fireplace, a polished brass bed, and French doors opening onto a sylvan view of meadows, trees, and sparkling blue swimming pool.

"It's a toss-up as to which is more delightful—a night's sleep in the peaceful bliss of the countryside, or the full farm breakfast that awaits you in the morning. The latter is served on an airy sun porch (woodstove-heated in the winter), and usually consists of home-grown foods. The eggs and bacon originate in the barn, and the honey comes from the farm's hive. All breads and muffins are home-baked and piping hot. And the coffee, Ann Mills's special blend, is the best we've ever tasted.

"If you can tear yourself away from the farm's tranquillity, the bustling, antique-gorged village of Lahaska is two minutes up the road. Fifteen minutes farther is New Hope, with its canals, characters, crowds, curios, and culinary crowns."   —*Gigi and Alan Dash*

Open from first weekend in March to weekend before Christmas.
9 rooms, 6 with private bath.
Rates $40–$85, including breakfast.
No credit cards.
French spoken.

West Hunterdon Transit bus to Doylestown stops 2 minutes from the inn. Conrail trains from Philadelphia to Doylestown.
Innkeepers: Ann and Don Mills.

_____*Lancaster*

Nissly's Olde Home Inns
624 and 632 West Chestnut Street
Lancaster, Pennsylvania 17603
Telephone (717) 392-2311; 866-4926

The boom in tourism surrounding (but usually not including) the Mennonite and Amish farming people of Lancaster County has not yet produced many old-hotel restorations, though the area certainly had its share of staging posts. Many visitors to the area find themselves stuck with little but a choice of motels. In Lancaster itself, however, there is one alternative. Here Esther Nissly and James Henry, who own the Tulpehocken Manor Inn in Myerstown, have opened a collection of seven restored Victorian houses to guests. Because these did not qualify strictly as inns, the Nissly houses were dropped from the last edition of this book. The outcry from former guests was immediate. And so, because of the dearth of Lancaster County inns of character, this accommodation service is herewith restored for travelers' use.

Two of the Nissly buildings are of special interest. The Menno Fry Mansion at 624 West Chestnut Street was built between 1894 and 1896 in the style of a French château. Its designer was C. Emlen Urban, an architect known locally for Watt & Shand's Department Store on Penn Square and the Southern Market at Vine and South Queen streets. The other notable building is the Steigerwalt Mansion, next door at 632 West Chestnut. It is almost a mirror of the adjacent house, but it is not known whether Urban designed it too. There is one story that the architect here used the same plans, but simply reversed them. Both mansions are marked by complex rooflines, stepped gables, high-quality masonry, and elaborate porches. In both structures the entry halls and staircases are focal points.

"I recently went back to my hometown of Lancaster to show a friend around. I stayed by chance at the Menno Fry house, just two blocks from where I grew up. When I arrived, expecting to occupy a bedroom with bath down the hall, I found that the people who had planned to take an efficiency apartment on the same floor—complete with kitchen, bath, and bedroom—had canceled, and I was given their place at my single-room rate. Wish that I had had more time to lounge in the parlor among the carved wood and Oriental rugs. For those of your readers who want to stay close to the historical landmarks of Lancaster and in the atmosphere of an old-city residential neighborhood, I highly recommend this service."

—*Donna Sue Gibson*

Open all year.
16 rooms and apartments.
Rates $21–$106.
No credit cards.
Innkeepers: Esther Nissly and James Henry.

Lititz

General Sutter Inn
14 East Main Street
On the Square
Lititz, Pennsylvania 17543
Telephone (717) 626-2115

"Founded by members of the Moravian Church more than 200 years ago, Lititz retains the dignity and charm of that early settlement. An active historical society, long before it was fashionable, plus a real sense of civic pride has aided in the preservation of the town, and today many of the original buildings, including the Moravian church, are still in use. Among those early buildings is an inn on the town square, built in 1764 and first known as Zum Anchor. It was later renamed for General Sutter, on whose land in California the gold rush began and who later, as the story has it, came to Lititz a poor and crippled man who hoped to find a cure for arthritis in the town's mineral springs. He died here in 1880, and is buried in the local Moravian cemetery.

"The General Sutter Inn combines the past with today's conveniences. If one is planning to visit the many historical places and attractions in Lancaster County, and likes the charm of a delightful, friendly small town, and does not feel a strong, compelling need to stay in stereotype lodgings, then Lititz and the General Sutter will provide a delightful stay."
—*Richard M. Cloney*

"The dining room was excellent."
—*Mark L. Goodman*

"The downstairs is lovely, the food is very good, and the staff delightful. However we had dismal rooms with cruddy shag carpets. This is not a country inn, but at the intersection of two busy roads: people should be told."
—*Holly Willsey-Walker*

Open all year.
13 rooms, all with private bath.
Rates $45–$54.
Credit cards: American Express, MasterCard, Visa.
Inn will meet guests at Lancaster airport.
Innkeepers: Joan and Richard Vetter.

_____*Lumberville*

Black Bass Hotel
Route 32
Lumberville, Pennsylvania 18933
Telephone (215) 297-5770

"One of the oldest of Bucks County inns is the Black Bass on the bank of the Delaware River in the small town of Lumberville. Clinging to the road like a wayside inn of Europe, the Black Bass (built in the 1740s) displays the wrought-iron ornamentation that marked the river towns. Inside it is a jumble of old wood, fireplaces, comforting bars (one with a pewter bar top from Maxim's), and seven wonderful richly furnished old rooms with names like Grover Cleveland, Victoria, and Vendôme. There is also a suite overlooking the river. The Black Bass has been a weekend escape for New Yorkers and Philadelphians for years. Its dining rooms—one a porch stretching along the canal bank and river—are also popular, and packed as a local pub on Saturday nights.

"Like a lot of old hotels, this one has its quirks. One early spring night the heating failed, and several guests decamped to a neighborhood establishment. The dining room menu can be overambitious; we have been disappointed on more than one occasion. But on the whole this inn is a classic of its genre and period."

—*B.C.*

"A peaceful, beautiful, and friendly hotel."   —*Mark L. Goodman*

Open all year, except Christmas Day.
8 rooms, 1 suite.
Rates $50 rooms, $110 suite, including continental breakfast.
Credit cards: American Express, Diners Club, MasterCard, Visa.
Nearest bus service at Frenchtown, New Jersey.
Manager: Dean Stephens.

Do you know a hotel in your state that we have overlooked? Write *now*.

1740 House
River Road
Lumberville, Pennsylvania 18933
Telephone (215) 297-5661

"Prepare yourself for Harry Nessler. If all innkeepers are characters, this is one writ large. 'We only serve things I like here,' he told me on my first visit to the 1740 House. 'And we only cook them the way I like them.' There are rumors (nay, legends) about how he preselects guests for a lot of quirky (though strictly legal) reasons. But when he hung out a sign (a fine screen print by artist Allen Sallburg, by the way), he adopted as his motto: 'If you can't be a houseguest in Bucks County, be ours.' And he meant it.

"Harry Nessler and his wife stumbled into innkeeping—he had been in real estate in New York City—when they bought a summer home and discovered that the real estate office, on the bank of the Delaware, was for sale, too. He'd always wanted to be an innkeeper, so he bought the place. A couple of core buildings in his now strung-out inn are very old (one room has a stone-walled bathroom that goes well back into the eighteenth century); the rest were skillfully added with no violence done to Lumberville's lazy, lovely main street—well, its only street actually. The 1740 House now has twenty-four rooms, a private dining room for hotel guests, with a comfortable parlor and library. Harry won't have a bar: he doesn't want the crowds to roll in off the streets and cramp his guests. He serves a very satisfying breakfast in his brick-floored dining room along the canal bank. If you're lucky, you'll catch him padding through his domain early in the morning in his lounge slippers (dogs at heel), feeling talkative."   —B.C.

"I've been to the 1740 House twice—once by myself and, because I was so impressed with the inn, the food, and the surroundings, later with my wife, whom I took with me so she could share my pleasure. Lumberville, about six miles north of New Hope along the Delaware River and Canal, is a lovely one-street town practically carved into a hillside along the river, with many charming old houses. The 1740 House is jammed between the road and the canal; it practically overhangs the latter! All rooms face the river. My room (number 14—simple, but quite comfortable) had large windows for a lovely view. The darkness is so total that I was able to leave the blinds open at night and let the beautiful view of the sunrise on the

New Jersey side of the river awaken me. Our room on the next visit was a stone-walled room, whitewashed (it had been part of a barn) and quite cozy and warm. Little view from that room—it was snowing anyway. One of my strongest memories is of the very old pine-paneled parlor with a huge stone fireplace, the room furnished quite comfortably with antiques. The whole complex is comfortable and old-shoe and well worth going out of your way for."

—*Michael B. Patterson*

Open all year.
24 rooms, 1 suite with kitchen, all with private bath.
Rates $54–$60, including buffet breakfast.
No credit cards.
Innkeeper: Harry Nessler.

_____*Mount Joy*

Cameron Estate Inn
RD 1 (Box 305)
Mount Joy, Pennsylvania 17552
Telephone (717) 653-1773

The building is a classic Pennsylvania Dutch brick structure, though it was built in 1805 for a statesman named Simon Cameron, who served the United States as a senator, ambassador, and Abraham Lincoln's first Secretary of War. The owners, Abram and Betty Groff, are Mennonite farmers who restored the home and opened it as an inn. Betty Groff was already known for her skill with the local cuisine. The author of *Betty Groff's Country Goodness Cookbook,* she and her husband run Groff's Farm Restaurant in a 1756 house about four miles away. The Cameron Estate offers a rare combination of true Pennsylvania Dutch heritage and a touch of Federal-style elegance not normally associated with a people so devoted to simplicity as the Mennonites and nearby Amish.

"The inn, located on wooded farmland, looks like the old country estate that it was. There is a warm parlor, a cozy dining room, and a pleasant veranda overlooking a rolling lawn and small stream. Our room (number 4), while large and fairly well done, was uncomfortably close to the dining room and too exposed to the outside. On further visits we will ask for a second- or third-floor room.
"Most people visit the Mount Joy area, between Lancaster and Harrisburg, for antique and factory-outlet shopping. We enjoyed

that also, but found more satisfaction in the country dining. Cameron Estate Inn served a very good dinner, and is popular locally. But two other places were superior. One was the Accomac Inn, in a remote spot overlooking the Susquehanna River near the town of Wrightsville. The food there was excellent, although the service was careless. Best of all was the Groff Farm Restaurant near Mount Joy. Between the excellent Pennsylvania Dutch cooking and the contagious exuberance of Betty Groff—who plays the cornet for diners celebrating birthdays—this restaurant served up an evening we will never forget."

—Bill and Jill Neugent

Open all year.
18 rooms, 16 with private bath.
Rates $45–$80, including continental breakfast.
Credit cards: American Express, MasterCard, Visa.
Restaurant, with liquor license, in inn.
Innkeeper: Carol Mutzel.

Myerstown

Lantern Lodge
411 North College Street
Myerstown, Pennsylvania 17067
Telephone (717) 866-6536

Lantern Lodge, a newish motor hotel, was built in 1974 around an early nineteenth-century farm with a stone barn and farmhouse. Accommodations surround a courtyard with a fountain and flowers. Myerstown is in Pennsylvania Dutch country, near Hershey, Lancaster, and Reading, with its popular factory-outlet stores. A Mennonite couple created this inn; they have since sold it to a Danish innkeeper.

"Immaculately clean and lavishly decorated, it stands in the quiet countryside. Sensitive, artistic taste was put to use in the beautiful rooms and the country garden with hundreds of bulbs and shade trees and a waterwheel. Absolutely superb."

—Susan and Nick Fox

34 rooms, all with private bath.
Rates $36–$64.
Credit cards: American Express, MasterCard, Visa.
Trailways bus stops 4 blocks from inn.
Innkeeper: Jaj K. Skov.

Tulpehocken Manor Inn and Plantation
650 West Lincoln Avenue
Myerstown, Pennsylvania 17067
Telephone (717) 866-4926; 392-2311

Tulpehocken Manor was one of the early land grants made by the Penn family. A man from the Palatinate who signed himself "Georg Cristoph Lay" took over the land in 1732 and built himself a Swiss-style stone farmhouse. Tulpehocken was the Indian name for the fertile valley where he settled; the plantation took its name. Christopher Ley (as he then came to spell it) died in 1741 and his son, Michael, eventually took over the property, building a newer, larger house. A third, smaller frame house, added in the nineteenth century, is called the Cyrus Sherk Pipe Smoke House, the place the owner's father could go to smoke his favorite corncob. By then the Michael Ley mansion had been expanded from an eight-room house to a twenty-seven-room Victorian residence with wide porches and a mansard roof. A small springhouse became part of the Tulpehocken collection when the adjoining land was bought in the mid-nineteenth century. All the buildings now offer accommodations to guests. (The Pipe Smoke House can hold up to six people in its three bedrooms.) The surrounding lush meadowland is still farmed, and grazed by a herd of Angus cattle.

"Tulpehocken Manor is an unusual collection of inn, museum, home, and farm. On occasion it is also a meeting place for craftsmen showing off their art, or a rally point for antique-car buffs. The recreated historic Hanover Rifle Battalion made Tulpehocken its headquarters, and the lucky visitor can sometimes see a Sunday afternoon maneuver, inspect the old front-loaded rifles and admire the uniforms. Besides the main manor house, there are several old stone buildings erected in the early 1700s and converted into cozy apartments of various styles and sizes. Almost any need for an overnight or longer accommodation can be met. But the main mansion is, of course, the focal point. Tools of early settlers are displayed. Locally made and imported historical furniture can be seen, and different periods of architecture studied. Woodwork, especially on the arched doorways, and stained-glass windows catch the eye.

"To sleep at Tulpehocken is not just getting a night's rest. It is an experience in the past. In case you are interested in the historical details, try to engage innkeeper Jim Henry in conversation. But

don't ask too many questions or you will be up well past midnight, fascinated by the stories of your host."   —*Wolfgang Kutter;*
also recommended by James and Winifred Mclachlan,
Wilda Hendrickson, and Henriette Meyer

Open all year.
13 rooms, several cottages and apartments, all sharing baths.
Rates $53–$265, depending on size of accommodation.
No meals.
No credit cards.
Innkeepers: Esther Nissly and James Henry.

_____*New Hope*

Centre Bridge Inn
River Road (Box 74, Star Route)
New Hope, Pennsylvania 18938
Telephone (215) 862-2048

"The handsome building is perched on the canalside, with a wide view of the Delaware River beyond. The bar and public dining room open on a canal-bank terrace where groups arriving by barge from nearby New Hope disembark for waterside parties."

—*B.C.*

"This was the most pleasant inn we visited. The bedrooms had all been remodeled so were new. We had a lovely corner room with canopy bed, Schumacher fabric bedspread and curtains, antiques, a view of the river and canal, and a big tiled bathroom with clipped ceiling and Schumacher wallpaper. We had fun eating and drinking in the dining room and bar below. It was very interesting to look around. I'd go back."   —*Melanie Omohundro*

Open all year.
7 rooms, 2 suites, all with private bath.
Rates $50–$100.
Credit cards: MasterCard, Visa.
West Hunterdon buses from New York City to New Hope. Airports at Trenton, New Jersey, 25 minutes away, and Doylestown.
Innkeeper: Stephen R. Dugan.

Turn to the back of this book for pages inviting *your* comments.

Hotel du Village
North River Road and Phillips Mill Road
New Hope, Pennsylvania 18938
Telephone (215) 862-9911; 862-5164

"In 1976, Omar and Barbara Arbani, who were already known in the area as the managers of the Inn at Phillips Mill, bought a turn-of-the-century country mansion and its nearby converted stable and have been working ever since to complete a comfortable hotel in a setting vaguely reminiscent of a French country house. The mansion, once called White Oaks, is now the restaurant at the Hotel du Village. Its fine wood paneling and stone fireplace survived more than half a century of boarding school children—the mansion had become a school, first for girls, then for boys, within twenty years of its completion. The stable, Appledore, is the hotel, with large, rebuilt rooms overlooking pastures, trees, and the inn's pool. Rooms are furnished in country style with quilts and crisp prints on sheets and curtains. Unlike many of the canalside hotels in the area, this inn has a spacious feeling, with ample grounds for strolling or for sitting under trees. The drive to New Hope itself takes a few minutes. There one can find many entertainments from restaurants to bookshops to a mule barge ride along the historic canal or a steam train excursion."   —B.C.

Open all year.
20 rooms, all with private bath.
Rates $45–$65 double, including continental breakfast.
Credit card: American Express.
French spoken.
Bus service to New Hope; local taxi service.
Innkeepers: Barbara and Omar Arbani.

The Inn at Phillips Mill
North River Road
New Hope, Pennsylvania 18938
Telephone (215) 862-9919; 862-2984

"Phillips Mill is no more than a bend in the road near the better-known town of New Hope. It is still a center for artists, with an annual show in the mill itself, a 1756 stone building that, with the similar structures around it, gives the tiny cluster the look of a Cotswold hamlet. The inn started life as a barn in the middle of the eighteenth century and did time as a girls' school before becoming, consecutively, a tea shop, a restaurant, and now an inn. Its small dining rooms are beautifully decorated to enhance the dark wood and stone of the building. Ceilings are low, fires blaze: the whole atmosphere gives off a warm welcome, especially in winter. Like all the inns along the Delaware River and the canal that parallels it, this hostelry is close to miles of towpath walks—the canal flows for more than fifty miles and its banks are state parkland."

—*B.C.*

"The inn was as delightful as we had been led to believe. We particularly enjoyed the breakfast of hot buttered rolls delivered to the room in a wicker basket. A word of caution, however: Rooms 4 and 5 are significantly less desirable than 1 and 3. Other nearby accommodation would be preferable." —*R. W. Morgan;*
also recommended by Mark L. Goodman

Open all year, except from first week in January to first week in February.
4 rooms, 1 suite, 1 cottage, all with private bath.
Rates $49 room, $59 suite, $75 cottage.
No credit cards.
Public restaurant, no bar.
French spoken.
West Hunterdon Transit buses from New York to New Hope.
Innkeepers: Brooks and Joyce Kaufman.

Logan Inn
10 West Ferry Street
New Hope, Pennsylvania 18938
Telephone (215) 862-5134

"New Hope was once little more than a ferry slip on the old York Road linking pre-Revolutionary Philadelphia with New York. It later became a mill town of some prosperity. But it was the discovery of it early in this century by artists and literati that has given New Hope a special flavor and a certain notoriety: a kind of country retreat for the Algonquin set, the home of artists and writers and the site of the Bucks County Playhouse. Get a hold of innkeeper Carl Lutz and persuade him to tell a few stories about New Hope's golden years and the crazy people who have passed through this hotel trailing the glitter of Broadway and Hollywood.

"New Hope has changed much over the last decade or two with the introduction of more commerce, which has elbowed some of the craft shops aside and draws dreadful crowds. But some people in town are working hard to hold the line, and to restore its quiet and brassy/classy/*haute bohémienne* ambience. Local gallery owners say that a new generation of artists and writers is discovering New Hope anew."
                                                                    —*B.C.*

"The Logan Inn combines historical interest (George Washington probably slept here) with luxurious upstairs rooms—canopied beds and cathouse divans—and a lovely garden room for lunch and dinner. The meals are a little expensive, but the atmosphere makes up for it. The service combines the best of both worlds—friendly if you're feeling sociable, but polite, allowing you plenty of room if you like to get away from it all. The fireside tables across from the bar are an ideal place to relax with cocktails in the evening, but media junkies beware: there isn't a television set in the place. It is, however, convenient to the local bookstore and the many fine restaurants, bars, antique stores, and shops selling wicker furniture and handmade quilts.

"All of that, and the frost-on-the-pumpkin New England atmosphere of the place (Washington tossed his famous coin across the Delaware River minutes away), make this resting-place almost irresistible."
                                                                —*Paul Wilner*

Open all year, except January 1 to February 10.
10 rooms, 8 with private bath; 1 stone cottage.
Rates $45–$55.
Credit cards: MasterCard, Visa.
West Hunterdon Transit bus from New York to New Hope.
Innkeepers: Carl Lutz and Arthur Sanders.

The Wedgwood Inn
111 West Bridge Street
New Hope, Pennsylvania 18938
Telephone (215) 862-2570

"We had intended to stay at the Logan Inn, but it was full, and Carl Lutz recommended the Wedgwood. This is a large Victorian house looking down Bridge Street to the lazy blue Delaware River, and the heart of New Hope only two blocks away. Its wide, wraparound veranda is a delight, as is the tree-shaded gazebo. The innkeepers are young and enthusiastic, ready to help houseguests select from the area's attractions: history, unusual shops, live theater, and music. One nice feature was the collection of local menus we made use of—aided by innkeeper Nadine Silnutzer's personal knowledge of the restaurants, and the comments of former guests."

—*Sharon and Marc Zucker*

Open all year.
8 rooms, 3 with private bath.
Rates $40–$65 double, including breakfast.
No credit cards.
No restaurant, but within walking distance of several.
Dutch and Spanish spoken.
Innkeepers: Nadine Silnutzer and Carl Glassman.

Philadelphia

The Barclay Hotel
237 South 18th Street
Philadelphia, Pennsylvania 19103
Telephone (215) 545-0300

"If you aren't invited to stop in a restored town house on Society Hill, the next best thing is the Barclay. Rittenhouse Square is the best address downtown, and the hotel lives up to expectations. There are attentive bellhops, a dark-green-carpeted, crystal-chandeliered lobby, and spacious, comfortable rooms with Early American reproductions. You'll be at the heart of Philadelphia's shopping and business district and a short cab ride away from museums and Independence Mall."   —*George Herzog*

"I have made a pastime out of looking for good hotel weekends away from New York City. This is my favorite. The atmosphere is elegant, the service excellent—and there are good weekend deals. We recently had a suite for two for $75 per night. That included Sunday brunch, or anything you wanted from the breakfast menu. You wouldn't believe the breakfast I had! This is a very classy hotel."   —*Steve Chazen*

Open all year.
285 rooms, all with private bath.
Rates $80–$125 single, $95–$140 double, $175–$350 suites. Weekend package, $75 per night for 2 people.
Credit cards: American Express, Carte Blanche, Diners Club, MasterCard, Visa.
Managing Director: Doreen Hamilton.

Four Seasons Hotel
1 Logan Square
Philadelphia, Pennsylvania 19103
Telephone (215) 963-1500

"Parisians would not scoff at the view from Four Seasons Hotel—across Logan Square, with its heroic Calder statuary, to the columned facades of the public library and the courthouse, and up majestically broad Parkway to the fabulous neoclassical spectacle of the Philadelphia Art Museum. The hotel itself is neo-Hittite, but handsome, and indoors it is little short of beautiful. Everywhere are rare woods, marble (seven different kinds), and pretty carpeting. The colors are soft. All is understated and generally elegant. The same goes for the service. There are two attractive dining rooms; the less formal of the two has a pink marble bar so imposing that a pope could celebrate high mass on it. We found our dinners good but not up to the decor; the buffet was terrific, however. In the green, spacious outdoor courtyard is a rushing cataract up which one could imagine (smoked?) salmon leaping. There is a spa with a lovely pool, exercise facilities, and saunas.

"This hotel, opened in July 1983, is not a small hotel, but in its grace and restful atmosphere and the attentiveness of its service, it seems like one. A luxurious place from which to explore this underrated city, with its extraordinary museums and historical sites and its bounty of restored eighteenth- and nineteenth-century neighborhoods."   —*Tom Congdon*

Open all year.
363 rooms, all with private bath.
Rates $95–$125 single, $115–$145 double; higher for suites.
Credit cards: American Express, Visa, MasterCard, Diners Club.
General Manager: James Fitzgibbon.

Latham Hotel
135 South 17th Street
Philadelphia, Pennsylvania 19103
Telephone (215) 563-7474

"After twelve hours on the train in the blizzard of 1983, the doorman of the Latham in his trademark high boots was a welcome sight.

The Latham is cozy, with period furnishings among modern accessories. Its restaurant, Bogart's is one of Philadelphia's best, casually elegant, with fine food and service."   —*George Herzog*

Open all year.
144 rooms, all with private bath.
Rates $90–$95.
Credit cards: American Express, Carte Blanche, Diners Club, MasterCard, Visa.
Manager: Barnet Steinmetz.

Society Hill Hotel
Third and Chestnut Streets
Philadelphia, Pennsylvania 19106
Telephone (215) 925-1394

"If W. C. Fields had ever stayed here he might have had a better opinion of Philadelphia. With only ten or a dozen rooms on three or four floors (I've only stayed on the second floor, so I'm not sure), it's a real find, cozy and quite elegant. The decor is topnotch: the style is colonial to a degree, with high ceilings and crown molding, and stencils along the top of the walls. Somebody spent a lot of money restoring what was, I believe, a home for longshoremen; the furniture is well made, the beds are firm, there are even brass doorknobs, not the tacky hollow-metal junk of most modern inns. There is plenty of hot water at all hours (I take a lot of showers because Philly is sultry in the summer) and real glasses instead of plastic ones, although I thought the towels a little skimpy. There's color TV, but I didn't use it.

"As the founding editor of *Fine Homebuilding* magazine, I travel a lot, and appreciate the fact that the hotel is centrally located, whether you're gawking at the Liberty Bell, ferreting out antiques, or pursuing that most perfect gastronomical art form, the sub sandwich. Downstairs is the hotel bar, which has planter's punches with Meyers's dark rum, Bass ale, and other patrician libations. It really is a good bar and seems to be the hangout of Philly's after-work smart set. There's live music many nights; one combo did Cole Porter's 'Love for Sale' as well as it's ever been done. The menu is modest, but what they do have is fairly good: try the potato skins, and the walnut-and-apple pie in season. All prices are quite reasonable, and the lodgings themselves were less expensive than any large hotel of similar trappings."   —*Mike Litchfield;*
also recommended by Judy Donovan

Open all year.
12 rooms and suites, all with private bath.
Rates $56–$90, including continental breakfast.
Credit cards: American Express, Carte Blanche, Diners Club, MasterCard, Visa.
Innkeepers: David DeGraff and Judith Baird Campbell.

_____*Plumsteadville*

Plumsteadville Inn
P.O. Box 388
Plumsteadville, Pennsylvania 18949
Telephone (215) 766-7500

"Long before the American Revolution, a small community had grown up about five miles north of Doylestown, now the county seat of Bucks County, on the land of an absentee English landlord named John Plumsted, a London ironmonger. For a long time the village was known as Hart's Tavern, after its best-known landmark. Nearly three centuries later the best-known landmark is still the tavern, now called the Plumsteadville Inn. The inn had suffered some rough years: the slump of Prohibition, vandalism, fire. But a careful restoration of the original inn and the skillful addition of a new wing over the last decade or so have probably given the inn more grace than it ever had during those early years when Plumsteadville was the home of Kratz wagon and sleigh works and the carbarn for the Philadelphia-to-Easton trolleys.

"The Plumsteadville Inn is more commercial and splashy than most of Bucks County's country inns. There is, for example, cabaret. While not to be recommended so highly as the country inns closer to the Delaware River, this inn can in a pinch serve as a base for exploring the historic county, the site of the first of Pennsylvania's frontier settlements, and the American home of the Penn family. The area around Plumsteadville is still populated by Mennonite farmers, who now live side by side with rich urbanites who have turned colonial farms into summer homes and the area's addresses into a Who's Who of writers and artists."   —*B.C.*

Open all year.
16 rooms, all with private bath.
Rates $25–$35 single, $35–$45 double.
Credit cards: American Express, MasterCard, Visa.
Bus and train service to Doylestown, 5 miles south. Greyhound buses between Easton and Philadelphia will stop at inn on request.
Manager: Edward Burns.

Point Pleasant

Innisfree
Cafferty Road (P.O. Box 108)
Point Pleasant, Pennsylvania 18950
Telephone (215) 297-8329

"Here is a country inn right out of Henry Fielding. Built in the mid-eighteenth century as a millhouse, it has settled into its private valley undisturbed: down a dip of a gravel lane off Cafferty Road opposite Point Pleasant Community Baptist Church. The building has thick stone walls, ancient timbers, and Dutch doors. The mill-stream still runs by its windows. Public areas are full of old furniture, and something of the clutter of home. This couldn't be much farther away from it all, even in this quiet corner of Bucks County.

"Point Pleasant has a special following. It is here that the best-known river-equipment rentals can be found, at Point Pleasant Canoes. Here (and at the company's branch locations along the Delaware) one can hire rafts, giant inner tubes, or canoes for float-ing down the wide Delaware, a popular summer pastime in these parts."

—_B.C._

Open all year.
19 rooms, 7 with private bath.
Rates $50–$80, including sit-down gourmet breakfast.
Credit card: American Express.
Nearest public transportation: West Hunterdon bus from New York to New Hope or Frenchtown, New Jersey.
Innkeeper: John R. Huestis.

Quakertown

The Sign of the Sorrel Horse
Old Bethlehem Road
Quakertown, Pennsylvania 18957
Telephone (215) 536-4651

"Tucked away just a few miles north of Lake Nockamixon, a state park area newly developed for boating and fishing, the Sign of the Sorrel Horse is housed in what was originally a tavern run by a soldier of the Revolution. A fine stone structure typical of solid eighteenth-century Bucks County architecture, the inn sits not two steps off a quiet two-lane country road which once served as the major thoroughfare between Bethlehem and Philadelphia. The

Sorrel Horse boasts a swimming pool and a terrace from which garden and lawn roll off into woodland.

"Inside, the dining room is traditional and elegant, white-table-clothed and certainly appropriate for the carefully prepared dinners and brunches of Ron Strouse, chef and owner. The bar is subdued and peaceful. Upstairs, six country bedrooms, each with an antique four-poster complete with quilt, await the tired traveler. A common parlor stocked with books, magazines, and sherry occupies the landing at the top of the stairs."   —*Jonathan Crossette*

Open all year, except the last two weeks of January and most of February.
6 rooms, 4 with private bath.
Rates $42–$50 double, including continental breakfast.
Credit cards: MasterCard, Visa.
Limousine service can be arranged from Philadelphia International Airport, Allentown-Bethlehem-Easton airport, or Amtrak's two Philadelphia stations, about 25 miles away.
Innkeepers: Ronald L. Strouse and Frederick L. Cresson.

_____*Riegelsville*

Riegelsville Hotel
10–12 Delaware Road (Box 157)
Riegelsville, Pennsylvania 18077
Telephone (215) 749-2469

"The better-known Delaware River inns used to be farther south in Lumberville and New Hope. But the popularity of upper Bucks County is growing rapidly, and with it the popularity of the Riegelsville Hotel. It can be missed by visitors because, while the inns farther south are on the River Road itself, the Riegelsville Hotel is one block off Route 611, several miles north of the end of River Road and tucked discreetly around a corner.

"The hotel, which dates from 1828, has been restored by Fran and Harry Cregar, and they have made an excellent job of the dining room, where they have exposed the stone walls, wooden beams, and fireplaces. It is now quiet and elegant. Harry, a host with a nice sense of humor, will bring out his wallet and show you photographs of what the room looked like before they started work on it. In the bar, light meals are always available. A canalside terrace has just been added by the Cregars, who are also planning to screen a second-floor porch for waterside dining."   —*David Wigg*

"The mule barges don't tie up outside anymore, but the towpath of the Delaware Canal makes a fine hiking path north or south from the hotel. Any traveler can look forward to the treat of an overnight stay in one of the 1828 guest rooms overlooking a Roebling bridge and the river. There is no front desk. Just sidle up to the bar and Harry will fix you a drink while Fran checks you in."

—*George Herzog*

Open all year.
12 rooms, 3 with private bath.
Rates $30–$50.
Credit cards: American Express, MasterCard, Visa.
Riegelsville is served by Greyhound buses.
Innkeepers: Fran and Harry Cregar.

_____*Scenery Hill*

Century Inn
Route 40
Scenery Hill, Pennsylvania 15360
Telephone (412) 945-6600; 945-5180

Century Inn, a National Landmark, was built in 1794 by the family that founded the village known today as Scenery Hill. The inn was on the Nemacolin Indian Trail, a route used during the French and Indian War. The trail later became the National Road, linking the new United States on the Eastern Seaboard to the unexplored lands of the West. Scenery Hill was part of the Whiskey Rebellion of the late eighteenth century, and a rare flag used by the insurgents can be seen at the inn, along with the building's original kitchen with its hand-forged crane and handmade cooking utensils. The front parlor contains a collection of Monongahela glass from the Gallatin Kramer glassworks in New Geneva.

"We were sorry we had only one night to spend at the Century Inn. What a delightful place it was! Our room was quaint and charming. The couple in charge were friendly and professional. We had dinner and breakfast, and both were delicious."   —*Patricia J. Lukens*

"What a delightful setting, rooms, and food. The very, very best."
—*Munroe W. Palestrant*

Open mid-March to mid-December.
6 rooms and suites, all with private bath.
Rates $40–$60 double.
No credit cards.

Public restaurant and bar.
Innkeepers: Megin and Gordon Harrington.

_____ *Shartlesville*

Haag's Hotel
Main Street
Shartlesville, Pennsylvania 19554
Telephone (215) 488-6692

"This is the place to sample traditional and authentic Pennsylvania Dutch food. Haag's is famous for its vast family-style meals, and people come from miles around, particularly on Sunday, to gorge themselves. The meals include twenty different dishes; you are invited to eat as much as you can from the white bowls set out all over the table in front of you. It is easy to forget one or two dishes on the perimeter as you skim from one to the next. A typical dinner might include chicken, ham or beef, gravy, potato stuffing, sweet potatoes, lima beans, chickpeas, dried corn, garden peas, pickled beets, pepper cabbage, chowchow, chicken salad, olives, pickles, celery, mustard beans, piccalilli, applesauce, tapioca pudding, dried apricots, old-fashioned homemade sugar cookies, home-baked pies (lemon sponge or shoofly), ice cream, bread, milk, tea and coffee.

"The dining room seats 250 people and is, as you would expect in Pennsylvania Dutch country, plain and practical (like the hotel rooms). Many of the ingredients for the meals come from the family's 125-acre farm. You can look into the kitchen from the sidewalk to watch the frenzy of activity as the family and local staff prepare the food on old gas and coal-fired stoves.

"The town of Shartlesville, founded in 1765 and named for a Revolutionary War hero, Colonel Peter Shartle, is not very pretty; at least the main street is not—an example of roadside America with all its faults."   *—David Wigg*

Open all year, except Christmas Day.
7 rooms, all with private bath.
Rates $10 single, $15 double.
No credit cards.
Public restaurant and bar.
German and Pennsylvania Dutch spoken.
Innkeeper: John J. Seitzinger.

Do you know a hotel in your state that we have overlooked? Write *now.*

Skytop

Skytop Lodge
Skytop, Pennsylvania 18357
Telephone (717) 595-7401

Skytop is in Pennsylvania's Pocono Mountains, one of the East Coast's oldest resort areas.

"It's style is something very rare for the 1980s. It is fancy, elegant —gives you the things you don't find in a modern hotel. I love the swimming pool, and the bike riding on the trails is wonderful. The meals were great. The price of a weekend here is not expensive. This is an exceptional place."   —*Steve Chazen*

Open all year.
166 rooms, most with private bath.
Rates from $78 single, $116 double, AP; higher in peak months.
   Weekend packages available in some seasons.
Credit cards: MasterCard, Visa.
President and General Manager: Donald Biles.

Uniontown

Mount Summit Inn
P.O. Drawer T
Uniontown, Pennsylvania 15401
Telephone (412) 438-8594

"Not so little but certainly historic, judging from its guest register, the inn is five and a half miles east of Uniontown on U.S. 40, on a summit with a marvelous view of southwestern Penn's Woods. U.S. 40 was the first national road westward from the coastal colonies. Probably the most interesting nearby historical attraction is Fort Necessity, the site of the first battle of the French and Indian War, and George Washington's only defeat—by the French from Fort Duquesne, now Pittsburgh. The fort has been reconstructed and a small museum is maintained by the National Park Service. Also nearby is Fallingwater, a house built by Frank Lloyd Wright, now open, except in winter, to tours by the public.

   "Mount Summit was a resort in its heyday. We were intrigued by the guest register."   —*Margaret R. Bellows*

Open May 1 to November 1.
126 rooms, all with private bath.

Rates $30–$48 per person double occupancy, including breakfast
and dinner. Reduced rates for children.
No credit cards.
Greyhound bus service to Uniontown.
Innkeepers: Donald and Eunice Shoemaker.

_____ *Upper Black Eddy*

Bridgeton House
River Road
Upper Black Eddy, Pennsylvania 18972
Telephone (215) 982-5856

"The traveler could be fooled into thinking that this recently
opened inn is a restoration of a riverside tavern of yesterday. The
1835 building was, in fact, a home, and then apartments and a real
estate office before being rescued from further misuse by Beatrice
and Charles Briggs, who have made it into a very pleasing small
hotel. Eschewing the penchant for Victoriana that is gripping much
of this historic area at the moment, the Briggses chose a simple
country style, with all materials carefully chosen to be faithful to the
building's architectural period. They have also opened their roadside inn to the river, which flows behind it, adding wide windows
and encouraging guests to make the most of a fine view of the old
gristmill at Milford across the water."   —*B.C.*

Open all year.
7 rooms, all with private bath.
Rates $55–$65, including continental breakfast.
Credit cards: American Express, MasterCard, Visa.
No bar or restaurant.
West Hunterdon Transit buses from New York stop in front of the
inn once a day on weekday evenings; more extensive bus service
at Frenchtown, New Jersey, a few miles downriver.
Innkeepers: Beatrice and Charles Briggs.

_____

Upper Black Eddy Inn
River Road
Upper Black Eddy, Pennsylvania 18972
Telephone (215) 982-5554

"One of the less-known pleasures of Pennsylvania's Bucks County is the stretch of walking territory along the Delaware Canal towpath north of the tourist center at New Hope. A string of inns marches through this quieter corner of the county, and here it is possible to hike for twenty or thirty miles, staying at a different historic hotel each night. Beginning at Lumberville, for example, one can move north at less than the speed of the old canal barges and their plodding mules to the Golden Pheasant at Erwinna, the Upper Black Eddy Inn, and the Riegelsville Hotel. All served the nineteenth-century canal trade.

"The Upper Black Eddy inn, facing the Delaware, serves European food—with a few Northern Italian specialties—and fresh seafood. The atmosphere is quiet here; the inn is also a family home. The hotel's guest rooms have recently been refurnished in antiques."
—*B.C.*

Open all year.
6 rooms.
Rates $25–$30.
Credit cards: American Express, MasterCard, Visa.
Innkeeper: Beverly Thompson.

Would you be so kind as to share discoveries you may have of charming, well-run places to stay in Europe? Please write to *Europe's Wonderful Little Hotels and Inns*, c/o Congdon & Weed, 298 Fifth Avenue, New York, New York 10001. (By the way, a new and greatly expanded edition of this splendid guide is now available at your bookseller's.)

Virginia

Abingdon

Martha Washington Inn
150 West Main Street
Abingdon, Virginia 24210
Telephone (703) 628-3161

"A women's college until 1937, the restored buildings of this inn bring elegance to the small town of Abingdon. We arrived late one Sunday night to find a spacious and simple inn, across the street from the Barter Theater—a must for entertainment. Flowers blooming beautifully in front of the inn welcomed us. The dining room here has been well noted, but we did not have a chance to enjoy an evening meal because of our arrival time. Breakfast was good, although they could use a new biscuit recipe. There was tea in the afternoon. It was all very relaxing and well worth returning to."
—_Lesha Kathryn B. Nix_

"This one is a must. The food was the best we have had anywhere. The antiques, the service, and the lovely town are superb."
—_Ann McSwain_

Open all year.
70 rooms, all with private bath.
Rates $50 single, $60 double.
Credit cards: American Express, Diners Club, MasterCard, Visa.
Restaurant and bar.
Innkeeper: Ellison Ketchum.

_____*Charlottesville*

The Boar's Head Inn
P.O. Box 5185
Charlottesville, Virginia 22905
Telephone (804) 296-2181

"Charlottesville is a pleasant, well-ordered place, even if architecturally unremarkable. It looks culturally undistinguished, except for
two bookshops within feet of each other on the pedestrianized shopping mall downtown. The Boar's Head Inn, though new, is a nice
place to stay. The main block, a reproduction three-story Georgian
building, is supplemented by large two-story wings where most of
the rooms are. The rooms are large, and have spacious balconies.
The setting on the outskirts of town is superb, with views to the
foothills of the Shenandoah range. The wooded grounds have
flower gardens and a large pond with ducks and geese. A full range
of facilities—swimming pool, bars, restaurants—make it a conventional hotel, but everything is scrupulously maintained and in no
way brash. Room furnishings are reproduction Victorian: chests of
drawers with big wooden knobs and other pieces in the same vein.
There is a splendid new visitors' center in Charlottesville, with a
large exhibition area and two auditoriums."   —*Clive Johnstone
and Winifred Weston*

Open all year.
175 rooms, including 13 suites, all with private bath.
Rates $59–$65 single, $69–$75 double, $100–$200 suites. Christ-
    mas and winter fitness packages available.
Credit cards: American Express, Carte Blanche, Diners Club, Mas-
    terCard, Visa.
Public dining rooms and bars.
Taxi from Charlottesville.
General Manager: Jerrod Godin.

Turn to the back of this book for pages inviting *your* comments.

_____ *Chincoteague*

Channel Bass Inn
100 Church Street
Chincoteague, Virginia 23336
Telephone (804) 336-6148

"Chincoteague has changed. What used to be a solid, hardworking fishing town has become more artsy-craftsy. There were several gallerylike places on Main Street that sell batiks, pottery, Baluchi rugs, and jewelry. But there are still those old clothing stores with the wooden floors and cabinets, too. And boats still come in loaded with fresh seafood that is sold right at the dock.

"The Channel Bass is an unassuming building from the outside —like a big, well-kept summer house. Inside it is beautiful, with a sitting room furnished in antiques. The hotel rooms are simple, but well appointed; the new wing has some queen- and king-size beds. The dining room, which specializes in Spanish and Basque food, is highly regarded (four stars from Mobil) but very expensive."

—Beverly Nelson

Open all year, except December and January.
10 rooms, 8 with private bath.
Rates $45–$115. Cooking school vacation packages available.
Credit cards: MasterCard, Visa.
Bus and plane service to Salisbury, Maryland, 45 miles north. Car rentals available there. Bus to J's Corner, 10 miles away, then taxi.
Innkeeper: James S. Hanretta.

_____

Refuge Motor Inn
Beach Road (P.O. Box 378)
Chincoteague, Virginia 23336
Telephone (804) 336-5511

"Yes, it is a motor inn. And yes, especially by the yardstick of the Eastern Shore, it is new. But the Refuge, nestled off the road just before the entrance to the Assateague Island National Seashore wildlife reserve and beach, has the feeling of being a part of that wild setting. The inn's weathered wood camouflages rooms of modern motel decor. Each of these rooms opens to the woods or grasslands around, and from them it is possible to glimpse seabirds or wild ponies (as well as some tame ones). The protected seashore with its excellent sandy beach is a short drive—or longer hike—across a small bridge, past a lighthouse, and along a road winding through the marshlands where the Chincoteague ponies and thousands of other wild things live, run, swim, and fly. It is also possible to tour the inland waters by boat. And at the end of the day, Chincoteague town has some of the best seafood to be found anywhere."

—B.C.

"Thank you so much for recommending this. The Refuge is top rate for a motel. We loved it."   *—Ann McSwain*

Open all year.
68 rooms, all with private bath.
Rates from $49 double June through September. Lower rates at other times. Up to two children free in room with parents.
No meals served.
Credit cards: American Express, MasterCard, Visa.
Innkeepers: Donald and Martha Leonard.

_____*Front Royal*

Constant Spring Inn
413 South Royal Avenue
Front Royal, Virginia 22630
Telephone (703) 635-7010

"After arriving at the inn, only a quarter of a mile from the Skyline Drive, we settled our belongings in our room and walked to the restaurant at the foot of the hill, which is also owned by the inn-keeper. Our meal, served family style, was meat loaf, potatoes, six vegetables, and rolls. When we returned to the inn later, the inn-keeper's mother met us and asked us to join her for lemonade on the porch. As we sat in enormous rockers, she told us how the house had been converted to an inn. The view of the mountains was so beautiful, and her stories so interesting, that we didn't think of the time until nearly midnight."   *—Betty A. Dufraine Bolinger*

"We were indeed treated as special guests at Constant Spring. The proprietress and her mother were most kind. The food at every meal was tasty, ample, and regional. My only complaint is that the room appointments were a bit shopworn and our bathroom badly needed repair and redoing. I wanted to redecorate and fix the minor flaws."
—Mrs. E. L. Yungk; also recommended by Gayle Bolinger

Open all year, except December 24 and 25.
5 rooms and 3 suites, all with private bath.

Rates $22–$30 per person, including breakfast and dinner.
No credit cards.
Trailways bus from Washington, D.C., stops a half-block away.
Innkeepers: Gary Iden and Mary Ann Wood.

_____*Hot Springs*

Vine Cottage Inn
P.O. Box 205
Hot Springs, Virginia 24445
Telephone (703) 839-2422

Bath County once had twenty-two therapeutic springs open for public use. There are now only three, those at Bolar Springs, Warm Springs, and Hot Springs, best known for the venerable Homestead. But the amenities of Hot Springs are not limited to the guests of the larger hotel.

"I found this quaint country inn just two blocks from the Homestead. Guests staying at Vine Cottage may use the Homestead's facilities, including tennis, golf, horseback riding, and skiing."
—*Tammy Buerkett*

"The Vine Cottage, where I have stayed for more than seven years, has recently been renovated, and the present owners' touches are delightful. It's an ideal location for all points of interest. A very welcoming and relaxing atmosphere prevails, and the food is excellent."
—*Mrs. A. Z. Alvis*

"The continental breakfast—with fruits, homemade rolls, breads, and all the coffee you could drink—was superb. We are recommending the inn to our friends; we wish we could have stayed longer."
—*Martha Littlefield; also recommended by Jobert Powers and George G. Weiss*

Open all year, except two weeks in December and two weeks in March.
17 rooms, 11 with private bath.
Rates $35–$45, including breakfast.
Credit cards: MasterCard, Visa.
French spoken.
Greyhound bus to Covington; Amtrak to Clifton Forge.
Innkeepers: Douglas and Jacqueline O'Brien.

Where are the good little hotels in Boston? Philadelphia? Omaha? Dallas? If you have found one, don't keep it a secret. Write *now.*

_____*Leesburg*

Laurel Brigade Inn
20 West Market Street
Leesburg, Virginia 22075
Telephone (703) 777-1010

"It was here that the Marquis de Lafayette was entertained by President James Monroe in 1825, and in many ways it still seems like 1825 at this old stone inn. The antique furnishings are immaculately clean and polished. The large staircase leading upstairs to the overnight rooms is smooth to the touch from so many years of dusting and waxing. The dining room, whose one wall is all glass doors, looks out over a beautiful lawn. The opposite side of the house is flanked by an English garden, and the entire inn fronts on one of the main streets of this historic northern Virginia town. The overnight accommodations on the second floor are roomy and very quiet. This is a great stopping-off place en route from Washington, D.C., to other parts of Virginia. The nicest thing about this little place is that you feel you are in your own home—having dinner and then slipping, unnoticed and happily, upstairs for a good night's sleep."
—*Rikki Stapleton*

"It doesn't try to be European elegant; it is kind of "country" and everyone is pleasant. The rooms are lovely, like at your grandmother's house where the gingham curtains were kept crisp and everything was polished. The dinner menu is extensive and reasonable."
—*Beverly Nelson*

Open all year, except January and early February.
6 rooms, all with private bath.
Rates $25 single, $37 double.
No credit cards.
Public restaurant.
Greyhound buses from Washington, D.C.
Innkeeper: Ellen Flippo Wall.

_____*Lexington*

The Alexander Withrow House
3 West Washington Street
Lexington, Virginia 24450
Telephone (703) 463-2044

The Withrow House has expanded in the last year or two to take in the old Central Hotel across the street. The owners have renamed it the McCampbell House, and it has more than doubled the capacity of the accommodations provided by this well-known hostelry.

"Lexington is a delightful town—old houses, quaint streets, Southern charm. The Alexander Withrow House is a restored 1789 home near the Washington and Lee University campus. Our suite, number 3, was a gem to find after a long journey. The multiwindowed sitting room had an antique sideboard, comfortable wing chairs, and oil paintings. The bedroom had a reading nook by the window. You enter the inn through a piazza overlooking a small bricked courtyard into a hall with Oriental rugs. Try the doughnuts in the little coffee shop around the corner; this is the way doughnuts should taste. We took two dozen home with us, but I'm afraid they never made it to Pittsburgh—we ate most of them on the way."
—*Mrs. Edward Sverdrut*

"Our cool October honeymoon evening was spent in this lovely, interesting town. Suite 2 was quaint, and had at hand all the information we needed about the town. The balconied porch was grand. Many restaurants in the town are closed Mondays, so choose the time of a visit wisely. ('Tis true about the doughnuts.)"
—*Lesha Kathryn B. Nix; also recommended by Rikki Stapleton*

Open all year.
15 rooms, 8 suites, all with private bath.
Rates $40–$55 per person.
Credit cards: MasterCard, Visa.
Bus service to Lexington.
Innkeeper: Beth Thompson.

_____*Middleburg*

The Red Fox
2 East Washington Street (P.O. Box 385)
Middleburg, Virginia 22117
Telephone (703) 687-6301

The Red Fox—known in its early years as Chinn's Ordinary—has been a busy town tavern for more than 250 years, not a bucolic country inn. Guests who understand that will find in it a sense of living history no museum can reproduce. On the other hand, if the bustle of a village tavern is not what the traveler wants—especially on a lively Saturday night—the Red Fox now has something new to offer. Tucked away on a quieter street is the Stray Fox, which became part of the inn a little over a year ago. The Stray Fox, though an inn for some years between the two world wars, was built and used for most of its existence as a private home. The building was once known as the Stray Shot, after being hit by a misfired Civil War cannonball. The Stray Fox, with eight guest rooms, has been redone in eighteenth-century style, right down to documented wall coverings and stenciling. When you call or write for reservations, be sure to specify which Fox you want.

"The Red Fox is only fifty minutes from downtown Washington, D.C., and twenty-five minutes from Dulles Airport. But once I am at its front door, light-years seem to separate this place from the bustling metropolitan area. The inn, a four-story fieldstone structure built in 1728, is right on the main street of a town filled with lots of lovely old-fashioned shops. Middleburg is in the middle of Virginia's horse country, and all around there is talk of horses and hunts and meets. There are several good local restaurants, but much of the town's activity seems to center on the Red Fox. The Night Fox pub in back of the tavern is a great spot for drinks in the evening. In warm weather there is an outdoor patio for drinking and dining.

"The main part of the inn has been completely renovated, but everything has been done to preserve the look and sense of times past. The downstairs is primarily the dining room and bar, all woody and filled with pewter. The lunch and dinner menus feature some local yummies like bourbon apple pie. The real beamed ceilings and the white stone fireplace in the main dining room make eating here a cozy pleasure. Upstairs there is the J.E.B. Stuart dining room, built around several huge fireplaces. There is always the smell of wood burning. The rooms are decorated to the period, most with canopied beds so high you almost need a stool to crawl into them. Every bedroom has its own fireplace with a generous supply of firewood."

—*Rikki Stapleton*

"The help was congenial and friendly, and the food superb. But our room was dusty. The upholstered chair and footstool looked so dirty that we put bath towels over them to sit down. One lamp was broken. The air conditioner didn't cool the room, the bathroom was musty, and our canopy bed had two twin-size mattress pads, making it uncomfortable. We would go back to eat, but not to sleep."

—*Mrs. W. L. Turpin*

Open all year.
13 rooms, 4 suites, 1 cottage, all with private bath.
Rates $65–$175.
Credit cards: American Express, MasterCard, Visa.
Greyhound bus from Washington, D.C.
Innkeeper: Turner Reuter, Jr.

Middletown

Wayside Inn
7783 Main Street
Middletown, Virginia 22645
Telephone (703) 869-1797

"The Wayside Inn sits comfortably in the northern end of the Shenandoah Valley. For the traveler that means easy access from the modern pace of I-81 to the quiet charm of the 1700s. Entry to the dining area is through a parlor furnished with period pieces. I still don't know how many rooms there are in which one may eat, but I know which are my two favorites. The Slave Kitchen lends itself to a cozy meal, with no more than four tables in the room. The Senseny Room, with its large stone fireplace, is ideal for parties and larger dinners. The menu includes a variety of Southern meals.

"The most exciting time to come to this part of Virginia is the first weekend in May. This is the time the Apple Blossom Festival is held in nearby Winchester, the apple capital, only a twenty-minute drive from the inn. As a native of the area, my favorite season is Christmas. Old-time decorations are hung at the Wayside in the Williamsburg manner, and there is a contest for homemade Christmas tree ornaments."
                                          —*Mary Henkel*

"Everyone knows about this inn. What they might not know is that the food can be horrendous."
                          —*Bill and Jill Neugent*

Open all year.
21 rooms, all with private bath.
Rates $40–$90.
Credit cards: American Express, MasterCard, Visa.
Public restaurant.
German spoken.
Greyhound bus service to Middletown.
Innkeeper: Charles H. Alverson III.

North Garden

Crossroads Inn
Route 692 (P.O. Box 36)
North Garden, Virginia 22959
Telephone (804) 293-6382

"This is the real McCoy: an old restored inn in the Charlottesville area of Virginia. We stayed in the two-story Summer Kitchen, now a cottage. Breakfast was Virginia ham, eggs, pumpkin muffins, and coffee. Such a treat!"

—*Ann McSwain*

Open all year.
4 rooms, 3 with private bath; 1 suite, 1 cottage.
Rates $45–$65, including breakfast.
No credit cards.
No restaurant or bar.
Spanish spoken.
Inn will meet guests at Charlottesville.
Innkeepers: Stephen and Shirley Ramsey.

Roanoke

Hotel Roanoke
19 North Jefferson Street
Roanoke, Virginia 24026
Telephone (703) 343-6992 or toll-free, in Virginia, (800) 542-5898; outside Virginia, (800) 336-9684

The Roanoke, which recently celebrated its centenary, describes itself as a "grand old hotel of the South," and prides itself on a staff of second- or even third-generation families. The hotel, at the southern entrance to the Shenandoah Valley, caters to vacation travelers as well as conference guests, but the old-fashioned interior of the place prevents a commercial atmosphere from developing. Built for the Norfolk and Western railroad in 1832, the hotel has a railway motif in some of its public rooms: the Whistle Stop is a turn-of-the-century depot recreated. The hotel is surrounded by ten acres of parkland.

"This is a miniature Hot Springs or Greenbrier. The interior has an old-fashioned flair. There is an indoor pool. The guest rooms are functional, but to see the restored ballrooms is to go back to when the South was in its glory."

—*Les M. Graziosi*

Open all year.
350 rooms, 25 suites, all with private bath.
Rates $42–$200.
Credit cards: American Express, Carte Blanche, Diners Club, MasterCard, Visa.
French and German spoken.
General Manager: Peter W. Kipp.

_____Smithfield

The Smithfield Inn
112 Main Street
Smithfield, Virginia 23430
Telephone (804) 357-4358

"Smithfield is the home of America's answer to prosciutto—sugar-cured Smithfield ham. The Smithfield Inn, built when George Washington was twenty years old, is the place to try this delicacy. This part of Virginia is also a good place to absorb early American history. Wander through restored Colonial Williamsburg, conjure up hoopskirted Southern women along Jamestown's Plantation Row, or refight the climactic battle of the Revolutionary War at Yorktown. If history isn't your thing, you can bike or hike through the 2,300 acres of greenbelt surrounding Williamsburg or even hit Busch Gardens, an amusement park with an old-world theme.

"When you get hungry, head for Jamestown dock and car ferry; enjoy the view on board as you cross the James River to Surry, about eighteen miles from Smithfield. You'll easily recognize Smithfield Inn by its white-columned porch stretching the length of the building, a great place to sit and smell the roses in the side garden. The inn's Williamsburg blue living room has some interesting antiques and books. There are several small dining rooms on the first floor done in colonial style. The one I ate in had a huge bouquet of flowers on an antique sideboard.

Having underestimated ferry times, I found the dining room closing as I arrived. But the congenial staff put together a 'plate' for me. It was terrific. The salty, paper-thin slices of Smithfield ham were deliciously complemented by sweet stewed tomatoes, spicy snap beans, corn fritters, and on and on until peach cobbler à la mode. The Sunday brunch menu looked great, too.

"My room upstairs in the main building was a disappointment, of characterless, boardinghouse vintage. It was clean, comfortable, and had a sink, but my decorating mind went straight to work redoing the whole upstairs—which is apparently in the works."
                                                    —*Catherine A. Crawford*

Open all year.
8 rooms.
Rates $30 single, $40 double.
Credit cards: American Express, MasterCard.
Restaurant and bar.
Innkeeper: James Abbott.

Sperryville

Conyers House
Sperryville, Virginia 22740
Telephone (703) 987-8025

The innkeepers bought this old country home, less than two hours' driving time from Washington, in 1979. The original part of the house dates from the early eighteenth century; it was known for generations as Conyers' Old Store and then as Finks' General Store. A new addition was built in 1979 to incorporate a new plumbing system; the house is still heated mostly by fireplaces, however. The inn's main house has six rooms, all with names, and two small cottages—one a springhouse once used to cool food and dairy products. The innkeepers emphasize that they are keeping this place essentially as a country house—L. L. Bean territory, they call it, "with mud in the spring." Their cockapoo, Pepper, "in his enthusiam to greet you, will be unable to differentiate between jeans and your elegant wool or silk slacks," they say. But in return for the experience of roughing it a bit, there are antiques on all sides, breakfast in front of a fire—or out in the sun—and a day of outdoor or indoor activities in Virginia's historic Rappahannock County.

"Conyers House is really more of a bed-and-breakfast house than an inn. But it has some very good rooms. The best reason to stay here, we think, is to dine eight miles away at the extraordinary Inn at Little Washington." —*Bill and Jill Neugent*

Open all year.
8 rooms, 3 baths.
Rates $75–$100 June to December, $65–$100 January through May, including large breakfast and afternoon tea.
No public bar or restaurant, but innkeepers will prepare a meal on advance notice.
French, German, Italian, and some Arabic spoken.
Innkeepers: Sandra and Norman Cartwright-Brown.

Syria

Graves' Mountain Lodge
General Delivery
Syria, Virginia 22743
Telephone (703) 923-4231

There is a certain kind of mountain lodge-cum-camp-cum-motel that has been a part of rural Americana for many, many years. Accommodation is usually basic, sometimes very comfortable, and there are things like family-style meals and a general spirit of heartiness that are not to everyone's taste. Graves' Mountain Lodge, a collection of buildings spread over hill and dale, is in that category. The accommodations here vary from rustic cabins and Appalachian-style houses to motel and lodge rooms. This is not the classic country inn a traveler finds in a cozy New England town, but the setting is superb, and there is much to do outdoors in the Blue Ridge Mountains of Virginia.

"The inn is often overrated, but it is in a beautiful mountain location."
—*Bill and Jill Neugent*

Open April through November.
45 rooms in cabins, cottages, and two motel-style buildings; all buildings with baths.
Rates $34–$50 per person per day, AP.
Credit cards: MasterCard, Visa.
Restaurant; no bar.
Innkeepers: Jim and Rachel Graves.

Tangier Island

Hilda Crockett's Chesapeake House
Tangier Island, Virginia 23440
Telephone (804) 891-2331

"I went to Tangier Island to see for myself that it was worth more than Manhattan. Discovered in 1605 by Captain John Smith of Pocahontas fame, Tangier was bought from the local Indians in 1650 for two overcoats. Manhattan went for a few trinkets, I believe. Well, there are certainly some things on Tangier that money won't buy on Manhattan. Peace and quiet for one, and narrow streets designed for walking; there are no cars, no pollution, and small houses with family graves in the front yard. People nod and say hello when you pass by.

"I thoroughly enjoyed walking around this one-by-three-and-a-half-mile island, crisscrossed by footbridges over the salt swamp. At the end of each road, I found a footpath leading to the sea. You can also rent bicycles, visit the museum, swim, fish, or—why not?—just relax.

"I got to Tangier by mail boat from Crisfield, Maryland, and enjoyed the hour-long trip in spite of a thunderstorm. A local teacher showed me the way to the Chesapeake House, which reminded me of summer camp more than anything. There are two white frame buildings with red shutters, several large dining rooms, with long oilcloth-covered tables, soft beds with metal frames, and bathrooms down the hall.

"Dinner was served family style, with everything on big white platters—crabcakes, clam fritters, ham, real cream corn pudding, lots of veggies, homemade rolls, a very rich pound cake, iced tea and coffee. Breakfast was designed for someone about to do a hard day's work, but scheduled for people like me who catch the 8 A.M. mail boat back across Tangier Sound."   —*Catherine A. Crawford*

Open April 1 to November 1.
8 rooms with shared baths.
Rates $25 per adult, $7.95–$13 per child, depending on age, including dinner and breakfast.
No credit cards.
Access to the island by boat from Crisfield, Maryland, or Onancock, Virginia. Call (804) 891-2240 or (703) 333-4656 for information.
Innkeeper: Hilda Crockett.

Trevilians

Prospect Hill
Trevilians, Virginia 23170
Telephone (703) 967-0844

The original home at Prospect Hill was built in 1732. The property remained a farm until after the Civil War, when William Overton, the owner's son, returned from battle and found the land overgrown and the slaves gone. The Overtons did what many Southern families did: took in guests.

"Prospect Hill is only a few miles from the busy college town of Charlottesville, but a visit here whirls you back to the time of the university's founder, Thomas Jefferson's eighteenth century. Monticello is the adjoining plantation. This beautiful old home, which was visited by relatives of our third president, stands as it must have then, at the end of an avenue of trees and tremendous boxwoods. The inn has been decorated with paintings and handsome old furniture, much of the period. Two dining rooms, one of them smaller and more intimate, draw one at night to small tables with blue tablecloths, candles, and quiet dinners, all overlooking a magnificent lawn."   —*Mr. and Mrs. W. Reid Thompson*

"Around the old yellow-and-white plantation house are three former slave quarters, a smokehouse, and a carriage house. The innkeeper is Bill Sheehan, a former sales executive who, with his French-born wife, Mireille, has come to prefer the ninety-hour-a-week life of an innkeeper. He led us to our room, the second floor of one of the converted slave quarters—Uncle Guy's. It had a small fireplace, with a fire laid, haunched ceilings, lots of windows, and a small but adequate bath. Another small slave cabin has a hot tub. The main house has a large, comfortable parlor with a big fireplace, where dinner guests gather until the host rings the dinner bell."

—*Michael Patterson*

Open all year.
7 rooms, 5 with private bath.
Rate $55 per person, including breakfast and dinner.
Credit cards: MasterCard, Visa.
French spoken.
Charlottesville airport 20 miles away.
Innkeepers: Bill and Mireille Sheehan.

_____ *Warm Springs*

The Inn at Gristmill Square
Box 359
Warm Springs, Virginia 24484
Telephone (703) 839-2231

The rooms in this restoration project are mostly suites, each with a name linking the inn to its history. The cluster of buildings also includes a country store, gallery, and restaurant. Gristmill Square's setting is pastoral: in a green valley surrounded by wooded, rolling hills. Fishing, golf, skiing and, of course, "the waters" are nearby.

"The countryside here is beautiful, and there are interesting things to visit on every side. We have come often in the spring and fall; we think those times of year are particularly appealing. The inn is small but self-sufficient. The staff does everything possible to make our family feel at home. The rooms could hardly be more attractive. Taste and imagination have played important parts in the development and restoration of these old buildings. Our suite had a washer/dryer and a small but remarkably complete kitchen alcove. But where food was concerned, we preferred to eat in the Waterwheel Restaurant just across the courtyard. The converted mill in which meals are served is full of atmosphere."

—*The Rev. William Hill Brown III*

Open all year, except the first two weeks in March.
12 rooms and suites, all with private bath.
Rates $55–$80 double, including continental breakfast.
Credit cards: American Express, MasterCard, Visa.
Innkeepers: Jack and Janice McWilliams.

_____ *Williamsburg*

Hospitality House
415 Richmond Road
Williamsburg, Virginia 23185
Telephone (804) 229-4020 or toll-free (800) 446-9204

Colonial Williamsburg is famous as a restoration of early American life, depicting life in the settlement of Williamsburg more than 350 years ago. It took over half a century of work and more than $100 million to complete; no wonder it is this country's most successful large-scale restoration project. Its success, however, has brought it huge crowds and the expected commercialism around the restored seventeenth- and eighteenth-century core. Many travelers recommend a winter or early spring visit, others say the town is worth seeing regardless of seasonal inconvenience.

"Our unexpectedly pleasant night here came about by accident. We could not get into any of the motels in Williamsburg and refused to pay the prices of the four hotels pushed by the information bureau. Someone suggested the Hospitality House. We were glad we took that advice! The rooms were the best we had stayed in on a long trip, the restaurant was excellent (our boys had excellent attention from room service, too), and the location was ideal for walking to the preserved center of town. The price was lower than what some big-name motels were asking." —*Gilbert Ross*

Open all year.
223 rooms, all with private bath.
Rates $93–103 double, $10 less for single occupancy.
Credit cards: American Express, MasterCard, Visa.
Restaurant and bar.
Manager: David Barrington.

Turn to the back of this book for pages inviting *your* comments.

West Virginia

Harpers Ferry

Hilltop House
Ridge Street
Harpers Ferry, West Virginia 25425
Telephone (304) 535-6321

"Overlooking the site of John Brown's daring 1859 raid on the United States arsenal, this quaint pile of native stone and timber welcomes guests to dine or stay the night. Thomas Jefferson thought its view of two rivers and three states was worth a European traveler's trip across the Atlantic. The National Park Service has done a careful restoration of the old, flood-ravaged village. The town now has many antique shops.

"The hotel staff is low-keyed yet attentive, engaging, and totally without airs. Their smiles go a long way to make up for much neglected—and, in the fifties, somewhat abused—decor. Whether or not you spend the night, do have a meal here. Food is hearty, with some down-home touches, and often served buffet style. What a relief to meet some honest country food in an age when every formula motel boasts an incompetent 'French' menu. The only false

touch was a chemical creamer, but this was cheerfully and promptly replaced by real milk."
                                        —*George Herzog*

Open all year.
60 rooms, 58 with private bath.
Rates $26 single, $36 double.
No credit cards.
Trains stop at the base of the hill, 3 blocks away; the trip from Washington takes 1½ hours.
Innkeeper: D. D. Kilham.

―――――――――――――――――――――*Lewisburg*

General Lewis Motor Inn
301 East Washington Street
Lewisburg, West Virginia 24901
Telephone (304) 645-2600

"This is an old-fashioned inn in the heart of the county seat of Greenbrier County. This is beautiful farm country, where you will find Morlunda Farm, one of the top Hereford breeders in the country. The climate is very pleasant, with cool nights and warm days from April through November. Lewisburg, 2,300 feet above sea level, is an old town full of lovely houses with spacious, well-kept grounds. The countryside is traversed by the lively Greenbrier River, a truly clean river where swimming, fishing, and canoeing are most enjoyable. The inn is named for General Andrew Lewis. Lewis gathered a force of frontiersmen and won one of the early battles of the American Revolution at Point Pleasant on the Ohio River in 1774.

"The inn has a good dining room, with family-style service. The lobby is full of relics. Take time to browse in memory hall."
                                        —*S. Cooper Dawson, Jr.*

"We had one of the worst meals of a recent trip here. The inn was delightful, but the food should definitely not be recommended."
                                        —*Rina C. Nydall*

Open all year.
28 rooms, all with private bath.
Rates $30–$50.
Credit cards: American Express, MasterCard, Visa.
Train service 9 miles away; Greyhound buses to Lewisburg. Piedmont Airlines from Roanoke, Huntington, Richmond, and Washington.
Innkeeper: John McIlheny.

Part Three

_____

South

Alabama

Mobile

Malaga Inn
359 Church Street
Mobile, Alabama 36602
Telephone (205) 438-4701

"The Malaga Inn, in the historic downtown district of Mobile, has been created from two splendid 1850s town houses joined around a quiet courtyard garden. Each of the rooms has been furnished with a great deal of individuality; all have private baths and color television. The tiny, dark bar is frequented by local artists and theater personalities who may be performing at the Civic Auditorium behind the inn. Meals are usually well prepared and courteously served. The Malaga is unique in Mobile for those who wish to stay away from large, carbon-copy, impersonal motels and hotels."

—*Robert Hochhauser*

Open all year.
41 rooms, 3 suites, all with private bath.
Rates $38–$44 single, $44–$52 double.
Credit cards: American Express, Diners Club, MasterCard, Visa.
Public restaurant and bar.
Innkeeper: Mayme M. Sinclair.

_____ *Florida*

Amelia Island

The 1735 House
584 South Fletcher
Amelia Island, Florida 32034
Telephone (904) 261-5878

"There are many wonderful inns in this country. But who would believe that one of the best of them is in Florida, best known for its busy attractions and even busier beaches. The 1735 House, on the northern Florida island of Amelia, only thirty minutes from Jacksonville airport, is a New England–style inn with Southern hospitality on a pleasantly unpopulated beach. Imagine waking up in Florida to nothing but the sound of softly rolling surf and the scent of the inn's freshly baked pastry.

"There are five suites in the main house, all with antiques and live plants. For the more adventurous, there is a lighthouse with room for six people."   —*Walter C. Plachta*

"Artists and writers would appreciate the inn's solitude as well as its spacious quarters. Each suite is really a small apartment, with kitchenette and dining area. While the inn does not have a restaurant—though breakfast in a basket, complete with newspaper, is brought to each room—there are good places to eat on the island."

—Beverly Robertson

Open all year.
5 suites, each sleeping up to 5 or 6 people, all with private bath and ocean view. 2 bedrooms, 2 baths in 4-story lighthouse.
Rates $45–$65, depending on season; lighthouse $80 double, including breakfast.
Credit cards: American Express, MasterCard, Visa.
Innkeepers: Susan and David Caples.

Englewood

Manasota Beach Club
7660 Manasota Key Road
Englewood, Florida 33533
Telephone (813) 474-2614

Owned and run by the same people who own the Weekapaug Inn in Rhode Island, the Manasota is a collection of cottages on a hill overlooking seventeen miles of beach in a conservation district along the Gulf of Mexico.

"On a quiet bay, with the Gulf on one side and the inland waterway on the other, the grounds are very attractive. The atmosphere is friendly, relaxed, informal. Many guests, like us, return winter after winter. It is a place where one can enjoy reading, walking on the beach, bird watching, swimming, or playing tennis—mixed with good conversation if one wants it."   *—Susan C. Walcott*

Open mid-January until first week in April.
28 rooms, all with private bath.
Rates $110–$115 per person, twin occupancy; $130–$160 single, AP.
No credit cards.
Air service to Tampa or Sarasota, then limousine to Englewood.
Innkeeper: Robert C. Buffum.

Where are the good little hotels in Boston? Philadelphia? Omaha? Dallas? If you have found one, don't keep it a secret. Write *now*.

_____*Fernandina Beach*

The Bailey House
28 South 7th Street (P.O. Box 805)
Fernandina Beach, Florida 32034
Telephone (904) 261-5390

"This is a first-rate bed-and-breakfast with beautiful accommodations and friendly, helpful people. My husband and I could not have wanted for anything during our stay. We hope to return here next time we are on Amelia Island."
—*Susan Nuckols*

"A house tastefully presented in a clean line of Victorian decor. Innkeepers Diane and Tom Hay are helpful guides about the town and its history."
—*Stan and Barbara Cook*

Open all year.
4 rooms, all with private bath.
Rates $55–$85, including continental breakfast.
Credit card: American Express.
No restaurant, but within walking distance of restaurants in historic downtown area.
Innkeepers: Tom and Diane Hay.

_____*Inverness*

The Crown Hotel
109 North Seminole Avenue
Inverness, Florida 32650
Telephone (904) 344-5555

Inverness, in west central Florida, was settled in the mid-nineteenth century, when Citrus County was still known mostly as Indian territory. The core of the building that now houses the Crown was once a peripatetic general store—the building was moved from Line Street to Main Street before becoming an inn. The town, originally Tompkinsville, took its name of Inverness from a homesick expatriate Scot. The hotel, once known as the Orange Hotel and then the Colonial, in turn has taken its name from its new British owners, who spent two million dollars over the last few years in restoring and reconstructing the place. Alas, for American tastes, the management goes a little heavy on the Britishness—an old London bus, for example, and a lot of talk about "European" service at a time when American innkeeping is rapidly overtaking it. But guests seem to like the atmosphere.

"The majestic Crown, nestled in the little town of Inverness, manages to bring a bit of Britain to Florida. I have never been more content with a hotel's facilities than on this trip. Imagine being received like visiting royalty. Or being ushered into a room that remarkably does not resemble the room across the hall. Or being served a three-hour dinner in a romantic atmosphere of candlelight and soft music. Never have I spent so little on a vacation and felt that I got more than my money's worth." —*Rae Anne Campellone*

Open all year.
34 rooms, all with private bath.
Rates from $45 single, $57 double.
Credit cards: American Express, Diners Club, MasterCard, Visa.
Public restaurant and tavern.
French, German, and Italian spoken.
Innkeeper: Ian Young.

Key West

"Key West is one of the more charming towns in the United States, a little tatty in places like a dowager with mud on her high-topped boots. The vegetation is lush tropical. It is a town full of lovely Conch (that's native Key West) houses with tin roofs and gingerbread trim, an occasional widow's walk, and now and then guy wires to hold down homes in case of a hurricane. It is a city where garbage trucks carry such signs as "Catering for Weddings" or "Call Us for Snow Removal." It is a city where a fire station was closed because so many firefighters had been arrested on marijuana charges, a city where an official eager to try out a new bus wrecked it before it could be put into service. It is a city where sunset is the principal daily social event, with hundreds of people lining the pier at Old Mallory Square to applaud the end of the day." —*Walter Logan*

The Banyan
323 Whitehead
Key West, Florida 33040
Telephone (305) 294-9573

"Although my reservation at another Key West inn was for three nights, I was packed and ready to leave at dawn's early light after one night of sleep-destroying activity. Fortunately I found another very nice guesthouse just down the road—the Banyan. There a suitable room was available, and I passed the next two days with such pleasant goodwill that the earlier nightmare had faded from memory by the time I left Key West."   —*William D. Masland*

Open all year.
12 rooms, 10 with private bath, many with kitchen facilities.
Rates $60–$140 winter, $45–$90 summer.
Credit cards: American Express, MasterCard, Visa.
Innkeeper: Vance Kier.

Eaton Lodge
511 Eaton Street
Key West, Florida 33040
Telephone (305) 294-3800

"Eaton Lodge offers a central location in Key West, but buildings and gardens are so placed that one has complete privacy and freedom from traffic nuisance. The interior garden is delightful, a haven for reading and relaxing in the sun. Management is first class: hoteliers who maintain a low profile but give top service. Furnishings are elegant. Parking is no problem. I rate the lodge as exceptional."
—*Howard Weinberger*

"One of the most relaxing places I have been to in years. I felt well looked after."
—*Keith Biggar*

Open late October to early September.
9 rooms, 2 suites, all with private bath.
Rates $55–75 summer, $70–$90 winter, including continental
   breakfast.
Credit cards: American Express, MasterCard, Visa.
No restaurant.
Courtesy car meets guests at Key West airport.
Innkeepers: Denison Tempel and Sam Maxwell.

Lake Wales

Chalet Suzanne
1 West Starr Avenue (P.O. Drawer AC)
Lake Wales, Florida 33853
Telephone (813) 676-1477

This extraordinary and unexpected inn was the creation of Bertha Hinshaw, a culinary expert and world traveler who turned to inn-keeping in 1931 to support her two children after the death of her husband and the loss of a family fortune in the Depression. The inn had acquired a wide reputation by the 1940s, when a fire destroyed much of it and there was no building material available in wartime to reconstruct. So the enterprising Mrs. Hinshaw simply recycled what she had: abandoned stables, rabbit hutches, and chicken-house frames were cobbled together and added to a circular game room by the lake. As the years passed, other bits and pieces were added. The inn now rambles in every direction over fourteen floor levels.

"From the moment you drive through the orange groves and smell the unbelievable blossoms, until you leave, Chalet Suzanne is a fairytale land. Delicious oranges and candy were in our room when we arrived on our most recent visit. As we were being shown the tower suite, I asked if it was new. "Nothing is new here, Mr. Good-man," was the reply. That is true. Everything here is old, made when quality counted and beauty was important.

"The proximity to central Florida's attractions, including Cypress Gardens and Disney World, makes the Chalet an ideal place to stay. The meals here are the best I have ever eaten, and that's quite an endorsement. The dining rooms are over the lake, and the dishes and glassware are different at each table."   —*Mark L. Goodman*

"The exterior architecture is a cross between Tinkerbell's castle and Watts towers. Post-Victorian 'antiques' are assembled with a certain flair in the bedrooms. Baths may have a pastiche of Spanish tiles in unexpected and imaginative combinations. The place looks terrific at twenty feet, but on closer inspection it can be disappointing. The hot and cold water faucets are sometimes reversed; I hate brushing my teeth with hot water! Some of the charming bathroom tiles are installed so that they do not drain properly, sometimes someone has to bathe in the remains of your water. A swinging light at bedside means there is no nightstand—and the lamp may hit you in the head when you get up. The celebrated restaurant is interesting for one night. If you stay a second, you have to insist on another menu to avoid a rerun. For me, too much sugar was used in all the dishes."
                                                        —*Camille J. Cook*

Open all year.
30 rooms, 3 efficiencies, all with private bath.
Rates $50–$80. Special AP packages available in summer.
Credit cards: American Express, Diners Club, MasterCard, Visa.
Public bar and restaurant.

Private grass airstrip.
Innkeepers: Carl and Vita Hinshaw.

St. Augustine

Founded in 1565 by the Spanish, St. Augustine offers a visitor the experience of seeing a New World town with more than 400 unbroken years of settlement. The architecture of 300 of those years has been preserved or restored here, complemented by museum collections and the publications of active educational and historical organizations that aid the visitor in understanding the region's special place in American history. At the same time, St. Augustine also offers beaches and inland waterways for recreation; it is a town for many tastes.

The Kenwood Inn
38 Marine Street
St. Augustine, Florida 32084
Telephone (904) 824-2116

The Kenwood is a success story of renovation in progress. The innkeepers are nearly finished restoring—but at the same time discreetly modernizing—a hotel that had been taking guests for almost 100 years, but that had lost much of its Victorian glory. Reopened only a few years, the hotel is already attracting a loyal following among experienced travelers.

"Pass between the columns and carved gingerbread woodwork of 100 years ago, cross the porch, and you will be greeted by Elsie Hedetniemi, who runs the Kenwood with the warmth of an accomplished hostess and the professionalism of a keen businesswoman. She positively gushes with pride over her lovely, restored city version of a vanishing breed: Florida plantation architecture. The four-cornered building is set among the quaint gardens and narrow streets of the Spanish and English colonial periods. It is furnished throughout with comfortable family pieces and antiques. Rooms are all different and delightful, full of floral fabrics and towels. Breakfast in the dining room is a chance to meet other travelers, and a treat for anyone who enjoys fruitcake with coffee and juice.

"Once settled in and refreshed, I walked to the ancient Spanish fortress, then drove a little way for an alligator dinner—now that's an adventure—before turning in."
—*George Herzog*

Open all year.
16 rooms, 14 with private bath.
Rates $25–$55, including continental breakfast.
Credit cards: MasterCard, Visa.
No restaurant.
Greyhound bus service; airports at Daytona Beach and Jacksonville.
Innkeepers: Elsie Hedetniemi and Robert Carr.

St. Francis Inn
279 St. George Street
St. Augustine, Florida 32084
Telephone (904) 824-6068

The St. Francis has been part of St. Augustine's history for nearly 200 years. The house was built in 1791 by Gaspar Garcia, who had received a grant to the land from the Spanish crown, which still owned Florida. It remained a private home for many years, then served as a school and a boardinghouse before becoming a proper hotel after World War I. This inn is among that puzzling and intriguing group of establishments about which this book receives widely differing comments, from the glowing to the shocked and angry. Weighing them all together, it seems safe to say that accommodations here are not consistent—or even predictable. But the place, built around a Spanish-style courtyard, is undeniably interesting.

"A Spanish iron gate creaks on your arrival. St. Francis himself, in stone, greets each traveler to this triple-story, 200-year-old inn in which one would have been at home with Spanish explorers, French settlers, English governors, and American Indians. This circumnavigator has found nothing like it in any of seventeen countries from north of the Arctic Circle to the foot of South America's Angel Falls."   —Dorothy Wms. Davis-Dodge

"It is in the old Spanish quarter, but the old Spanish quarter means two things. One end of St. George Street, where the inn stands, is a long pedestrian thoroughfare with shops and tourists. The inn, at the other end of the street away from all this activity, enjoys all the seclusion one could seek. There is nothing else like it in St. Augustine. We looked."   —Clive Johnstone and Winifred Weston

"The inn has been described as being full of antiques. That is exaggerated. I think of Victorian as marginally valuable and anything more recent as just old—and that is what much of the St.

Francis contains. It is assembled with happy abandon and gives you the feeling of stepping into an eccentric aunt's parlor—you know, the aunt who never throws anything away. The inn is cluttered; the stairwell is layered with paintings of the inn by admiring amateurs. But the place exudes a naive charm that can be appreciated and enjoyed, and enjoy it we did.

"Renting a suite does not necessarily mean opting for luxury here. The sitting room will most likely have a sofa that converts to an extra bed and a cooking corner for budget-conscious travelers. Some plumbing is antiquated and some updated. If this matters, specify your needs when reserving."   —*Camille J. Cook*

"When we first got there, we didn't like it. The place grew on us though, and we got to enjoy it. After eating out a lot, the kitchen facilities in our room (2-C) gave us an opportunity to prepare our own food. I don't know if I would go back, but just about any place is worth experiencing for one night."   —*Mark L. Goodman*

Open all year.
5 rooms, 3 suites, 1 apartment, 1 cottage, all with private bath.
Rates $30–$60. Weekly and monthly rates available.
No credit cards.
No restaurant or bar.
Innkeeper: Elizabeth H. Davis.

American hotels and inns generally list rates by the room, assuming one person in a single, two in a double. Extra people in rooms normally incur extra charges. Where rates are quoted per person per day, at least one meal is probably included under a Modified American plan (MAP). A full American Plan (AP) would include three meals.

Georgia

Cumberland Island

Greyfield Inn
Cumberland Island, Georgia
Mailing address: Drawer B
Fernandina Beach, Florida 32034
Telephone (904) 356-9509

Cumberland Island, the largest and probably least well known of Georgia's Sea Islands, or Golden Isles, is accessible only by boat or plane. It has retained its wilderness, thanks to its isolation. Deer, wild turkey, raccoons, and ducks wander the woods and the seventeen miles of beaches. Greyfield, built in 1902, was the home of Thomas Carnegie's granddaughter Lucy Ferguson, who made it into an inn. Much of the feeling of the old home has been retained. Guests tend to find Greyfield through word of mouth. There is no tennis court, golf course, or swimming pool at Greyfield. The innkeepers offer instead clam digging, seining, oyster roasts, kite fishing, and bird watching.

"Greyfield, still owned by the Fergusons, is very special."
—*Alexandra E. Whitney*

233

Open all year.

9 rooms, 1 with private bath; 1 efficiency apartment.

Rate $75 per person per day, AP. Children under 3 free, 10 percent discount for children 3–10.

Credit card: Visa.

Bar for guests' use. Dining room features local seafood, homemade breads, and desserts.

One ferry daily except Wednesday from Fernandina Beach, Florida. No cars, bicycles, or pets on ferries. Schedules available from the inn.

Innkeeper: Janet Ferguson.

_____*Dahlonega*

The Smith House
202 South Chestatee Street
Dahlonega, Georgia 30533
Telephone (404) 864-3566

The town of Dahlonega, about seventy miles north of Atlanta, took its name from the Cherokee word for "precious yellow color." Gold was discovered here, on what had been Indian lands, in 1828, and by 1860 it is estimated that millions of dollars worth of the metal had been taken from the surrounding hills. A United States mint was built here in 1838; it minted over $6 million in gold pieces in fewer than thirty years. The old mint is now part of North Georgia College.

"The inn's reputation was built on its home-style cooking, firmly in the Southern tradition (fried chicken, biscuits, corn bread, and local vegetables). This is an extremely well kept and comfortable lodging place, a block or so from the restored town square where fiddlers still play for their own enjoyment. Antique, craft, and other small shops surround the square, which has not yet become too commercialized.

"Because Dahlonega was a gold-mining center until California drew the prospectors away, you can still see some of the old mines, and buy locally made gold jewelry."   —*Beverly Nelson-Brown*

Open all year; closed Mondays.

20 rooms, 4 suites, all with private bath.

Rates $30 single, $36 double, $40–$48 suites.

Credit cards: American Express, MasterCard, Visa.

Public restaurant featuring family-style or cafeteria-style country meals of three meats and ten vegetables.

Manager: Margie Saine.

Jasper

The Woodbridge Inn
Jasper, Georgia 30143
Telephone (404) 692-6293

This mountain inn, formerly the Lenning Hotel, has had a wide reputation in the South since the mid-nineteenth century. Owned for many generations by the descendants of James Lenning, who built the hotel, it first served traveling salesmen, then vacationers from Georgia and neighboring states. The inn is now owned by Joe and Brenda Rueffert. Joe, trained as a chef in Bavaria, has given his inn a statewide reputation for cuisine.

"Jasper is a very small town in the north Georgia mountains, but its inn is widely known for its food, which is spectacular. The *Atlanta Journal and Constitution* raved that it was the only restaurant from Tennessee to Atlanta that didn't serve fried chicken. One problem with the inn is that the owners live in the main 1848 building, and guests stay in a small, modern lodge (motel is too harsh a word for it). All the rooms overlook the mountains, however, with a few bilevel suites that have sitting rooms on the mezzanine. The inn-keepers' personalities and energies dominate the place. A year or so ago, they helped overturn the county's dry laws, a remnant of Prohibition. The food really is wonderful—meat, seafood, bread, and vegetables, all fresh and seasoned with finesse."

—*Beverly Nelson-Brown*

Open all year.
12 rooms, all with private bath.
Rates $34–$58.
Credit cards: American Express, MasterCard, Visa.
Public restaurant featuring European cuisine.
French, German, and Spanish spoken.
Innkeepers: Joe and Brenda Rueffert.

Lakemont

Lake Rabun Hotel
Route 1 (Box 101A)
Lakemont, Georgia 30552
Telephone (404) 782-4946

"This rustic, two-story structure is on a hillside in the Chattahoo-chee National Forest on the shore of Lake Rabun, though the view of the lake is obscured by trees. Rooms vary in size, but are mainly on the smallish side. They are comfortably furnished with items indigenous to this mountain area. Innkeeper Barbara Gray's continental breakfast includes her own excellent doughnuts. The atmosphere is congenial: the innkeepers introduce guests to each other on a first-name basis. The inn seems to be popular with the Atlanta legal and advertising set. Autumn foliage weekends are booked a year in advance."   —*George G. Weiss*

Open April 15 to October 30.
16 rooms, 1 with half-bath, others with shared baths.
Rates $16.50 single, $22.50 double, $4 per child, including buffet breakfast.
No credit cards.
Restaurant across the street.
Innkeepers: Dick and Barbara Gray.

_____*St. Simons Island*

The King and Prince
201 Arnold Road (P.O. Box 798)
St. Simons Island, Georgia 31522
Telephone (912) 638-3631

This hotel, originally a beach club, was built in a graceful Spanish colonial style at the edge of the sea on one of the most attractive of Georgia's Sea Isles. The island has been inhabited since colonial times, so visitors have the unique experience of enjoying a magnificent geographical setting while being surrounded by history: forts, churches, plantations.

"This grand old hotel has a long history, boasts an excellent dining room, and is right on the beach. The hotel provides swings and beach chairs and even lights for an evening dip."
                                                    —*Beverly Nelson-Brown*

Open all year.
94 rooms and suites in main hotel and 3 houses, all with private bath.
Rates $45–$80 rooms, depending on view; $90 suites; $50–$130 houses, depending on season.
Credit cards: American Express, Diners Club, MasterCard, Visa.
Public bar and restaurant.
French, German, and Spanish spoken.
General Manager: Richard E. Tucker.

_____*Savannah*

The old city of Savannah, founded and designed by General James Edward Oglethorpe in the eighteenth century, remains true to its plan two and a half centuries later. It was here that Oglethorpe brought his English colonists to settle a new territory he named for King George II. Savannah today is rich in historic squares and public buildings and homes, a large number of them carefully preserved or restored. The city is increasingly popular with tourists looking for a grander early America. Each year the number of inns and old homes open to travelers grows, giving visitors a chance to become, briefly, part of the city's history.

_____

Ballastone Inn
14 East Oglethorpe Avenue
Savannah, Georgia 31401
Telephone (912) 236-1484

To the people of colonial port cities, the name Ballastone had a special meaning. This city and others—among them San Juan, Puerto Rico—were paved and built of the stones European ships carried in their holds as ballast when they came to the New World to pick up treasure or, in the case of Savannah, bales of cotton.

"The inn is in the heart of the historic city, probably one of the most beautiful downtown areas anywhere. The house was built in 1835 for a family named Anderson. Tarby Bryant and his associates restored it in a Victorian manner, but with an eclectic touch. Southern hospitality is evident here. Serenity reigns."
—*Mr. and Mrs. William C. Beckenhauer, Jr.*

"The Ballastone is everything an inn is supposed to be: a glass of sherry when you check in, bathrobes in the bathrooms, rooms for every taste, and a snifter of brandy and a candy by your bedside at night. There are canopied and brass beds, an open bar by a gas fireplace in the sitting room downstairs, and breakfast served in your room. There was even a card waiting for us when we got home, thanking us for staying at the Ballastone. This is a class inn."
—*Mark L. Goodman*

Open all year.
19 rooms, all with private bath.

Rates from $70 single, $85 double, including Southern continental
 breakfast.
Credit cards: American Express, MasterCard, Visa.
Cash bar for guests only. No restaurant.
Manager: Brad Holloway.

Charlton Court
403 East Charlton Street
Savannah, Georgia 31401
Telephone (912) 236-2895

"It is very difficult to encapsulate in one short entry all that Savannah means. It's a city with the flavor of Edinburgh, Dublin, and Bath, but with rather more verve and color. And cleaner—one can never understand Americans' fascination for grubby old Britain. To do justice to this old town, one should stay here at least three days. There is greenery in abundance in this kind climate. Brick-paved and cobbled streets are plentiful—someone must have the highway engineer on a tight rein. From the broad river—Savannah is still an important port—there are seven-day inshore cruises as far as Charleston and back. There is no shortage of information to make the visitor's trip happy and rewarding. No roadside clutter. Savannah seems to avoid all the obvious tourist traps and pitfalls. People live here, and getting to know you seems to be what it is all about.

"Home accommodations are of the most astonishingly high quality. Inside Inns is a wonderful scheme operated by the Chamber of Commerce that offers the visitor a less pretentious and certainly more agreeable way to savor the flavor of the old town. Beautifully restored private houses rent apartments: we sampled two. At one of them, Charlton Court, the home of Isabella and Jerry Reeves, we had a garden suite with a separate courtyard entrance—a bedroom with double bed, living room, bath, and kitchen."
—*Clive Johnstone and Winifred Weston*

"As someone who spends four nights a week on average on the road, I would like to say that this particular place is absolutely superb. Instead of coming into a hotel, which requires a certain degree of endurance and offers stark boredom, going to Charlton Court is like visiting a second home."   —*Mike Nicholes*

Open all year.
1 carriage house.
Rate $65, including continental breakfast and free use of bicycles.
 Children under 12 free.

No credit cards.
Innkeepers: Mr. and Mrs. J. H. Reeves.

Four Seventeen: The Haslam-Fort House
417 East Charlton Street
Savannah, Georgia 31401
Telephone (912) 233-6380

This 1872 house has had a theatrical life: it was built for John Haslam, an entrepreneur who produced minstrel shows after the Civil War, and is now owned by Alan Fort, who, among other things, has been an actor. Mr. Fort, one of the first to join what is now a fast-growing trend in the city, opened a garden suite to guests several years ago.

"The garden apartment is furnished with a distinctive array of comfortable antiques. One immediately becomes a house guest while enjoying the uncommon luxury of complete privacy. Evenings in the side yard can be shared with the conversational host, who offers a wealth of in-town information. Alan is ably assisted by his staff— Myrna, Maude, Rhonda, and Humphrey—who, while pets, are no less discreet and considerate than their owner."
—Sue and Don Wood; also recommended by John L. Herbert,
Jeanne and Eldon Winkler, and Percy Rowe

Open all year.
1 suite with 2 bedrooms, country kitchen, and bath; 3 one-bedroom cottage suites with kitchen; 2 guest rooms.
Rates $60 single–$125 for 4 people, including breakfast, soft drinks, and liqueurs.
Credit card: American Express.
German, Norwegian, and Spanish spoken.
Innkeeper: Alan Fort.

Gasthaus Gunkel
409 East Charlton Street
Savannah, Georgia 31401
Telephone (912) 234-6218

"This is the home of Kay and Dieter Gunkel. They offer similar accommodations to Charlton Court. These Inside Inns are far better than the best motels; everything is crisp, clean, fresh, and of high quality. The Gunkels have a lovely rosewood piano in the living room, and a perfectly splendid garden courtyard at the rear. There is street parking, so there is no long haul with baggage."

—*Clive Johnstone and Winifred Weston*

Open all year.
1 suite.
Rates $60 double, $80 for three people, $90 for four, including continental breakfast.
No credit cards.
German spoken.
Innkeeper: Kay Gunkel.

The Stoddard-Cooper House
19 West Perry Street
Savannah, Georgia 31401
Telephone (912) 233-6809; 234-5305

When Barbara and David Hershey bought this 1854 town house on Chippewa Square in 1978, it had been abandoned and misused: the pine floors were covered with linoleum, fluorescent lights festooned the ceilings, the kitchen had been gutted to serve as storage space for a local bank, and the plumbing and heating systems had vanished along with the marble mantels. The restoration of the house, where once New York's DeWitt Clinton family had lived, took two years. The Hersheys now offer guests a basement-level suite, with street entrance and a garden at the rear.

"The inn, strategically located in the heart of historic Savannah, has been restored to conform to its surroundings, and is furnished with a blend of antiques and modern conveniences. There is a private walled garden where guests may enjoy an ample supply of pastries and coffee each morning—or they can prepare a full breakfast in the kitchen. Guests are furnished with complete information about the city."

—*Steven and Waneta Anderson*

Open all year.
One 2-bedroom suite, with full kitchen.
Rates $75 for two people, $95 for three, $125 for four, including continental breakfast, wine, and fruit.

Turn to the back of this book for pages inviting *your* comments.

*Old Talbott Tavern,
Bardstown*

Kentucky

Bardstown

Old Talbott Tavern
107 West Stephen Foster Avenue
Bardstown, Kentucky 40004
telephone (502) 348-3494

This tavern, known for many years as the Old Stone Inn, has been in operation since 1779, when the post roads from all directions passed by, making it an important stop for stagecoaches. Accommodation originally was a large loft divided in two for men and women; cooking was done in the fireplaces. Naturally, stories of famous guests are part of the place: an exiled Louis Philippe whiling away his time in an upstairs room in 1800, Abraham Lincoln's family in residence while a trial to settle the title to a farm was under way. During restoration work not long ago, the stripping away of wallpaper in a large second-floor room revealed wall paintings thought to have been done by companions of Louis Philippe, since the work is French in style and subject.

"Sights worth seeing in the area are Stephen Foster's 'Old Kentucky Home,' the Barton Museum of Whiskey History and, in nearby Loretto, Maker's Mark distillery, with its first-class, family-run tour.

This is highly recommended over the mass-produced big distillery tours. Bardstown also has an Olympic-size swimming pool, refreshing in the hot and muggy summertime.

"We stayed in Room 14 at the tavern. It was roomy but we thought it needed repair. The tavern's food was excellent, however: the filet mignon was very tender and the corn pudding had an unusual hint of cinnamon. The hostess brought us a soft drink before retiring. It was on the house."   —*Nancy Heckman*

"I love my big old bed in 14—the room number a concession to progress. The furnishings are the Old Talbott and so is the fire in the old fireplace, the link for me between the warmth of yesterday's Old Talbott and the Talbott of today."   —*Herbert Pender, Jr.*

Open all year.
6 rooms, all with private bath.
Rate $35 double.
Credit cards: American Express, MasterCard, Visa.
Public restaurant and bar.
Bus service to Bardstown.
Innkeeper: Peggy Downs.

_____*Berea*

Boone Tavern Hotel
Main and Prospect (C.P.O. 2345)
Berea, Kentucky 40403
Telephone (606) 986-9358

"Berea College provides educational opportunity to the isolated young people of the Appalachian Mountains. For sixty years, all the students have shared in a labor program, working ten hours a week to help defray bills. For countless young mountain people, this has meant the difference between a college degree and no college at all. The students who run Boone Tavern are part of this work program.

"Each room of the hotel is furnished with handcrafted pieces from the college's woodwork shops. Crafts of the southern Appalachian highlands are to be found in the shops of Boone Tavern Square. The inventories come from recognized production centers and from individual artists and craftspeople—potters, jewelers, sculptors, weavers, dollmakers, blacksmiths, chairmakers, printmakers, and dulcimer craftsmen.

"Boone Tavern's restaurant is acclaimed for its regional food, and 'no tipping' is the rule. Overnight guests find individualized rooms, with windows that open to let in the fresh mountain air.

Spotless baths are supplied with an abundance of linen, including the old familiar huckaback hand towels."

—Alice and E. G. Getman

"Tours of the college are arranged on request, and I have found them extremely rewarding. There is also summer drama presented by the students. Berea is an excellent location if one is interested in the beautiful state of Kentucky. It is about twenty minutes from Lexington, and less than an hour from Cincinnati."

—Ruth J. Cranford; also recommended by Senator Wendell H. Ford

Open all year.
57 rooms, all with private bath.
Rates $20–$42.
Credit cards: American Express, Diners Club, MasterCard, Visa.
Restaurant, no bar. College activities open to guests.
Innkeeper: Miriam R. Pride.

_____*Brandenburg*

Doe Run Inn
Route 2
Brandenburg, Kentucky 40108
Telephone (502) 422-2042; 422-2982

The land on which Doe Run was built in 1800 was owned by Daniel Boone's brother, who was known locally as Squire Boone. Doe Run, with stone walls two and a half feet thick, was the first building to be raised on the squire's land. Abraham Lincoln's father is thought to have worked as a stonemason here. The building was first used as a woolen mill, then a gristmill. Next it became a flour and grain mill, operated by the ancestors of the present owners. By the turn of the twentieth century, Doe Run had become a summer camp to which boarders came for the mineral waters. In 1927 it became a proper inn, full of antiques that tell the craft history of the area.

"The inn is back from the road, beside a creek in which watercress grows in abundance. The creek, Doe Run, gave the inn its name. Some of the rooms are furnished in antique pieces, such as hand-carved walnut headboards and marble-topped dressers. The meals —good examples of Kentucky country cooking—are served on the screened porch overlooking the stream and the waterfalls."

—Bob and Marilyn Prescott

Open all year.
14 rooms, 5 with private bath.

Rate $22.
Credit cards: MasterCard, Visa.
Public restaurant, with smorgasbord Friday night and Sunday noon till 9 P.M.
Innkeeper: Lucille S. Brown.

_____*Harrodsburg*

Beaumont Inn
Harrodsburg, Kentucky 40330
Telephone (606) 734-3381

Harrodsburg, in bluegrass country, is reputed to be Kentucky's oldest town. The Beaumont has been part of its history since 1845, when it was opened as a school for young ladies. It served as a school and college until 1917, when the family of the present owner bought it and converted it into an inn. Annie Bell Goddard and her husband, Glave, were the first owners of the inn. She had been a pupil there when it was a school, and had taught there when it was Beaumont College. The present innkeeper is the fourth generation of that family to run the inn. The inn's twenty-nine rooms are scattered through four buildings now: the Main Building, Goddard Hall (1935), Greystone House (1931), and Bell Cottage (1921).

"At Beaumont Inn, Southern cooking at its best awaits the tourist who can beat the local citizens to the table. The menu features mouth-watering Kentucky country ham, Kentucky fried chicken even the Colonel would admire, and tasty corn pudding. A marvelous gift shop is another part of the treat."
—*Senator Wendell H. Ford*

Open March through November.
29 rooms, all with private bath.
Rates $28–$46 single, $46–$52 double.
Credit cards: MasterCard, Visa.
Restaurant.
Innkeeper: Charles M. Dedman.

The Inn at Pleasant Hill
Route 4
Harrodsburg, Kentucky 40330
Telephone (606) 734-5411

"Southern hospitality, Southern cooking, and American scenery at its loveliest. Set amid the rolling hills of Kentucky, a Shaker community has been restored here to the way it appeared before the Civil War. Accommodations are available throughout the settlement, in structures faithfully restored down to the reproduction furniture and wall-to-wall hanging wooden pegs. Most often we request lodgings in the 1839 Trustees' House, with its lovely twin-spiral staircases reaching to the third floor. Although each building is a museum in itself, the Center Family House serves as the principal Pleasant Hill museum. Meals are served in the Trustees' house: the breakfast buffet is a specialty. There is as much or as little to do here as you desire. After strolling through the village, watching craftspeople at work, you might walk a mile or two down to the Kentucky River. Or you might look again at the Shaker cemetery, where most headstones are marked with only worn initials, true to the Shaker way."   —*Joanne and Nick Apple*

"Here you can find some of the most delicious victuals, homegrown right in view on the grounds, that you could ever put in your mouth. You can feel the spirit at the same time. Browsing the grounds, the visitor learns the history and heritage of the Shakers, sees their unequaled carpentry and skillfully accomplished crafts."
    —*Senator Wendell H. Ford; also recommended by Nancy Heckman*

Open all year.
61 rooms, all with private bath.
Rates $30–$50 single, $40–$60 double.
No credit cards.
Innkeeper: Ann Voris.

Details of special features offered by an inn or hotel vary according to information supplied by the hotels themselves. The absence here of a recreational amenity, a bar, or a restaurant doesn't necessarily mean one of these doesn't exist. Ask the innkeeper when booking your room.

Louisiana

New Orleans

French Quarter Maisonettes
1130 Chartres Street
New Orleans, Louisiana 70116
Telephone (504) 524-9918

"Innkeeper Mrs. Junius Underwood and her two cats make a stay here an absolute delight. Inside the clean apartment and snug courtyard it was hard to imagine we were in the heart of the French Quarter. Mrs. Underwood gives each guest an excellent folder that includes suggestions for restaurants, things to do, and tours."

—Jack and Sue Lane

Open all year, except July.
7 rooms and suites, all with private bath.
Rates $38–$44.
No credit cards.
Innkeeper: Mrs. Junius Underwood.

Rates quoted were the latest available. But they may not reflect unexpected increases or local and state taxes. Be sure to verify when you book.

Lafitte Guest House
1003 Bourbon Street
New Orleans, Louisiana 70116
Telephone (504) 581-2678

Acquired by its present owners in 1980, the house had been taking in guests for many years with what the manager, Steve Guyton, calls "varying degrees of success and popularity." Mr. Guyton has been at work for several years on restoration and redecoration of the house, which was built in the French style in 1849 for Paul Joseph Geleises—a wealthy man, judging by the costs of construction. The house, in the city's historic district, the Vieux Carré, was built on a site that had been occupied by one building or another since 1795.

"Nestled in the heart of this beautiful and historic city amid some of the most popular nightspots in America, the Lafitte Guest House seems none the less miles from the clamor and buzz of the French Quarter. This old building offers the finest lodgings we have found in the city. Decor is exquisite: a fine eclectic mixture of lovely Victorian antiques and contemporary textures and tones.

"Just outside the door is Bourbon Street and all you have ever heard about it. Within easy walking distance are some of the world's greatest restaurants, the city's business district, and the Mississippi River. Canal Street separates the old from the older. A streetcar ride up St. Charles Avenue passes some of the most splendid Greek Revival palaces of the South."   —*Catherine and Bill Bailey Carter*

Open all year.
14 rooms, all with private bath.
Rates $58–$85 single, $68–$95 double, including continental breakfast.
Credit cards: American Express, MasterCard, Visa.
No restaurant or bar.
Airport limousine service available.
Manager: Steve Guyton.

Lamothe House
621 Esplanade Avenue
New Orleans, Louisiana 70116
Telephone (504) 947-1161

This house was built in about 1800 for Jean Lamothe, a wealthy French sugar planter from Santo Domingo, who was seeking a safe place for his family because of disturbances on the island. It became a guesthouse in the 1950s.

"Walking through the entrance hall, you are confronted by a patio with three stories of balconies, a fishpond, and lots of plants. Ascending the curved stair, you are welcomed by the innkeeper or a member of the staff. A visit to the French Quarter is much enhanced by a visit to this inn."
—*James K. Mellow*

"The continental breakfast in the dining room was a daily high point, since we met and chatted with some very interesting guests. Offstreet parking here is another boon."
—*Marion Smith*

Open all year.
16 rooms and suites, all with private bath.
Rates $75–$100, including continental breakfast.
Credit cards: American Express, MasterCard, Visa.
Airport limousine service; local buses for touring city.
Innkeepers: Frieda and Ralph Lutin.

Maison de Ville
727 Toulouse Street
New Orleans, Louisiana 70130
Telephone (504) 561-5858

"It is easy to overlook the sign at 727 Toulouse Street. Maybe that is as it should be. Once inside, it is even easier to overlook the fact that you are in a hotel. The building was a home from the early nineteenth century until the late 1930s. The conversion to a well-maintained hotel offering modern comforts was achieved without changes in appearance. Furnishings are authentic to private homes in early nineteenth-century New Orleans. The courtyard, with its fountain in the center and its slave quarters that have been converted to guest rooms, is a delightful spot for your breakfast, afternoon tea, or evening port.

"The sightseer could not find a more convenient location. A half-block to the left and you are in the fine shopping area of Royal Street. A half-block to the right and you are in the heart of Bourbon Street night life, which really is in full swing around the clock. Some of the finest restaurants are within three blocks. The staff can make reservations for dining: they seem to be on a first-name basis with the restaurants, and get you a good table."

—John B. Parramore, Jr.

"The variety of the restaurants is exceptional. Across the street from the Maison de Ville is a pub called Molly's, where we enjoyed barbecue and beans. More elegant is the food at Le Ruth's in Gretna, across the river—but reservations are needed long in advance. Another favorite is the Caribbean Room at the Hotel Ponchartrain. Try Crozier's, too. And the K-Paul is fun."

—Art and Susan Bachrach

"We had a gorgeous suite in the Audubon cottage—a heavenly oasis." *—Camille J. Cook*

Open all year.
21 rooms, all with private bath.
Rates $80–$95 single, $90–$105 double, including continental breakfast.
No credit cards.
Manager: William W. Prentiss.

Olivier House
828 Toulouse Street
New Orleans, Louisiana 70112
Telephone (504) 525-8456

"The Olivier House is in the French Quarter, the old Franco-Spanish city of the Creoles. Most tourist attractions—as well as historic sites such as St. Louis Cathedral, Jackson Square, the Cabildo Museum, the Jazz Museum, and the Pontalba Apartments—are within a four-block range. The hotel was built in 1836 as a town house for the widow of Nicolas Olivier, a wealthy plantation owner. The major part of the hotel consists of the old Olivier home with the slave quarters in the back." *—John and Jeannette Holt*

"My husband and I spent a marvelous four days here. The room we had was furnished with antiques, and the staff left it spick-and-span every morning. There were rolls and coffee for breakfast and a crème de menthe candy on each pillow at night. The atmosphere was one of a home. The resident cat even had kittens during our stay. Our visit spoiled us as to what kind of hotels we will stay in from now on." *—Nancy L. Kuethe*

"We selected the Olivier House from this book, made reservations two months in advance, and were confirmed for a brass bed, balcony, and so on. The airport limo dropped us there on a Friday night, and what were we shown? A back room with a two-by-four window and an unmade bed. Our first evening in New Orleans was spent walking the streets looking for another place to stay. We suggest removing this one."

—Jack and Sue Lane

Open all year.
40 rooms, including 7 suites, all with private bath.
Rates $50–$95.
Credit cards: American Express, MasterCard, Visa.
No restaurant or bar.
Spanish spoken.
Innkeepers: Jim and Kathy Danner.

St. Francisville

The Cottage Plantation
Route 5 (P.O. Box 425)
St. Francisville, Louisiana 70775
Telephone (504) 635-3674

The owners of this estate, built over a period from 1795 to 1850, believe that it is one of only a few antebellum plantations in the South to have remained intact in the post–Civil War period.

"The entire area up the Mississippi from Baton Rouge is full of history, and the Cottage Plantation is part of it. The annual Audubon Pilgrimage in St. Francisville includes this home, where Andrew Jackson and his men stayed en route to Natchez from the Battle of New Orleans. Hanging moss from giant live oak branches envelops the front gallery. At night the silence can be heard."

—Charles L. Hoke

"This is one of only a few plantation homes to take guests. Much intelligence has been used to retain the plantation's air of having been lived in, rather than done over and put back together. Every morning at 8, demitasses are brought to your room. Breakfast at 8:30 is taken in the beautiful dining room, overlooking the shaded veranda and lawn. No other food is available here, but lunch can be managed at one or two little places on the outskirts of St. Francisville. Dinner (and lunch, too) can be found at a nice old thirties sort of roadhouse called South of the Border—the Mississippi border, it turns out—or at Asphodel, about twenty miles back through town.

"The area has many rehabilitated plantation houses open to the public. One of the nicest is Oakley House, now a museum and state park. It is a large house where John J. Audubon lived and tutored for some years, while doing many of his famous bird paintings."

—*Will and Tedda Sternberg; also recommended by Marion Smith and Genevieve and Morrell Feltus Trimble*

Open all year, except Christmas Day.
5 rooms, all with private bath.
Rates $40 single, $60 twin or double, including morning coffee and full plantation breakfast.
No restaurant or bar.
Innkeeper: Mrs. Robert H. Weller.

Propinquity
523 Royal Street (P.O. Box 814)
St. Francisville, Louisiana 70775
Telephone (504) 635-6855

"St. Francisville, quiet and sleepy, is one of the most charming old towns of the South. The majority of the old homes are lived in, and if the owners wish to show them to the public, they place an 'Open' sign on the building. That's how we found Propinquity. The house is of Spanish design, built high, with two porches across the east exposure to catch the breeze. This was innkeeper Gladys Seif's childhood home."   —*Mr. and Mrs. Ralph E. Heasley*

"We occupied the entire upstairs suite and were delighted with both our hosts and our accommodations. The Seifs are very active octogenarians who, when we visited, were preparing a crawfish party for 300 guests. We went on from here to Natchez, then on our return stayed again with the Seifs. Mrs. Seif gave us a tour of her home, and Mr. Seif took our picture, a practice by which they remember all their guests."   —*Marion Smith*

Open all year, except Christmas and New Year's Day.
1 two-bedroom suite, with large bath.
Rate $50 double for each bedroom, including continental breakfast.
No credit cards.
No restaurant or bar.
Innkeepers: Charles and Gladys Seif.

Do you know a hotel in your state that we have overlooked? Write *now*.

Mississippi

Natchez

Natchez, a city of superior early nineteenth-century Southern architecture, is also a city engaged in restoration. Travelers report that a number of homes have begun to take guests, especially during the annual spring Pilgrimage in March and April, when more than thirty architecturally interesting houses are on display for tour groups. Marion Smith, a contributor to this book, wrote this about the experience she and her husband had in finding accommodations: "The antebellum homes that take guests were booked for the Pilgrimage months in advance. But we found that many other local people had opened their homes to tourists, by arrangement with the Pilgrimage committee, and we were totally delighted with the time spent with our hosts, Mr. and Mrs. D. Corlew. We were given our own key to the house. Continental breakfast was included in the reasonable fee, but our hosts also invited us to lunch and dinner. They made reservations for us to see the Confederate Pageant—a must to see, with young people performing dances of the Old South in gorgeous antebellum costumes." Information on the Pilgrimage is available from the Natchez Garden Club, P.O. Box 537, or the Pilgrimage Garden Club, Box 1585, Natchez, Mississippi 39120.

The Burn
712 North Union Street
Natchez, Mississippi 39120
Telephone (601) 445-8566

One of Natchez's finest houses is The Burn, which as an inn continues to be recommended by readers of this book. Built as a home in 1832 in Greek Revival style, with Doric columns supporting a front portico, The Burn is now owned by Natchez's mayor, Tony Byrne.

"Natchez was a legend in its own time, the queen of the Mississippi for over a century, known for the grandeur on the bluff and the bawdy under the hill, the meeting place of dukes and thieves. Nestled on a rise of lawn in the shade of majestic oaks and pines, The Burn first appears to be a small cottage. Inside, one sees the error of the first impression, for the house is large and beautifully appointed with antiques of various periods. The garden and grounds could entice even a recluse out to walk the hidden paths or laze by the pool."   —*Valette Randall*

"The Burn, meaning 'the brook,' was given its name by its Scottish builder 150 years ago. It survived the Civil War—as headquarters for Union soldiers and then as a hospital—and years of postwar neglect until it was bought and restored in 1978. What makes The Burn unique in a city of antebellum homes is that you don't have to admire its antiques from behind a velvet rope. When you are shown your room in the house or the nearby *garçonnière,* you will find a beautifully draped four-poster bed, perhaps one carved in New Orleans by Prudent Mallard. You will find a fireplace with candelabra, comfortable velvet or tapestry chairs, real flowers on your Empire table, and every lamp a gem. You are free to walk the Aubusson carpets or to sit on a brocade sofa."
                                        —*Mrs. William J. Simmons*

Open all year.
6 rooms, all with private bath.
Rates $65 single, $75 double, with full plantation breakfast.
Credit cards: MasterCard, Visa.
No restaurant, but dinner can be arranged for small groups.
Innkeepers: Mr. and Mrs. Tony Byrne.

If you would like to amend, update, or disagree with any entry, write *now.*

Ravenside
601 South Union Street
Natchez, Mississippi 39120
Telephone (601) 442-8015

"Ravenside, built by a Mr. and Mrs. James S. Fleming in the 1800s as a 'party house' strictly for entertainment, later became the home of their daughter Roane Fleming Byrnes. The house was bought in 1973 by Mr. and Mrs. John Van Hook. A great many of the original furnishings have been retained, and the woodwork has been restored to its natural beauty. The numerous Louisiana and Mississippi antebellum homes we toured paled in comparison to the lovingly and carefully restored Ravenside. Staying here was a marvelous experience."   —*Jack and Sue Lane*

Open all year, except July and August.
5 rooms, all with private bath.
Rates $55–$60, including full breakfast and evening cocktails.
No credit cards.
Innkeepers: Verda and John Van Hook.

Silver Street Inn
1 Silver Street
Natchez, Mississippi 39120
Telephone (601) 442-4221

"Visitors to Natchez can now stay under the Hill, in the neighborhood once inhabited by boatmen, trappers, gamblers, and prostitutes—an area once known as the cesspool of the South. Silver Street Ltd., a teeming bawdy house in the 1840s, is now elegantly refurbished as a specialty shop on the lower level and an inn upstairs. Guests enter by an outside stairway into a keeping room with a fireplace and country antiques: an early pewter cupboard, a cypress dry sink, and a rare Mississippi huntboard. There are four guest rooms, two of them opening onto the upper gallery overlooking Silver Street and the Mississippi.

"After settling in, stroll down Silver Street and along the riverbank to the Cock of the Walk to dine on the Southern delicacy of catfish with all the trimmings: greens, corn bread, fried dill pickles,

fried onions, and potatoes. On your way back, you may want to visit the Saloon, another restored building from Natchez-Under-the-Hill."
—*Janie W. McGuffie*

Open all year.
4 rooms, 2 with private bath.
Rate $65 double, including continental breakfast.
Credit cards: American Express, Diners Club, MasterCard, Visa.
No restaurant or bar.
Innkeepers: Lu Barraza and Peggie Herrington.

Port Gibson

Oak Square
1207 Church Street
Port Gibson, Mississippi 39150
Telephone (601) 437-4350; 437-5771; 437-5300

"Port Gibson is a small western Mississippi town about five miles from the river. Along its main street are many restored antebellum homes. Their architecture, their beautiful gardens, and the lush foliage everywhere make this community a worthwhile stop. On the main street of Port Gibson, restored to its mid-nineteenth-century elegance, is Oak Square. The mansion is the home of Bill and Martha Lum, who with great care and attention have restored this once-neglected building. The restoration includes antique furnishings, many of which are period pieces. The Lums' families have been part of Mississippi for more than 200 years.

"On the grounds of Oak Square is a nineteenth-century town house that was moved to Port Gibson from Vicksburg. This is also used as a guesthouse, furnished in the same way as the main house. Breakfast is usually served in the main house. It is a typical Southern breakfast, plentiful and served on beautiful old china. Despite all the elegance, one feels very much at home, very comfortable. We have stayed in many inns in the United States and Britain, and Oak Square is one of the best.

"If one has an interest in the Civil War and the evolution of Southern society, the combination of this fine inn, the town, and the abundant historical sites in the area make a trip to Port Gibson an unforgettable experience."
—*Louis and Karen Parvey*

Open all year.
10 rooms, 7 with private bath.

Rates $50 single, $55–$65 double, including full Southern break-
fast.
Credit cards: American Express, MasterCard, Visa.
Restaurant owned by innkeepers 2 blocks away.
Innkeepers: Martha and William D. Lum.

Would you be so kind as to share discoveries you may have of charming, well-run places to stay in Europe? Please write to *Europe's Wonderful Little Hotels and Inns,* c/o Congdon & Weed, 298 Fifth Avenue, New York, New York 10001. (By the way, a new and greatly expanded edition of this splendid guide is now available at your bookseller's.)

_____ *North Carolina*

Asheville

Flint Street Inn
116 Flint Street
Asheville, North Carolina 28801
Telephone (704) 253-6723

"I first read about the inn in the magazine of the National Trust for Historic Preservation. We thoroughly enjoyed our stay. Our hosts, Rick and Lynne Vogel, had just remodeled the 1915 Eva Clark House and had furnished it with American pieces from the early twentieth century: Art Nouveau and Art Deco sculpture and prints, wooden clocks, fine quilts. The Vogels made our visit to Asheville delightful. They recommended restaurants and sites to visit, gave us maps and brochures, and lent us picnic dishes for lunch in the park. They shared a wealth of information about their neighborhood, recently designated the Montford Historic District. The inn is a short walk from downtown, the Thomas Wolfe House, and the convention center. Each morning Lynne baked something fresh: blueberry muffins, biscuits, rolls. Coffee was excellent and the orange juice was fresh-squeezed. Anyone planning a drive along the

Blue Ridge Parkway or even a business trip to Asheville would find the Flint Street Inn a pleasant haven." —*Judith L. Johnston*

Open all year.
3 rooms, 2 shared baths.
Rates $35–$50, including breakfast.
No credit cards.
Innkeepers: Lynne and Rick Vogel.

_____*Black Mountain*

The Red Rocker Inn
136 North Dougherty Street
Black Mountain, North Carolina 28711
Telephone (704) 669-5991

This old inn, built in 1894 and given as a wedding present to the daughter of the owner, remained in that family—the Doughertys, for whom the street is named—until less than a decade ago. A few years ago, after the inn subsequently changed hands several times, it was bought by Fred Eshelman, who began the long job of restoring the building to its Victorian glory, while building a local reputation for his family-style restaurant, with its specialties like peanut butter pie and watermelon ice cream. Black Mountain is near the Blue Ridge Parkway and Asheville's Biltmore Mansion. It boasts the golf course with the world's longest (par six) seventeenth hole.

"We happen to be from North Carolina, and have known of the Red Rocker Inn in Black Mountain for many years. Recently, hearing that it was under new management, we decided to try it. We were thoroughly pleased, so pleased that we have taken friends there for dinner on two subsequent occasions. My wife has looked at all the guest rooms. She was impressed by their quaint decor and their general attractiveness. Also the price is right, most reasonable for this tourist area. We hope some of your readers will visit the inn to check it out for themselves." —*C. E. Anderson;*
also recommended by Mrs. Henry M. Ruppel

Open early May to end of October.
18 rooms, 10 with private bath, 8 with connecting baths; 2 suites.
Rates $30–$65. Packages available in some seasons for stays of two or more nights.
No credit cards.
Family-style restaurant.
Innkeepers: Patricia and Fred Eshelman.

Bryson City

Bryson City, the seat of Swain County, is at the edge of the Great Smoky Mountains National Park in an outdoor recreational area—with fishing, hiking, and white water canoeing—that is also becoming a crafts and antique center as well. This is also Cherokee territory, and there are Indian fairs and pageants as well as a Cherokee museum to visit.

Folkstone Lodge
West Deep Creek Road (Route 1, Box 310)
Bryson City, North Carolina 28713
Telephone (704) 488-2730

Folkstone was built as a farmhouse in 1926, and the owners have preserved some touches unique to that age—Art Deco stained glass, for example, and some period furniture and bathroom fixtures like claw-footed tubs. The building was constructed of stone, floors included, and these are also carefully maintained.

"While visiting the Smoky Mountains, we happened on this lovely inn. Its quaintness and location could be matched only by the friendliness and helpfulness the innkeepers offered us as we discovered the romance of the area. The food was delicious, and the rooms were white-glove clean."   —_Debbie and Larry Elizalde_

Open all year.
5 rooms, all with private bath.
Rate $22.50 per person per day, double occupancy, including breakfast.
Credit cards: MasterCard, Visa.
No restaurant or bar.
Innkeepers: Bob and Irene Kranich.

Fryemont Inn
Fryemont Road (P.O. Box 459)
Bryson City, North Carolina 28713
Telephone (704) 488-2159

The inn was built in 1921 for a timber-cutting king named Captain Amos Frye. Only the best chestnut, oak, and maple in the Smokies were chosen for the building. Local craftsmen carved furniture of cherry and walnut. Ironwork was done by the best blacksmith in the mountains. Stonemasons built fireplaces that could take ten-foot logs. The inn is covered in poplar bark, as sturdy as it is rustic.

"Found this one by accident—a rustic lodge sitting on a hillside. There is a large sitting room with a huge stone fireplace, and a porch full of rockers. The food was superb. Records from the forties were played during dinner. There is a pool and tennis court."

—*Judith Alford*

Open April through October.
31 rooms, 6 suites, all with private bath.
Rates $30–$50 double, EP; $62–$68, with breakfast and dinner.
Credit cards: MasterCard, Visa.
Public restaurant and wine bar; beer sold at package store on premises.
Nearest airport at Asheville, 60 miles away.
Innkeepers: Sue and George Brown.

Hemlock Inn
P.O. Drawer EE
Bryson City, North Carolina 28713
Telephone (704) 488-2885

"The excitement of springtime in the mountains is enhanced by a visit to this inn just outside Bryson City. In May the guests may be wildflower enthusiasts; family groups come in the summer; in the fall couples come to see the autumn colors. Innkeeper Ella Jo Shell takes care of the food, while John Shell oversees all other aspects of the operation. They like what they are doing, and their guests become friends. When asked how she liked running an inn, Ella Jo said, 'Why, it's just like having company all the time.'

"Meals are served family style at six large round tables. There are lots of fried chicken, country ham, fresh vegetables, and desserts. Guests assemble promptly for meals and remain standing while John gives a blessing. His prayers are short, earnest, and eloquent.

"One can hibernate here: just eat, sleep, rock, read, rest, and walk around the wooded grounds. Within fifty miles are the Great Smoky Mountains National Park, Nantahala Forest, Nantahala Gorge, Joyce Kilmer Memorial Forest, Fontana, Gatlinburg, the Blue Ridge

Parkway, Asheville, Waynesville, Hendersonville, Brevard—beautiful mountain country with waterfalls, hiking trails, and picnic areas." —*Willis Warnell*

"The building is no architectural gem, but rather a simple, brown, one-story board-and-batten structure that belongs to the land. Rooms are without the usual television set, radio, clock, or telephone. Air conditioning is the cross-ventilation provided by the gloriously unpolluted mountain breezes that can get nippy in the spring or fall, when they are countered by electric wall heaters.

"Only five miles from the inn is a Cherokee reservation, but be careful to avoid the profusion of shops selling made-in-Japan junk. One can drive over the Smokies to Gatlinburg to shop for mountain crafts—pottery, quilts, wood carvings. It is an easy drive to Asheville to the Biltmore House, said to be the largest private house ever built in America. Near Franklin, twenty-five miles south, you can join rock hounds digging for rubies and sapphires." —*John C. Roesel*

Open early May to early November.
25 rooms, 2 cottages, all with private bath.
Rates $68–$90, including breakfast and dinner.
No public restaurant or bar.
Innkeepers: Ella Jo and John Shell.

Burnsville

Nu-Wray Inn
On the Town Square (P.O. Box 156)
Burnsville, North Carolina 28714
Telephone (704) 682-2329

"Since 1838 the Wray family has glorified this lovely old place full of antiques, including a music box used to summon guests to dinner. Food is served family style, and it is extremely hearty Southern fare. People come to Burnsville from all over the South to enjoy the mountains, the artists' school, the craft shops, and the summer theater." —*Margaret Eskridge*

"Enough has been said about the Southern cooking. The hot breads —both cornmeal and biscuits—are accompanied by sourwood honey, which surpasses all jams and preserves. And tables groan, though I do detect efforts to conserve: when I last visited there were no longer two meats at dinner and the talked-of twenty additional dishes had been reduced to ten. But the tables were full, nonetheless.

"Mention should be made of the unusual collection of clocks—

all ticking away and chiming or cooing on schedule. There are many antique musical instruments as well: two beautiful grand pianos, one said to be 150 years old. An old player piano stands just outside the dining room and is played alternately with a magnificent old Reginaphone. Both seem to have an inexhaustible number of recordings."

—*Myrl Aldrich*

Open May 1 to December 1.
32 rooms, 25 with private bath.
Rates $25 single, $38 double.
No credit cards.
Public restaurant, no bar.
Innkeepers: Howard and Betty Souders.

_____ *Cashiers*

High Hampton Inn and Country Club
Highway 107 (P.O. Box 338)
Cashiers, North Carolina 28717
Telephone (704) 743-2411

This was for many years the summer home of the Hampton family of South Carolina. The best-known member of the family, General Wade Hampton, used to invite his friends to the Blue Mountain retreat for fishing and hunting. The inn has kept the rustic mountain look and an informal atmosphere: no discos, casinos, or bright lights. Instead, guests are invited to enjoy the mountain birds and flowers and the famous dahlia gardens of the inn, and to hike the hills.

"I lived the better part of my life in this state, and have traveled its length. To me, High Hampton has been a great old place. It has hosted presidents!"

—*Myrl Aldrich*

Open April 1 to November 1, and from Wednesday through Sunday of Thanksgiving weekend.
130 rooms, 9 suites, all with private bath.
Rates $48–$57 per day per person, including three buffet-style meals.
No credit cards.
No bar.
Guests can be met at Asheville airport on advance notice.
Innkeeper: William D. McKee.

Turn to the back of this book for pages inviting *your* comments.

_____*Dillsboro*

The Jarrett House
Dillsboro, North Carolina 28725
Telephone (704) 586-9964

"You would probably drive right by the Jarrett House, if someone
had not told you about it. Who ever heard of Dillsboro? Built in
1890, the inn, close to the North Carolina entrance to the Great
Smoky Mountains National Park, is three stories high, with a full-
length balcony on each floor. The inn's floors are concave in places
from years of use. The furnishings are antiques: we slept in a four-
poster bed. The bathroom had a claw-foot tub. To top it all off, the
dining room was great. For dinner, there were four entrées, served
Southern style, for only $6.50. Breakfast, at $2.95, was equally
good. We strongly recommend staying here instead of at the more
commercial town of Cherokee when in the area."

—*Dana Marble*

Open April 1 to October 31.
18 rooms, all with bath or shower.
Rate $25 per person, $3 extra each additional person.
No credit cards.
Bus service to Sylva, 5 miles away. Guests can be met there or at
    nearby airports.
Restaurant; alcoholic drinks available by arrangement.
Innkeepers: Jim and Jean Hartbarger.

_____*Edenton*

Mrs. J. W. White's Tourist Home
208 West Queen Street
Edenton, North Carolina 27932
Telephone (919) 482-2242

"This is a large white house with snowy white furnishings—curtains,
blinds, towels, bedcovers, and table mats: Mrs. White's name is
rather appropriate. Everything is of nearly Shaker simplicity, so if
you want a motel-type shower, do not come here—Mrs. White
would probably feel uneasy anyway. The one bathroom has two
doors, and there are firm instructions not to go away leaving either
locked—and don't splash the walls. Also, you might be hard-pressed
to find a shaver socket.

"Mrs. White is a lifelong inhabitant who knows and appreciates
the historic town of Edenton. She is frequently seen with her guests

at Mrs. Boswell's. You musn't miss Mrs. Boswell's, *the* place to eat.
Starting with a ten-seat local diner in 1940, Mrs. Boswell now at-
tracts customers from far and wide for breakfast, lunch, and supper.
The soups are unexcelled; clam chowder is a specialty. No less
delectable is the local seafood."   —*Clive Johnstone and*
Winifred Weston

Open all year.
6 rooms with shared baths.
Rates $12 single, $24 double.
No credit cards.
Manager: Mrs. J. W. White.

_____*Flat Rock*

Woodfield Inn
Flat Rock, North Carolina 28731
Telephone (704) 693-6016

This mid-nineteenth-century inn was called the Farmer Hotel in
stagecoach days. Squire Farmer was its builder; the laborers were
slaves. The inn was constructed of Carolina white pine, with a hand-
hewn foundation secured by wooden pegs. Inside the inn, the wood
is dark walnut. Furniture from the antebellum South graces the
rooms.

"This has operated as a travelers' hotel since before the Civil War.
It is just south of Asheville—you can see it from the highway: a
spectacular old place."   —*Myrl Aldrich*

Open all year.
19 rooms, 13 with private bath.
Rates $60–$65 single, $70–$75 double, $90 suites, including conti-
    nental breakfast.
Credit cards: American Express, MasterCard, Visa.
Air and bus service to Asheville.
Innkeeper: Peggy Olsen.

_____*Robbinsville*

Snowbird Mountain Lodge
Joyce Kilmer Forest Road
Robbinsville, North Carolina 28771
Telephone (704) 479-3433

The Snowbird Indians are a branch of the Cherokees who still live here on their ancestral lands. They have given their name to the Snowbird mountain range, and to this mountaintop inn that overlooks both the hills and Santeetlah Lake below. The lodge was built in 1941 to serve as a stopover for bus tours of the Smokies. All construction materials—a variety of rich woods and stone—came from the area. Local craftsmen carved the paneling and furniture.

"The lodge is delightful: plain but tastefully furnished rooms, a large living room, with tables set up for games, a huge fireplace with chairs clustered for conversation, and a desk that looks out over the mountains and lets you imagine you are in Switzerland. The lodge is in the Joyce Kilmer Forest area, so you can take a packed lunch from the inn and bike up the hill to picnic and look at nature. There is a game cabin for shuffleboard, Ping-Pong and such. We loved every bit of it."   —*Zora and Mel Rashkis*

Open late April to first weekend in November.
22 rooms, 20 with private bath.
Rates $85–$90 double, AP.
Credit cards: American Express, MasterCard, Visa, but payment by check preferred.
Restaurant open to public by reservation only. No bar; the county still observes Prohibition.
Taxi connection from Knoxville, Tennessee, can be arranged.
Innkeepers: Bob and Connie Rhudy.

_____ *Saluda*

The Woods House
Drawer E
Saluda, North Carolina 28773
Telephone (704) 749-9562

"Situated on a steep mountain grade halfway between the tourist meccas of Tryon and Hendersonville, is Saluda, a town untouched by commercialism. Here innkeeper Dorothy Eargle, owner of a successful antique shop in Alexandria, Virginia, has recently bought one of the fine old summer houses that abound in this area. She has restored the house and furnished the rooms with oak and wicker pieces of another century. My visit was in March, and cozy fireplaces and a modern heating system kept guests comfortable. Leave a morning call, and you will find hot coffee outside your door, announced by a discreet knock. When you come downstairs, there is an old-fashioned country breakfast to fortify you. Dotty can be persuaded to serve dinner, should you wish to linger another night."

—Joe Ambrust

Open May through October.
6 rooms with connecting baths; one 3-room cottage.
Rates $35–$50; cottage $65, including full country breakfast.
Credit cards: MasterCard, Visa.
Dinner for guests only, by reservation.
German spoken.
Innkeeper: Dorothy Eargle.

American hotels and inns generally list rates by the room, assuming one person in a single, two in a double. Extra people in rooms normally incur extra charges. Where rates are quoted per person per day, at least one meal is probably included under a Modified American plan (MAP). A full American Plan (AP) would include three meals.

Battery Carriage House, Charleston

South Carolina

Beaufort

Bay Street Inn
601 Bay Street
Beaufort, South Carolina 29902
Telephone (803) 524-7720

Beaufort is a historical town between Charleston and Savannah. The Bay Street Inn, built in 1852 as the Lewis Reeves Sams House, is in Beaufort's historic district. It is a home constructed in extravagant Greek Revival style: Doric columns on one floor, and Ionic on the next. The house, on the Beaufort waterfront, survived the great fire of 1907, which destroyed many of the town's historic buildings.

"The rooms in this antebellum inn are furnished in antiques of the period—except for the mattresses, which are modern and very comfortable. There was a bowl of fresh fruit for us in our room, and bicycles were provided for our use to explore the historic town. We were delighted with our stay, which was the high point of our trip to the coastal Carolinas and Georgia." —*Frank E. Jones*

"The two front rooms, with the best view, have old-fashioned tubs, one in a curtained cubbyhole and one surrounded by a pink silk

screen. We found a certain advantage to a tub rather than a shower: it is more relaxing—and you can take your drinks with you. The inn is within walking distance of shopping, historic houses, museums, a marina, and a landscaped waterfront. You can drive to the sea islands, with their beaches, marshes, lighthouse, and palmetto forests."
—*Betty and Don Edwards*

Open all year, except August.
5 rooms, all with private bath.
Rates $50–$65, including full breakfast.
Credit cards: MasterCard, Visa.
No restaurant.
Beaufort served by bus, or by train to Yemassee. Airports at Savannah and Charleston.
Innkeepers: Terry and David Murray.

Charleston

Charleston is, by wide acclaim, among the most gracious of American cities. The home of seventeenth-century aristocrats and a bustling port, it became a town of elegant houses, fine churches, and imposing public buildings set among winding streets and luxurious gardens. A number of the homes and public buildings are now open to the public in the spring and early summer. Boat tours of the harbor offer a view of the city's famous Battery.

Battery Carriage House
20 South Battery
Charleston, South Carolina 29401
Telephone (803) 723-9881

The Battery Carriage House is just that: a converted mid-nineteenth-century carriage house once attached to an impressive Battery mansion. Opened not long ago as an inn, it was so successful that its owner has since bought and converted two other properties: the Elliott House, in the heart of Historic Charleston, and the Meeting Street Inn, opposite Charleston's old city market.

"The little brass plate by the wrought-iron gate tells you that this five-story building behind four-story palms is the Battery Carriage House inn. Furnishings here are of eighteenth-century style. The rooms, with canopied beds, look like the sort you usually view from behind a rope. They are, however, equipped with kitchenettes, television, and a bottle of chilled wine. Bicycles are left leaning against a wall downstairs, for guests' use." —*Peggy Payne*

Open all year.
10 rooms, all with private bath.
Rates $65–$85, including continental breakfast on a silver tray.
Credit cards: American Express, MasterCard.
No restaurant or bar.
Innkeeper: Katherine A. Riopel.

Jasmine House
Pinckney and Meeting Streets (P.O. Box 991)
Charleston, South Carolina 29401
Telephone (803) 577-5900 or toll-free (800) 845-7639

The Jasmine House was known for a short time as the Indigo Inn, but the owners discovered this caused confusion with another building, so the name was quickly changed.

"This one is brand-new, but built and operated to accentuate the charms of the Historic Charleston district. A gray, windowless exterior surrounds a lovely little courtyard, onto which each room opens and in which breakfast is served. Rooms are furnished with Low Country antique reproductions. The lobby is a little gem of eighteenth-century colonial decor. The inn is in the midst of Charleston's famous markets, shops, and restaurants."
—*Margaret R. Eskridge*

Open all year.
40 rooms, all with private bath.
Rates $75–$85, lower off-season, including breakfast.
Credit cards: American Express, MasterCard, Visa.
Facilities for the handicapped.
Danish, French, German, Hindi, and Russian spoken.
Innkeepers: Mr. and Mrs. H. B. Limehouse.

Sweet Grass Inn
23 Vendue Range
Charleston, South Carolina 29401
Telephone (803) 723-9980

"At the edge of Charleston's historic district, within view of the mingling of the Cooper and Ashley rivers, sits the Sweet Grass Inn, built in about 1800. From the inn's rooftop patio the rivers and the rooftops of Charleston can be seen. Although the inn's exterior is not imposing, its six architecturally interesting fanned windows do provide a landmark. Once inside, you're immediately confronted by all that represents Southern hospitality. The fresh fruit, morning paper, loads of menus for restaurant selection, and beautifully decorated rooms (fresh flowers and four-posters) are the glories of being a guest. Good-byes are tough at the inn, but memories come quite easily."
—Lorraine Zitman

"A very nice breakfast is served from a common table, where you can enjoy meeting the other guests. When you return from an afternoon of shopping, tea or coffee is served in your room."
—Anne Powell

Open all year.
8 rooms, all with private bath.
Rates $68–$78, including breakfast.
No credit cards.
Manager: Beth Craven.

Sword Gate Inn
111 Tradd Street
Charleston, South Carolina 29401
Telephone (803) 723-8518

"The inn had just changed hands a week before we arrived. However, all the good things written about the Sword Gate in earlier editions of this book have not changed. It is a warm, hospitable place to stay. The new owner, Mr. Fisher, seems determined to keep the Sword Gate the quality establishment the previous owners created. We stayed in Room 4, and there was fresh fruit, a morning paper at our door, a nice breakfast, and 24-hour coffee and tea available. More rooms are being added upstairs. We look forward to returning."
—Mark L. Goodman

Open all year, except December 24–26.
7 rooms, all with private bath.
Rates $50–$125, including full breakfast.
No credit cards.
Innkeeper: Everell Fisher.

Vendue Inn
19 Vendue Range
Charleston, South Carolina 29401
Telephone (803) 577-7970

Vendue Inn was once an old warehouse a block from the waterfront. The inn, bounded on one side by an original cobblestone street, is within many historical points of interest, and not far from a new waterfront park.

"It made our visit during the American Spoleto Festival all the more enjoyable. There was complimentary wine and cheese and a continental breakfast served in our room. Most impressive were the warmth and helpfulness of the staff, who did their best to arrange tours and make reservations at restaurants around town. Vendue Inn, more like a private dwelling than a hotel, is a wonderful example of the restoration going on in America's most historic city."
    —*Robert Dedalus; also recommended by Margot Hamilton*

Open all year.
18 rooms, 2-bedroom carriage house, all with private bath.
Rates $63–$68 single, $73–$82 double, including continental
    breakfast and afternoon wine and cheese.
Credit cards: American Express, MasterCard, Visa.
No public bar or restaurant.
Hebrew and Spanish spoken.
Innkeepers: Evelyn and Morton Needle.

Where are the good little hotels in Boston? Philadelphia? Omaha? Dallas? If you have found one, don't keep it a secret. Write *now*.

Tennessee

Gatlinburg

LeConte Lodge
P.O. Box 350
Gatlinburg, Tennessee 37738
Telephone (615) 436-4473

LeConte Lodge is in an open glade 6,500 feet above sea level, just below the summit of Mount LeConte in the Great Smoky Mountains National Park. This is no destination for the casual traveler: no road reaches the lodge; you have to hike or ride in on horseback. The shortest hike is five and a half miles. Accommodations include both cabins and rooms in two lodges. Confirmed advance reservations are absolutely essential here.

"LeConte is like an old summer camp. Depending on where you get the horse, it can take the better part of a day to get there. LeConte isn't advertised much; people seem to hear about it by word of mouth. When you go there, you become conscious of going 'back' somehow into a time and place that are very, very remote."

—_Jai Cochran_

Open end of March through first week in November.
2 lodges, 8 cabins, sharing outdoor privies.

Rates $31.80 a day per adult, $21.20 each child under 10 years of age, including two meals and linens.
No public restaurant or bar.
Innkeeper: James Huff; Manager: Tim Line.

Mountain View Hotel
500 Parkway (Box 727)
Gatlinburg, Tennessee 37738
Telephone (615) 436-4132

There are two connected areas that together make up this hotel complex in Gatlinburg, at the gateway to the Smoky Mountains of Tennessee. One is the original mountain lodge, the other a spacious, but contemporary, motel. Rooms are very different in the two sections, so if you want pine paneling and real wooden furniture, be sure to ask for a room in the lodge.

"This is a big, old-time place, and it is everything a forest lodge is supposed to be. There is a great big fireplace near the door. The food is wonderful. There are no lunches, but the lodge made us a picnic."
—Jai Cochran

Open all year.
75 rooms in lodge, 40 in motor hotel, all with private bath.
Rates $30–$50.
Credit cards: American Express, Diners Club.
Restaurant.
Manager: Tom Woods.

_____*Pigeon Forge*

Kero Mountain Resort
Route 11 (Box 380)
Sevierville, Tennessee 37862
Telephone (615) 453-7514

"A truly beautiful place in the foothills of the Smoky Mountains, just twenty minutes from Gatlinburg. The owners and managers, two delightful ladies, maintain several charming cabin homes in forty acres of complete privacy. A plate of homemade brownies greeted us. There is a small lake, stocked with bass and bluegill. Hidden paths cut through the trees for hikers. Swimming in the deepwater lake from May through September is possible, though there is no beach. Uncrowded, tranquil, thoroughly tasteful."

—*Grace Streithorst*

Open all year.
1 three-bedroom and 2 two-bedroom cabins, all with private bath.
Rates from $30 double.
No credit cards.
No restaurant or bar.
Innkeeper: Jean Keough.

Red Boiling Springs

Donoho Hotel
East Main Street (P.O. Box 36)
Red Boiling Springs, Tennessee 37150
Telephone (615) 699-3141

Red Boiling Springs was once a flourishing spa in the Cumberland Mountains where people came to drink the sulfur waters and bathe in restorative pools of red, black, or white water—each color was believed to have its own curative qualities. There were many hotels in those days. Now, as a local resident says, "We are down to just three little ones"—and one of those has recently been made into the center for a summer camp. That leaves the Donoho and the Counts Hotel, both of which are now owned by Edith Walsh. Mrs. Walsh intends to make Counts into a year-round residential hotel—"what we call a boardinghouse," she says. The Donoho, a long, white, wood-frame building with wide verandas lined with rocking chairs, will serve tourists who pass this way in summer.

"The Donoho has family-style dining, and the food—all home cooking—is great. The hotel is old and beautiful. The people were very sweet, and the prices were reasonable."   —*Brenda Riley*

Open May through September.
45 rooms, 42 with private bath.
Rate $25 per person, AP.
No credit cards.
Public dining room.
Innkeeper: Edith Walsh.

All inkeepers appreciate reservations in advance; some require them.

Rogersville

Hale Springs Inn
110 West Main Street
Rogersville, Tennessee 37857
Telephone (615) 272-9967

This handsome, old, in-town curbside inn was built in 1824 to accommodate stagecoach travelers. It is now the oldest continuously operating inn in Tennessee; in its lifetime it has given shelter to presidents and many other distinguished Americans. The inn got its present name in 1884, when it was used as a stopover for tourists on their way to the Hale Springs Resort, a mineral-water spa fifteen miles north.

"It had just turned dark, and a traffic light brought me to a stop just at the front entrance of the inn. I could hardly believe my eyes. I decided immediately to investigate. The innkeeper was so pleased to have a guest interested in the inn's history that he showed me every room. The accommodations were comfortable and spacious. Having a fireplace and an ample supply of wood topped off everything beautifully." —*Robert Sillers*

"My husband and I travel frequently on business and whenever possible, seek out the extra-special spots. In all seriousness, our criteria are based on how well an establishment could cope with us if we were to collapse totally and need daily attention and wonderful food. Innkeepers Sheldon and Marlena Livesay would get all A's. On several visits, a loaf of Sheldon's fabulous raisin bread was tucked (still warm) into our case as we left." —*Sue Daugherty-Corline*

"I spent three nights here recently. The James K. Polk room was eloquent, comfortable, and relaxing. Along with the antique furniture and original fireplace, I was greeted by a fruit basket and ginger ale. Every evening I was served seasoned tea sweetened with honey. The inn can be recommended to any drummer (traveling salesman) or person traveling back into history." —*Tom H. Meadows; also recommended by Mary Louise Walker*

Open all year.
8 rooms, most with fireplaces, all with private bath.
Rates $45–$65 single, $50–$75 double, including continental breakfast.
Credit cards: American Express, MasterCard, Visa.
Greyhound bus service to Hale Springs.
Innkeepers: Sheldon and Marlena Livesay.

Part Four

_____

Midwest

Illinois
Indiana
Michigan
Minnesota
Ohio
Wisconsin

Hotel Nauvoo,
Nauvoo

Illinois

Chicago

Burton House
1454 North Dearborn Parkway
Chicago, Illinois 60610
Telephone (312) 787-9015

"This is a wonderful 1877 landmark Victorian house that has been in innkeeper Glenn Hjort's family for many years. It was Glenn's aunt's home for some time, and it is still very much an eccentric aunt's house. Breakfast is served on the family china. Guests are surrounded by fine furniture, linens, crystal, and porcelain. The location is ideal—right on Chicago's Gold Coast, near fine restaurants, Lincoln Park, and Lake Michigan. For business travelers this is much nicer than staying in a commercial hotel. They also offer afternoon tea and evening coffee or cocoa.   —*Joan Wells*

Open all year.
3 rooms, all with private bath.
Rate $90 double, including continental breakfast, afternoon tea or aperitif, and evening expresso, cappuccino, or cocoa.
Credit cards: MasterCard, Visa.
Innkeepers: Ralph Raby and Glenn Hjort.

The Raphael
201 East Delaware
Chicago, Illinois 60611
Telephone (312) 943-5000

"This is the counterpart to San Francisco's Raphael. Its location on the Gold Coast could not be better, just a block from the lake and the same distance from the varied shops on North Michigan's Magnificent Mile. The quality and diversity of Chicago's theater and dining have increased tremendously in the last several years, and the Raphael is a good place to start sampling the fruits of the rebirth. You can walk to small art galleries, the Museum of Contemporary Art, and Rush Street night life. The hotel has a delightful restaurant, where a complimentary breakfast is served to guests. It is good for dinner as well. The cozy bar, with piano music, is a nice spot for drinks."   —*Tonette J. Brougher*

"A charming European-style hotel on a quiet, picturesque street. The intimate dining room seats only forty-two. There is complimentary Perrier chilled in your room, and a turn-down service for the traditional six pillows, three sheets."   —*Marci Burger*

Open all year.
172 rooms, all with private bath.
Rates $70–$90 single, $80–$100 double, including breakfast.
Credit cards: American Express, Carte Blanche, Diners Club, MasterCard, Visa.
General Manager: Mark Pistilli.

Richmont Hotel
162 East Ontario Street
Chicago, Illinois 60611
Telephone (312) 787-3580 or toll-free outside Illinois
    (800) 621-8055

"Built in the twenties, the Richmont blends a liberal touch of Europe with friendly Midwestern hospitality and offers them at rather amazing prices in a city this large and a neighborhood this fashionable. When we saw the green-and-white canopy on the quiet street and were greeted by a doorman who seemed really glad to see us, we thought it was going to be a good place. The cool, high-ceilinged lobby with the lounge to the right and a continental-style writing room to the left, backed up this impression. When I saw the Neutrogena soap in the small but complete bathroom, I was sure.

"The double-glazed windows in the prettily papered room actually open, allowing a choice of fresh air as well as cooling or heating. There is plenty of lighting for makeup, the towels are really thick, and the mattresses the most comfortable I've slept on in any hotel on any continent. (Why do so many managements think that isn't important to a good night's sleep?)

"If there is a drawback, it is the lack of a restaurant (although there is a bar). But there is a delicious, buffet-style continental breakfast served on marble-topped tables under a lovely chandelier in the lounge. For lunch and dinner, there are a number of restaurants almost outside the door." —*Alys Bohn; also recommended by Estelle Frankel*

Open all year.
190 rooms and suites, all with private bath.
Rates from $55 single, $67 double, $90 suites, including continental breakfast. Weekend packages available.
Credit cards: American Express, Diners Club, Visa.
Bar, but no restaurant.
French spoken.
General Manager: Michael Harney.

The Tremont Hotel
100 East Chestnut Street
Chicago, Illinois 60611
Telephone (312) 280-1307 or toll-free (800) 621-8133

"Three charming hotels cluster within a block of the Water Tower Center on Chicago's Magnificent Mile. The Knickerbocker surrounds you with clubby elegance. The Whitehall pampers you with exquisite service. But the Tremont does both, on a more intimate scale than either of its neighbors. Rooms are furnished in the most tasteful reproductions and fabrics. Baths are appointed with Italian marble. And Cricket's, the bar and restaurant, is reminiscent of the Jockey Club and 21. Altogether, John. D. Coleman's achievement at the Tremont is a tour de force." —*George Herzog*

Open all year.
139 rooms, all with private bath.

Rates $105–$150 single, $125–$170 double, $275–$700 suites.
Credit cards: American Express, Carte Blanche, Diners Club, MasterCard, Visa.
Restaurant and bar.
French, German, Italian, and Spanish spoken.
Resident Manager: Michael Silberstein.

The Whitehall Hotel
105 East Delaware Place
Chicago, Illinois 60611
Telephone (312) 944-6300

"The Whitehall's minimum accommodation is a room with a king-size bed and enough floor space to do your yoga exercises. For a few dollars more, you can have an executive room that offers all the basic amenities—here that includes color television, two phones, a refrigerator, and even a bathroom scale—plus a wall separating the bed from a sitting area where TV may be watched, or meals taken in privacy. I know an executive from New York who personally supplements her hotel expense account to enjoy the luxury of an executive room. The Whitehall is crowned by price-is-no-object accommodations on the top floor. The ultimate is one of the four large apartments, each with special decor—Oriental chairs in the Churchill, Breuer chairs in the Contemporary. The most charming of these may be the Terrace Suite, which wraps around three exposures of the building. The large terrace—commanding a vista of Lake Michigan and awesome views of the urban sprawl, with jewel-like strings of lights defining the traffic arteries for miles into the distance—adjoins a sumptuously furnished dining room. The kitchen can be fitted with crockery, cutlery, and crystal and the large refrigerator stocked with meal makings. During a five-week theatrical engagement in Chicago, Katharine Hepburn once enjoyed her own cooking in the Terrace Suite. The living room has books on the shelves, a stereo, and large, living greenery. The bedroom has all the goodies of simpler sleeping quarters, including a small refrigerator so that you won't have to walk the length of the suite to the kitchen for a nightcap, plus a bidet and a third TV in the bath, so you won't miss the morning news while shaving. In all, a luxurious island in a city of surprises." —*Camille J. Cook*

Open all year.
223 rooms, all with private bath.

Rates $105–$150 single, $125–$170 double, $275–$900 suites.
Credit cards: American Express, Carte Blanche, Diners Club, MasterCard, Visa.
French and Spanish spoken.
General Manager: Michael Silberstein.

_____*Galena*

Victorian Mansion Guest House
301 South High Street
Galena, Illinois 61036
Telephone (815) 777-0675

"The Victorian Mansion Guest House was once the home of a lead miner, Augustus Estey. U. S. Grant was once a guest at a party there. The house, on two and a half acres, has been restored. There is no television, not even radio, in its high-ceilinged rooms—and the bathroom is down the hall. 'We have lots of artists as guests,' innkeeper Mrs. Primrose says, 'and they don't mind sharing the plumbing.'"
                                                              —*Jerry Klein*

Open all year.
6 rooms, 1 with private bath.
Rates $28–$40.
No credit cards.
Trains and buses serve Galena.
Innkeepers: Charles and Linda Primrose.

_____*Nauvoo*

Hotel Nauvoo
Mulholland Street
Nauvoo, Illinois 62354
Telephone (217) 453-2211

"There is much to see in Nauvoo, high on a bluff overlooking the Mississippi River. The town was founded by Joseph Smith and the Mormons, and operated for a time as an almost autonomous state. It was not only the largest city in Illinois at that time, but also the site of the first great Mormon temple. Largely deserted after the killing of Smith by an angry mob, the settlement is now being beautifully restored, complete with museums and places of historical interest.

"Few people are aware of the treasures that exist in the once-thriving little towns that line the rivers in the area. By taking the ferry at Nauvoo, one can cross the Mississippi and soon be driving along the winding Des Moines River, once among this nation's busiest water routes. We never miss the little town of Bonaparte and always look forward to a delicious lunch or dinner served with great imagination there in a restaurant housed in a huge picturesque mill that stands right at the river's edge. Another day's outing can be made along the Illinois side of the Mississippi. Hamilton is a great place for hunting geodes and fossils. There is Warsaw, a pleasant little town with a beautiful vista of the great river. Fantastic old storefronts face the treelined streets, and one can still find an old-fashioned chocolate soda here. Antiques shops are, of course, plentiful and if one is fortunate, a pleasant afternoon can be spent at an out-of-the-way farm auction.

"Each year when the trees begin to glow with their October colors, my husband and I drive to Nauvoo to relax after the summer tourists have gone. This would not be possible without the old Hotel Nauvoo. The hotel looks like the large residence it was back in 1841. The architecture is pure pioneer Mormon, a reflection of the devotion and vision of the Kraus family, who have owned it since 1946.

"The rooms are large, airy, and comfortable. Paintings by Lane Newberry adorn various rooms. The furniture is not fancy and there is no room service. But there is comfort and serenity. It is rewarding to spend a day sightseeing and then return to the Hotel Nauvoo for dinner. We not only drive leisurely, but also dine leisurely, and here we can indulge this wish. The Hotel Nauvoo is famous for its dining rooms, and is always busy. In October, however, the crowds thin out, and we benefit from this lull that comes just before winter. We always return home with a supply of blue cheese and wine made in Nauvoo, and enough memories to sustain us until next October."

—*Jeanne Purdom*

"For the money, the hotel is fine. But the rooms are small—very; the bathroom sink was in the bedroom, not the bath, because there was no room. The staff was not very warm. There were a few antiques in the dining room, but not in the rooms. My wife and I found little to recommend for those interested in a unique hotel or inn. The city of Nauvoo and the museum, however, are interesting and worth a visit."

—*Mike McLain*

Open April 1 to November 1.
10 rooms, 1 cottage, all with private bath.
Rates from $22.50 single, $26.50 double.
No credit cards.
Innkeeper: Elmer J. Kraus.

Indiana

Angola

Potawatomi Inn
Pokagon State Park
Route 2 (Box 37)
Angola, Indiana 46703
Telephone (219) 833-1077

Pokagon State Park, in the northeast corner of Indiana, was established in 1925. The inn was built two years later. Since then, the accommodations have been remodeled and expanded, with rooms in the original inn supplemented with cabins and a small motel. Conference facilities have also been added. Visitors may want to be specific in requesting accommodation here.

"Quietly situated on a rise overlooking Lake James, the Potawatomi Inn offers comfortable rooms, good food, Hoosier hospitality, and a bit of Indiana history in the winter wonderland of the park. Pokagon boasts one of the longest toboggan runs in the country. Cross-country skiing is also available, as well as skating the lake. Just a short trail away is the more secluded Lonidare Lake; take your snow shovel to clear the ice." —*James and Alice Price*

Open all year.
81 rooms, all with private bath.
Rates $25–$30
Credit cards: MasterCard, Visa.
Innkeeper: C. J. Helmsing.

_____*Churubusco*

Sycamore Spring Farm
Box 224
Churubusco, Indiana 46723
Telephone (219) 693-3603

"Just twelve miles northwest of Fort Wayne on U.S. Highway 33 is a small town with the improbable name of Churubusco. Beyond the town, at the second crossroad, is a small red-lettered sign that says 'The Farm.' Turn right, and exactly three miles down the road is Sycamore Spring Farm, identified by its split-rail fence.

"The farmhouse was copied from a Williamsburg tavern, rebuilt with painstaking care by the owner, Jerry McCoy. Inside, Janice McCoy has been equally dedicated in copying furnishings and decorations. The house is now as authentic a colonial reproduction as you can find in Williamsburg itself. The McCoys run a real farm, and the products of it provide the tables with meals Janice prepares herself. This is an ideal place to bring children who have never been exposed to farm life. There are pony rides, and children can get acquainted with farm animals, watch crop production, help with chores, and do some gardening.

"Ten minutes away is Chain O'Lakes State Park, where boating, fishing, and swimming are available. Within an hour's drive are Amish Acres at Nappanee, or the popular outdoor Wednesday flea market at Shipshewana. Indiana's two largest freshwater lakes, James and Wawasee, are easy drives." —*Myrl Aldrich*

Open January through October.
2 rooms, both with private bath.
Rates $50 single, $75 double, $25 child, AP. Minimum stay 2 days.
No credit cards.
Buses, trains, or planes met at Fort Wayne for $25 round trip.
Innkeepers: Jerry and Janice McCoy.

Rates quoted were the latest available. But they may not reflect unexpected increases or local and state taxes. Be sure to verify when you book.

Michigan City

Duneland Beach Inn
3311 Pottawattomie Trail
Michigan City, Indiana 46360
Telephone: (219) 874-7729

"An hour and a half from Chicago, there is a beautiful beach on Lake Michigan and miles of sand dunes to walk along. The inn, a good place to get away, sits amidst the northwest dune country. The innkeepers are most hospitable and their home-cooked food is the best I've had in years." —*William Foley*

Open all year.
10 rooms, all sharing baths.
Rates: $24 single, $29 double, $49 suite, including full breakfast.
Credit cards: MasterCard, Visa.
No restaurant, but the inn serves a public Sunday brunch.
Innkeepers: George and Kathleen Friedrich.

New Harmony

New Harmony Inn
North Street
New Harmony, Indiana 47631
Telephone (812) 682-4491

New Harmony, in Indiana's southwest corner, epitomizes a certain spirit that pervaded early American life. To it came first a group of Lutheran Separatists from the German city of Württemberg, who had earlier settled in what became known as Harmony, Pennsylvania. Their leader, George Rapp, wrote of New Harmony in 1815: "I cannot explain with words how gladly and well I live in this pleasant New World. Everything is moving to a new birth." Within ten years Father Rapp and his egalitarian and celibate community had developed marginal land into prosperous agricultural country and built a town that was the envy of the territory. When the Rappites moved back east, they sold their community on the Wabash River to Robert Owen, the Scottish industrialist and social reformer who sought to build a model society in a perfect environment free of competition but full of educational development. Scientists, naturalists, and writers from all over the world came to New Harmony, making it an early center of research and inquiry. New Harmony, still a small town, has preserved the core of its utopian past, and continues to carry out a large restoration effort while encouraging the best of contemporary architecture.

"The New Harmony Inn is a modern structure of unusual architecture. The halls are light and bright, with exterior light emanating from transparent areas in the ceilings. The rooms are unusual, with vaulted ceilings, a glass wall in some, wood floors beautifully finished, and new furniture in yesteryear's style. There are rocking chairs and brick fireplaces in the rooms. There is a picturesque small lake on the grounds with park benches here and there. The whole atmosphere is peaceful beyond belief, which makes possible perfect and wonderful relaxation."
—*Joe Solomon*

"After using other books describing country inns, I was apprehensive about what I would find in New Harmony. I was delighted to find exactly what you had described, and more so! The inn was within walking distance of most of the historic sites. The continental breakfast, included in the room cost, was excellent. The inn's Red Geranium restaurant was the best I had encountered so far in Indiana."
—*July Shettleroe*

Open all year.
45 rooms, several guesthouses, all with private bath.
Rates $31–$56 single, $38–$61 double, including continental breakfast.
Credit cards: American Express, Carte Blanche, Diners Club, MasterCard, Visa.
2 restaurants.
Innkeeper: Gary Gerard.

Would you be so kind as to share discoveries you may have of charming, well-run places to stay in Europe? Please write to *Europe's Wonderful Little Hotels and Inns,* c/o Congdon & Weed, 298 Fifth Avenue, New York, New York 10001. (By the way, a new and greatly expanded edition of this splendid guide is now available at your bookseller's.)

Michigan

Detroit

Hotel St. Regis
3071 West Grand Boulevard
Detroit, Michigan 48202
Telephone (313) 873-3000

"This luxury hotel, built and designed originally by mostly local people, is located in the New Center redevelopment area, ten minutes from downtown Detroit. Here in the 1970s, General Motors and others decided to renovate the neighborhood, which had deteriorated. General Motors has its new world headquarters here, the Detroit Medical Center complex is here and, most recently, a center of shops and retail spaces was dedicated. Houses have also been renovated, many beautiful ones from the post–World War I era. The area has one of Detroit's few theaters, the Fisher Theater. The police stables, which are historically interesting, have been located here since the last century.

"The hotel was originally decorated in French Regency style, but somehow this didn't seem to fit well into New Center. The hotel also changed management many times, and it then began to look like a lady whose glory had faded. Now there has been another renovation that began a few years ago under the management of Rank Hotels —best known for its London hotels such as the Athenaeum, Gloucester, and Royal Garden. The new owners have created something very beautiful. That heavy red-and-black feeling is gone; there is a new, drawing room–like lounge and a fine small restaurant, where you can almost never get in without a reservation. There is a relaxed, gentle atmosphere around the hotel; people seem to be there to make you more comfortable. Rooms have been renovated, some retaining antique-style furniture, others more contemporary. This is the only first-class hotel in New Center."

—*Carmelita Smirnes*

Open all year.

117 rooms and suites, all with private bath.

Rates $85 single, $100 double, $190–$250 suites. Weekend packages available.

Credit cards: American Express, Carte Blanche, Diners Club, MasterCard, Visa.

Sales Manager: Sandra Stone.

East Jordan

Jordan Inn
East Jordan, Michigan 49727
Telephone (616) 536-2631

"East Jordan is on the southern arm of Lake Charlevoix in the northwestern corner of Michigan. This end of the lake, virtually devoid of tourists, is beautiful, with many swans. Rooms at the Jordan Inn are modest, but very homey and comfortable. We have visited there several times while skiing in the Boyne Mountains eighteen miles away. They have excellent wines and good food. Another exceptional dining spot, Rowe Inn in Ellsworth, a few miles down the road, features among other delicacies fresh morels in season and homemade ice cream."   —*Sylvia Vangieson*

Open all year.

12 rooms, 4 with private bath.

Rate $24 double.

Credit cards: MasterCard, Visa.

Restaurant for dining by appointment only.

Innkeeper: Christina Dobrowolski.

Turn to the back of this book for pages inviting *your* comments.

_____*Farmington Hills*

Botsford Inn
28000 Grand River
Farmington Hills, Michigan 48024
Telephone (313) 474-4800

"Botsford Inn, in a suburb of Detroit, was built in 1836 and was a popular stopping place for drovers, farmers, and travelers to and from the city. Dances were held on the 'spring dance floor,' which is still part of the inn. Henry Ford attended these dances with his future wife. In 1924 he bought the inn from the Botsford family and restored it, adding antiques from his own collection. In the downstairs parlor there is still a square piano once owned by General Custer's sister, and there is also a buffet from General Lee's home. In 1951, after Mr. Ford's death, the Anhuts purchased the property. John Anhut has made five additions to the original inn, and has converted the coach house into a convention and banquet center. There is an Early American garden created by Mrs. Ford, and the dining room specializes in American dishes. The inn is surrounded by an extensive lawn, in which is set a State of Michigan historical marker telling of the inn's history."   —*Kathryn Briggs*

"The inn has extensive banquet facilities, and the garden area was booked every night of our weekend stay. Bands played until the early morning hours directly outside our window in the historic section, despite the complaints of guests."   —*James M. Gilchrist*

Open all year.
63 rooms, all with private bath.
Rates $35–$45 single, $45–$55 double; suites from $55.
Credit cards: American Express, Diners Club, MasterCard, Visa.
French and German spoken.
Innkeeper: John W. Anhut.

_____*Glen Arbor*

The Homestead
Glen Arbor, Michigan 49636
Telephone (616) 334-3041

"The Homestead is many things to many people: a second home or retreat for some, a vacation resort for others. The complex's original building dates from the early 1930s when it was a small hotel providing dining and lodging in the summer months. The building

—still called 'the Inn'—remains today the prime attraction as a dining facility for the year-round resort community that has grown up around it. Guests stay in luxurious, privately owned condominiums of varying size and style, the exteriors conforming and blending so as not to disturb this unsurpassed natural setting.

"The exclusive and extensive Homestead property, on the Leelanau Peninsula on the eastern shore of Lake Michigan, is bounded by water and natural parks. The Sleeping Bear sand dunes trail off to provide a beach of unusual beauty. The Leelanau Peninsula offers a variety of vistas. It is abundant in cherry orchards, and there are small harbors where boats offer excursions to islands that lie betwixt and between the shipping passages of the Great Lakes. This is the Great Lakes at their most splendid." —*Nancy Mayer*

Open all year, except November and April.
256 apartments.
Rates $33–$184, depending on size and location of accommodations.
Credit cards: American Express, MasterCard, Visa.
Restaurant and bar.
Manager: Bob Kuras.

Harrisville

Big Paw Resort
P.O. Box 187
Harrisville, Michigan 48740
Telephone (517) 724-6326

"On Michigan's Lake Huron shores, in the upper part of the Lower Peninsula, stands one of the great restorative beauty spots. Big Paw is this little gem's name, and while it isn't exactly an inn, it is similar in that it offers rest and relaxation in unique surroundings with delicious home cooking.

"Built in 1938 and owned and operated ever since by the Yokom family, Big Paw is a group of log cottages at the edge of a woods, each with lawn and gardens and private walks to the sandy beach that stretches for miles. Each unit has a woodburning fireplace with a woodpile—which is probably dusted by the elves who clean your cottage while you are consuming an enormous breakfast in the dining room. Walking on the beach, boating, and superb lake fishing are available. Lighted tennis courts, croquet, and shuffleboard are on the premises; golf is nearby. Occupancy here is limited to twenty-five or thirty. Privacy is the word." —*Lola Rothmann*

Open Memorial Day weekend to November 1.
4 rooms; 3 cottages with 1–3 bedrooms each.
Rate $60 per day per person, including breakfast and dinner.
Credit cards: MasterCard, Visa.
Dining room for guests only.
Greyhound bus service to Harrisville.
Innkeeper: Ronald A. Yokom.

_____ *Horton*

Wellman General Store
205 Main Street (P.O. Box 58)
Horton, Michigan 49246
Telephone (517) 563-2231; 787-3774

"Peace, charm, comfort, history, space, and luxury are what I found at Wellman General Store. This is a large and very complete apartment on the first floor of a totally rebuilt interior of a sturdy, two-story 1880s general store. Everything was furnished, from a lighted makeup mirror to the facilities for preparing meals or snacks at my convenience.

"The small town of Horton is approximately midstate, but near larger towns with colleges, shops, lakes, and so on. It is a great place to take a break in the travel routine or a weekend away from stress and responsibility."   —*Doris Warner*

Open all year.
1 apartment with private bath.
Rates $35–$100, depending on number of persons and meals taken.
No credit cards.
Meals available by advance arrangement.
Train, bus, and air service to Jackson.
Innkeeper: Karen D. Gauntlett.

_____ *Mackinac Island*

Grand Hotel
Mackinac Island, Michigan 49757
Telephone (906) 847-3331

"One of the great hotels of the railroad and Great Lakes steamer eras, the magnificent Grand has reigned over the Straits of Mackinac since the 1880s. It boasts the longest porch in the world, very fine dining, and a restoration program that has added comfort in the taste of W&J Sloane. Guests dress for dinner, which is quaint, but then the current clientele is closer to conventioneering Middle America than the name Grand might lead one to suppose. But one can savor the past when the orchestra plays for dinner or later for dancing. If you are feeling truly grand, ask for a room with a water view.

"The special charm that draws one to the island is the complete absence of cars. Horses pull buggies that serve as taxis; drays move anything from a ferryload of baggage to farm produce. One may rent a buggy of one's own (how rare!) or a trail horse. Riding here is a social event; one meets new people around every bend."

—*George Herzog*

Open mid-May to November.
266 rooms, 260 with private bath.
Rates from $82 per day per person, including two meals.
Reduced rates for children.
No credit cards.
Public bar and restaurant.
French, German, and Spanish spoken.
Seasonal ferry service to island from St. Ignace and Makinaw City.
   Air taxi service connects Mackinac Island to Pellston and St. Ignace airports 24 hours a day.
Innkeeper: John M. Hulett III.

Hotel Iroquois on-the-Beach
Makinac Island, Michigan 49757
Telephone (906) 847-3321

"The hotel was built as a private home in 1902, to which rooms have subsequently been added. As in past years, the superior quality of food and service is matched only by the excellent views from the guest rooms and two dining rooms.

"We love the drive across the Mackinac Bridge, so we take the Star Line boat from St. Ignace to the island. It docks right next to the Iroquois, and the porter meets your boat. The Star Line has day and overnight parking facilities in St. Ignace.

"There are many annual events that keep the island busy, such as the lilac festival in June and the Mackinac sailboat races in July. All historical sites are open from Memorial Day, and carriage tours start as early as May 15."

—*Becki Barnwell*

Open May 15 to late October.
44 rooms, 4 suites, all with private bath.
Rates $52–$110 off-season; $76–$185 June, July, and August.
Credit cards: MasterCard, Visa.
Public restaurant and bar.
French and Spanish spoken.
Innkeepers: Sam and Margaret McIntire.

Stonecliffe
101 Stonecliffe Road
Mackinac Island, Michigan 49757
Telephone (906) 847-3355

"For those who prefer a secluded retreat in hiking and horse country, this millionaire's 'cottage,' which now accepts guests, offers a lovely spot on a rocky crag. The Stonecliffe's enclosed coach is ready to meet you at Shepler's Dock or take you back and forth to town anytime. The driver is not only a skilled horseman, but also gives every appearance, from mustache to boots, of having been hired from the Dodge City of a century ago. Some people come up here from the village for dinner as much for the drive as for the food."   —*George Herzog*

Open mid-May to mid-October.
50 rooms, all with private bath.
Rates $50–$95.
Credit cards: MasterCard, Visa.
Innkeeper: George Staffan.

The Windermere
Mackinac Island, Michigan 49757
Telephone (906) 847-3301; 847-3491

"Right in town, the Windermere nestles under the protective guns of the colonial fort, right at the harbor and just a block from John Jacob Astor's fur-trading emporium. It is exceptionally well maintained, and very convenient for bicycling."   —*George Herzog*

Open May through October.
30 rooms, all with private bath.

Rates $65–$75.
Credit cards: MasterCard, Visa.
Innkeeper: Margaret Dowd.

_____ *Marshall*

The National House
102 South Parkview
Marshall, Michigan 49068
Telephone (616) 781-7374

"On the town square of Marshall stands a two-story brick building with large windows that beckons the traveler to come in. The door opens to reveal a wood-plank floor with old benches, crocks filled with flower arrangements, and a crackling fire. Each room in the inn is named after a prominent person from Michigan. Opening one door, there is a room that is Victorian from the massive bed to the marble-top dresser and the washstand with a bowl and pitcher. In the Country Room, the metal bed, quilt, and country oak dresser and blanket chest return a guest to the era of the brave homesteaders. The National House is habit-forming. We find excuses to make a trip to Marshall just to stay there."   —*Shirley and Sid Waggoner*

"The Federal-style inn was built in 1835. It has been recognized as a state historical site, and a marker detailing its history is on the front of the building. A former slave is among those figures from local history for whom the rooms are named. The inn is across the street from the local historical society's Honolulu House, and many of the town's 1,200 well-kept pre-1900 homes are within walking distance. Marshall, called 'the world's biggest showoff town,' holds a historic homes tour in September. It attracts thousands.

"The only meal served at the inn is a continental breakfast, but lunches and dinners are available at Win Schuler's restaurant, a few blocks away."   —*Kathryn Briggs*

Open all year, except Christmas Eve and Christmas Day.
15 rooms, 1 suite, all with private bath.
Rates $50–$80, including continental breakfast.
Credit cards: American Express, MasterCard, Visa.
Innkeepers: Beth and Michael McCarthy.

Do you know a hotel in your state that we have overlooked? Write *now*.

_____ _Plymouth_

The Mayflower Hotel
827 West Ann Arbor Trail
Plymouth, Michigan 48170
Telephone (313) 453-1620

There is a tradition, possibly unique to this country, of townspeople joining together to build themselves a hotel they can be proud of. The Mayflower is such a hotel. It took only half a day in 1926 to raise local money for its construction. It opened in 1927, just in time to be hit in its early years by the Depression. By 1939, however, the hotel's board of directors had found hope in a new manager: a local boy named Ralph Lorenz who had worked his way through Eastern Michigan University in the food department of the student union. He was given very explicit instructions to keep the hotel in the center of community affairs and not to let down the 234 stockholders who had faith in the hotel and the town. In 1964, Ralph Lorenz and his wife, Mabel, bought the hotel and, with the help of their six children, made it into a family operation. In 1981, in recognition of his services to the city of Plymouth, Mr. Lorenz was presented at the White House with the Small Business Association's National Senior Advocate of the Year award. In the following year, the Plymouth added a large new wing, built motel style, and further renovated the original hotel. The emphasis here is not so much on age or style as on up-to-date-ness. Ralph Lorenz has always prided himself on that: he began to air-condition rooms in 1946, he was the first in the area to add television and, after visiting Plymouth, England, in 1970, he came back and introduced the concept of bed-and-breakfast to Michigan. The hotel calls itself the first hotel to have Norman Rockwell paintings on the walls, Jacuzzis in every bath, and a supersophisticated fire alarm system. This is an American original, too, in its own way.

"My husband and I spent the most delightful night together since our honeymoon in this charming hotel. It should certainly be included in your book; everything about it is perfect."

—*Lana Shirzon*

Open all year.
100 rooms, all with private bath.
Rates $30–$45 single, $40–$58 double, including full breakfast.
Credit cards: American Express, Diners Club, MasterCard, Visa.
2 dining rooms and an English-style pub.
Innkeepers: Ralph G. Lorenz and R. Scott Lorenz.

_____*Saugatuck*

Wickwood Inn
510 Butler Street
Saugatuck, Michigan 49453
Telephone (616) 857-1097

"I am a hopeless romantic and hopelessly in love with the Wickwood. On the burned-out edge of middle-aged lunacy, I work on the average a sixteen- to eighteen-hour day seven and sometimes eight days a week. I can't steal away enough time to rejuvenate the way most people do. I need something else. At the Wickwood I can get back together again in an old-fashioned way in an old-fashioned inn. I can't imagine a more perfect inn. It is probably a typical example of Victorian architecture. I have stayed in three rooms and seen them all.

"I would liken Saugatuck to an abbreviated version of Fort Lauderdale, with its shops, art galleries, and private homes. It is a boating city, but unlike other resort towns because it is never overcrowded by tourists. The town and the inn are like nothing else in this part of the world."   —*David Zarka*

Open all year, except Christmas.
7 rooms, all with private bath.
Rates $55–$85; lower October through April. $45 per room for groups taking the whole inn for conferences; continental breakfast and afternoon setups included in all room rates.
Credit cards: American Express, MasterCard, Visa.
Owners: Sue and Stub Louis; innkeeper: Laura Statler.

American hotels and inns generally list rates by the room, assuming one person in a single, two in a double. Extra people in rooms normally incur extra charges. Where rates are quoted per person per day, at least one meal is probably included under a Modified American plan (MAP). A full American Plan (AP) would include three meals.

Minnesota

Baudette

Rainy River Lodge
Baudette, Minnesota 56623
Telephone (218) 634-2730

"When we go to the upper reaches of Minnesota, near the Canadian border, I choose the Rainy River Lodge, for two reasons: the hospitality of the place and the fishing. Not only are the food and cellar superb, but the rooms are also large and comfortable, commodious, and decorated, fortunately, with no interior decorators on the scene. Quality is the key word. As a fisherman, I think Rainy Lake is peerless."
—_Dale E. Barlage_

Open May 15 to December 1.
5 cabins, all with private bath.
Rates $18–$45 per night, $108–$270 per week, including boat.
Credit cards: MasterCard, Visa.
Meals provided to guests on request.
Innkeepers: Linda and Ron Gores.

Where are the good little hotels in Boston? Philadelphia? Omaha? Dallas? If you have found one, don't keep it a secret. Write _now_.

_____*Grand Marais*

Cascade Lodge
P.O. Box 693
Grand Marais, Minnesota 55604
Telephone (218) 387-1112

"While traveling on one of the continent's most scenic drives, from Duluth to Thunder Bay, Ontario, one must stop at Cascade Lodge, on the shores of Lake Superior. The activities here are varied, including hiking, stargazing, cross-country skiing, and searching for agates. And there is the mystique of the largest inland water in the world. The lodge, in existence for sixty years, does not allow liquor, and takes pride in its family atmosphere. The chef provides some of the best food between Duluth and Thunder Bay."

—*Dale E. Barlage*

Open all year.
13 rooms in lodge, 12 other units including 4 log cabins, all with
    private bath.
Rates $29–$49 single, $35–$55 double.
Credit cards: MasterCard, Visa.
Restaurant, but no bar.
Finnish and German spoken.
Triangle bus line connects to Duluth or Thunder Bay.
Innkeepers: Gene and Laurene Glader.

_____*Minneapolis*

Marquette
710 Marquette Avenue, at IDS Center
Minneapolis, Minnesota 55402
Telephone (612) 332-2351

"Minneapolis is a world-class city, a state-of-the-art city. In the heartland of America, it has attracted worldwide attention with its two art museums, its Orchestra Hall, its Tyrone Guthrie Theater, and its vanguard zoo.

"In the urban heart of Minneapolis is a great little hotel, frequented by symphony buffs, scholars, artists, and connoisseurs of good food. The hotel's capacious rooms and public areas were designed by Philip Johnson; thus the guest has the chic and elegance of the Bauhaus style merged with the later internationalism of David Webb and his associates. All fit remarkably well. One can breakfast on the terrace overlooking America's answer to Milan's Galleria. Lunch and dinner are in the Marquis, a French restaurant. Room service is remarkably fleet.

"Father Marquette, a putative trencherman and man of grace, would have been delighted."　　　　　　—*Dr. F. M. Hinkhouse*

Open all year.
282 rooms and suites, all with private bath.
Rates $85–$475.
Credit cards: American Express, Carte Blanche, Diners Club, MasterCard, Visa.
General Manager: Jephson Hilary.

_____*New Prague*

Schumacher's New Prague Hotel
212 West Main Street
New Prague, Minnesota 56071
Telephone (612) 758-2133

In a community with a largely Czech and German heritage, John and Nancy Schumacher have restored an 1898 hotel, decorating it with Bavarian folk art and giving the twelve rooms the names of the months of the year. Above the door of each room a glass medallion from Munich names the month.

"Only forty miles from Minneapolis, one feels one is in another part of the world. The clocks and woodcarvings are authentic Bavarian —it is like something out of a storybook.

"The food is excellent, all made with fresh eggs, pork, veal, vegetables, grains, and other ingredients from the surrounding area. The owner is also the chef. The specialties of the house are prepared with a German or Czech accent. Some of the entrées include sauerbraten, rabbit, wiener schnitzel, and many other wonderful veal dishes."　　　　　　—*Dale E. Barlage*

Open all year, except 3 days at Christmas.
12 rooms, all with private bath.
Rates $60–$80.
No credit cards.
Innkeeper: John Schumacher.

All inkeepers appreciate reservations in advance; some require them.

_____*Red Wing*

St. James Hotel
406 Main Street
Red Wing, Minnesota 55066
Telephone (612) 388-2846

The St. James was built in 1875 when Red Wing had become the largest wheat market in the world and eleven local businessmen wanted to celebrate the city's success. The hotel was run by the Lillyblad family for seventy-two years. Legend is that Clara Lillyblad's food was so good that trains stopped in Red Wing just for a meal. The hotel was bought in 1975 by the Red Wing Shoe Company, which paid for an extensive restoration. The renewed hotel reopened in 1979.

"Red Wing is a Mississippi River town with a long history and many interesting old homes. Amtrak stops here, so if you like riding trains, this is a good location. By car, it is a beautiful ride along river bluffs. The guest rooms at the St. James have been faithfully refurnished and decorated in elegant Victorian style, with brass beds, lace-trimmed sheets, and beautiful furniture. There are fresh flowers in every room, and the beds are turned down nightly. The lobby, staircase, hallways, dining room, and library contain many exquisite antiques. I went to the St. James for a rest and enjoyed everything from the sound of the trains and river traffic to the silence of an old hotel content with its new lease on life."

—*Eileen R. McCormack*

Open all year.
60 rooms, all with private bath.
Rates $55–$80.
Credit cards: American Express, MasterCard, Visa.
3 restaurants and bar.
Red Wing reachable by train, Greyhound bus, and boat.
Innkeeper: Gene Foster.

_____*St. Paul*

Bleick House
270 Fort Road West
St. Paul, Minnesota 55102
Telephone (612) 227-2800

"We were in St. Paul on business when we decided to stay over a few days and just happened on this bed-and-breakfast inn in an older part of town where many homes have been restored. Bleick House is on the National Register. Within a block is another Victorian house serving food. The inn is within walking distance of all downtown St. Paul's museums, theaters, and stores."

—*Carol Kendrick*

Open all year.
22 rooms with shared baths.
Rates $25 single, $35 double, including breakfast.
Credit cards: MasterCard, Visa.
Innkeeper: Eleanor Saunders.

_____ *Sauk Centre*

Palmer House Hotel
500 Sinclair Lewis Avenue
Sauk Centre, Minnesota 56378
Telephone (612) 352-3431

Sauk Centre, at the southern end of Big Sauk Lake, was the childhood home of Sinclair Lewis, who was later to satirize small-town America in *Main Street.* Sauk Centre became his Gopher Prairie. Later in life he mellowed: among his lesser-known books is *Work of Art,* which praised the keeper of a small hotel. When Lewis died in Rome, his ashes were returned to his birthplace here. Both the Lewis home and a center devoted to the works of the United States' first Nobel Prize-winning novelist are open to the public in summer. The Palmer House, where Lewis worked in 1902 while still a boy and which barely escaped demolition ten years ago, has recently been listed in the National Register of Historic Places.

"There is much here to recall *Main Street.* In the hotel are two private party rooms, the Kennicott and the Minniemashie, both reminiscent of Lewis. The hotel was bought in 1974 by two men—a former Methodist minister and an ex-printer—tired of metropolitan living, who restored the old place to the way it was in the early 1900s, when Lewis worked here.

"I checked into the hotel quite by chance. I found no elegant decor, but the lack of luxury was immediately overcome by the hospitality that prevailed. Frequently, eight-course dinners are served, and all other meals are good." —*Pauline Wilcox*

Open all year.
37 rooms, 4 with private bath.

Rates $15–$35.
No credit cards.
Restaurant; no bar, but beer and wine served.
German spoken.
Greyhound bus service.
Innkeepers: R. J. Schwartz and A. W. Tingley.

_____ *Stillwater*

Lowell Inn
102 North Second Street
Stillwater, Minnesota 55082
Telephone (612) 439-1100

Lowell Inn has been owned or managed by the Palmer family since it opened in 1924. Arthur and Nelle, pianist and actress with a good deal of experience on the road, were the first Palmers to run the hotel, which they bought in 1945. The second and third generations are now in charge.

"The inn is a special place to stay for that special weekend. My husband and I have spent more than ten anniversary weekends—not to mention a honeymoon—there. Stillwater, the 'birthplace of Minnesota,' is a beautiful little town north of St. Paul on the St. Croix River. It has a long history and is proud of it.

"The inn's lobby has generous overstuffed furniture arranged in comfortable groupings for conversation and cocktails while waiting for a table in one of the three dining rooms. The Washington Room is more formal, with white linen, silver, and china. The Garden Room has a stone floor, wrought-iron tables, and a natural spring waterfall. The third, the Matterhorn Room, is best of all: there is no menu, just fondue served with escargots, salad, dessert, and wine. All this is set in a room with exquisite Swiss wood carvings."

—*Margaret A. Levey*

Open all year.
17 rooms, 4 suites, all with private bath.
Rates $59–$109.
Credit cards: American Express, Diners Club, MasterCard, Visa.
Innkeepers: Arthur and Maureen Palmer.

If you would like to amend, update, or disagree with any entry, write *now*.

_____ *Wabasha*

Anderson House
333 West Main Street
Wabasha, Minnesota 55981
Telephone (612) 565-4003

"Established in 1856, the Anderson is Minnesota's oldest continuously operating hotel. It was recently designated a historic landmark. Except for a few years, the hotel has always been operated by the Anderson family, who came here from Pennsylvania. Over the years, they have wisely kept the hotel in its original state, with gorgeous furniture over a hundred years old. One room is called the Mayo, because doctors from the Mayo Clinic, forty miles away, frequently stayed there.

"Wabasha is an important city historically. It is seventy miles southeast of the Twin Cities, on the Mississippi River and on the direct route from Minneapolis to Chicago via Red Wing, Winona, LaCrosse, and Milwaukee. A bridge spans the Mississippi at Wabasha, so that one can drive on an equally fine highway to Chicago on the other side of the river. In the 1820s, Wabasha (or Wapasha, named for a Sioux chief) was an important fur-trading center. The unit of exchange—worth 5 cents—was the muskrat. The Grace Memorial Episcopal Church, given to the town by wealthy lumber people, is probably the most beautiful church in the world in a town this size. Designed by a New York architect, and possessing gorgeous Tiffany windows, the ninety-year-old church is in perfect condition. The *Delta Queen* and its new counterpart, the *Mississippi Queen,* make regular stops at Wabasha."   —*Dr. Harold C. Habein*

Open all year.
45 rooms, 20 with private bath.
Rates $16–$39. Package plans with meals available.
No credit cards.
Greyhound bus service.
Innkeeper: John Hall

Details of special features offered by an inn or hotel vary according to information supplied by the hotels themselves. The absence here of a recreational amenity, a bar, or a restaurant doesn't necessarily mean one of these doesn't exist. Ask the innkeeper when booking your room.

Granville

Buxton Inn
313 East Broadway
Granville, Ohio 43023
Telephone (614) 587-0001

"The inn was built in 1812 by Orin Granger, and was originally called The Tavern. After Mr. Granger died, the inn changed hands several times until it was bought by Major Buxton in 1865; he ran it for over forty years. Orville and Audrey Orr bought it in 1972 and have been restoring it ever since."   —*Nancy Michael*

"I think it is preferable to its better-known and larger neighbor, the Granville Inn. A nearby restaurant to be tried is in an old country home called Bryn Mawr. Granville is a lovely little town, the home of Denison University."   —*Jean Ogg*

Open all year.
3 rooms in inn, 10 rooms in annex, all with private bath.
Rates $40 single, $45 double.
Credit cards: MasterCard, Visa.
Restaurant and bar.

Bus daily from Columbus airport.
Innkeepers: Orville and Audrey Orr.

_____

Granville Inn
314 East Broadway
Granville, Ohio 43023
Telephone (614) 587-3333

"The Granville Inn, built in 1922, was purchased in 1976 by Robert Kent of Newark, Ohio, because he and his wife had been fond of the inn since they were students at Denison University. 'It had the feeling of an English castle,' he once said, 'and we heard that it was going to be turned into a nursing home or condominium.' Wanting to preserve the inn, the Kents began a five-year renovation program. The thirty-two guest rooms are now individually styled in the great country house tradition. We found the rooms of good size, with twin or double beds and massive wooden chest-dressers.

"On the ground floor, behind the main dining room that was once part of a huge lobby, is the Pub—a cozy, intimate lounge with a huge stone fireplace. The Pub was once the inn's dining room. Also on the ground floor is the Great Hall, often used for weddings and receptions as well as meetings. There are also several conference rooms on the second floor and in the basement.

"All of the sandstone for the inn was quarried east of town on the Bryn Du farm, which was once part of the estate. The hills behind the farmhouse were known then as the Welsh Hills because of the number of Welsh families living in the area. En route from the inn to the Bryn Du farmhouse, one passes the busy eighteen-hole golf course that is part of the inn's weekend golfing package. The course was designed by Donald Ross in the mid 1920s."

—*F. D. Nofziger*

Open all year.
27 rooms, all with private bath or shower.
Rates $41 single, $45 double.
Credit cards: American Express, MasterCard, Visa.
Bar and restaurant; banquet facilities.
Innkeeper: Jennifer Utrevis.

Turn to the back of this book for pages inviting *your* comments.

_____ *Lebanon*

The Golden Lamb
27 South Broadway
Lebanon, Ohio 45036
Telephone (513) 932-5065

"William Howard Taft, Warren G. Harding, Rutherford B. Hayes, U. S. Grant, James Garfield, and William McKinley were among the ten presidents of the United States who sought refuge under the sign of the Golden Lamb, Ohio's oldest inn. Henry Clay often visited. DeWitt Clinton, then governor of New York, stopped overnight on his way to inaugurate the Ohio canal system in 1825. The Golden Lamb began as a two-story log building on December 23, 1803, when Jonas Seaman obtained a license to operate an inn on the stage route between Cincinnati and Dayton. In 1815, a four-story brick building replaced the log structure. Originally, some of the second-floor rooms were dormitories, sleeping as many as eighteen people in a room.

"Guests still tote their luggage up the wooden stairway, but once in their rooms, they find some modern requirements: the antique four-poster beds have modern boxsprings and mattresses. There is electricity, a small TV, and air conditioning. Still, the feeling is one of life in another century. It is said that Charles Dickens complained that no spirits were available when he stopped at this inn. Today, the Black Horse Tavern at the back of the inn fills those needs.

"The Golden Lamb is recognized as a Shaker museum because of its fine collection of Shaker furniture, many of the pieces used every day. Antique cupboards with antique glassware and knick-knacks, line the inn's hallways. The rooms have rag carpets and Currier and Ives prints. Four public dining rooms, and five private ones, offer outstanding food and service in this historic setting."

—*F. D. Nofziger*

"One of the finest restorations among the many country inns I've visited, the Golden Lamb has spacious, comfortable rooms and a restaurant in which traditional American cooking reaches a very high standard. Ask to dine in the Shaker Room and you will combine the best of the inn's treats for eye and palate."   —*George Herzog*

Open all year, except Christmas Day.
18 rooms, all with private bath.
Rate $48 double.
Credit cards: American Express, Carte Blanche, Diners Club, MasterCard, Visa.
Innkeeper: Jackson B. Reynolds.

_____*Loudonville*

Blackfork Inn
303 North Water Street (P.O. Box 149)
Loudonville, Ohio 44842
Telephone (419) 994-3252

"For those of us in the Midwest, country inns can seem few and far between. This lovely spot should certainly be listed: nothing has been spared in the restoration of this house. The beautiful main rooms are furnished with antiques. A complimentary continental breakfast is served on lace tablecloths, with flowers on the table, in the dining room. No other meals are served, but menus from area restaurants are on hand. The places to eat include the Malabar Inn, another restored house near Malabar Farm, the home of the Pulitzer Prize-winning author Louis Bromfield. His house is open to the public for tours, incidentally. Also nearby is Mohican Lake State Park for hiking and picnicking. Loudonville is next to Holmes County, which has a larger Amish population than Lancaster County, Pennsylvania."   —*Christine and F. Harlan Flint, Jr.*

Open all year.
6 rooms, all with private bath.
Rates from $57 double, including continental or Amish cheese-and-apple-butter breakfast. Reduced rates midweek and for single people traveling on business.
Credit cards: MasterCard, Visa.
German, some Slavic languages spoken.
Guests met at Cleveland's Hopkins Airport or Mansfield Airport by prior arrangement. Greyhound buses serve Loudonville.
Innkeepers: Sue and Al Gorisek; Resident Manager: William Beaver.

_____*Marietta*

The Lafayette Motor Hotel
101 Front Street
Marietta, Ohio 45750
Telephone (614) 373-5522

Marietta, on the Ohio River, was founded in 1788 by General Rufus Putnam and a band of Revolutionary soldiers and accompanying citizens. It became the first settlement in the Northwest Territory; for that reason it is called Ohio's first city. Marietta has excellent museums, most notably the Ohio River Museum and Campus Martius, a collection of exhibits mounted by the Ohio Historical Society that includes General Putnam's restored home. There are also interesting walking tours through Marietta's historic neighborhoods, and a stern-wheeler to ride on the river.

The Lafayette Hotel was built in 1918, but has expanded and changed much over the years, so guests should not expect a traditional inn. But much memorabilia survives, and the motor hotel tries to make the most of its past.

"The hotel is close to the river, a bonus. But be sure to ask for rooms in the old section, which are small, attractive, and comfortable. The Gun Room has a good menu and excellent food and service." —*Jean Ogg*

Open all year.
98 rooms, all with private bath.
Rates $28–$45. Special packages including meals available. Discounts for AARP members.
Credit cards: American Express, Carte Blanche, Diners Club, MasterCard, Visa.
French and German spoken.
General Manager: Jean O'Grady.

Would you be so kind as to share discoveries you may have of charming, well-run places to stay in Europe? Please write to *Europe's Wonderful Little Hotels and Inns,* c/o Congdon & Weed, 298 Fifth Avenue, New York, New York 10001. (By the way, a new and greatly expanded edition of this splendid guide is now available at your bookseller's.)

Jamieson House,
Poynette

Wisconsin

Bayfield

The Mansion
7 Rice Avenue
Bayfield, Wisconsin 54814
Telephone (715) 779-5408

"Bayfield is a wonderful small town with crafts, antiques, and ferry rides across breathtaking Lake Superior. The Mansion, which overlooks the lake and the Apostle Islands, is a beautiful Queen Anne neoclassical home with fifty-three rooms of exquisite woodwork, carving, and paneling throughout three floors. The atmosphere throughout is warmed by Tiffany glass dating to 1911. The innkeepers believe meals are a pleasurable activity, and at mealtimes there is a mood of easy grace as guests relax at a Chippendale table by an open fire."
—*Judy Mitchell*

Open all year.
3 rooms with shared baths.
Rate $40.
No credit cards.
Meals available by special arrangement.
Innkeeper: Paul Turner.

_____*Milwaukee*

The Pfister Hotel
424 East Wisconsin Avenue
Milwaukee, Wisconsin 53202
Telephone (414) 273-8222 or toll-free (800) 323-7500

"This is an underrated city. The lake and the parks are lovely, and many old buildings downtown have been restored. Be sure to see some grand old homes, and stop at the Terrace Museum for the Decorative Arts. Try to see the Milwaukee County Museum, too; its European village is a delight. The Pfister's lobby is elegant, the rooms are adequate, and the view of the lake and downtown from the tower is nice. You are just a half-block from the pleasant atmosphere of Karl Ratsch's restaurant, an award-winner, where the food is good and the prices are reasonable. Milwaukee has a hearty, ethnic charm, and the Pfister is the place to enjoy it."

—*Tonette J. Brougher*

"The hotel's rooms are divided between the original eight-story 1893 hotel and a twenty-three-story tower built in 1966. The old building has more charm, the tower more convenience. The place is well located, just a few blocks from Lake Michigan. For the best views of the lake, ask for rooms 8, 9, or 10 as high as possible in the tower."

—*Paul Salsini*

Open all year.
333 rooms and suites, all with private bath.
Rates from $54 single, $80 double.
Credit cards: American Express, Carte Blanche, Diners Club, MasterCard, Visa.
General Manager: François-L. Nivaud.

_____*Poynette*

Jamieson House
329 North Franklin
Poynette, Wisconsin 53955
Telephone (608) 635-4100

"The homes of Hugh James and his eldest son, across the street from each other, now house the Jamieson House. When Jeff Smith began restoration of the 1878 Hugh Jamieson Mansion, it was a derelict Victorian ghost slated for razing. The eldest son's 1883 town house was a nursing home for elderly men. Today each glitters in its own special way. The restaurant occupies the Jamieson mansion; the son's town house is the guesthouse.

"Each of the restaurant's four dining rooms is decorated with reproduction Victorian wallpaper and lighting fixtures and contains part of the owner's extensive collection of Victorian furniture (including parlor organs) and Oriental rugs. A large Garden Room has been added and is used for dessert, coffee, and after-dinner liqueurs. The cuisine is outstanding; while basically French, it reflects the chef's interest in other cuisines. The mood is relaxed and congenial; the owner and his staff will guide you through the ever-changing menu and the wine list, which includes some of the best among European and California wines.

"Across the street in the guesthouse there are four suites, each with a luxurious private bath. Some have sitting rooms. Each room is papered in the large, boldly colored patterns of the Victorian era and is furnished with more of the owner's collection."

—*John C. Harvey*

Open all year.
7 rooms, all with private bath.
Rates $45–$65, including breakfast.
Credit card: American Express.
Innkeeper: Jeffrey Smith.

Rates quoted were the latest available. But they may not reflect unexpected increases or local and state taxes. Be sure to verify when you book.

Part Five

U.S. Territory
Puerto Rico

_____ *Puerto Rico*

Coamo

Baños de Coamo
P.O. Box 540
Coamo, Puerto Rico 00640
Telephone (809) 825-2239; 825-2186 or toll-free (800)
223-6530

"Even before the boom in hotel and inn restorations really took off
on the mainland, the island government in Puerto Rico had given
its blessing and its backing to a program called Paradores Puer-
toriqueños—a collection of small, historic, or otherwise especially
interesting country inns modeled on the *paradores* of Spain and the
pousadas of Portugal. There are six of them now, scattered around
the island.

"Baños de Coamo is a new resort built on the ruins of an old spa.
A hot mineral spring here attracted Franklin D. Roosevelt, among
others; guests can still enjoy its 109-degree water while overlooking
a tropical countryside. The restorers of the inn made much use of
local woods, and of bentwood furniture. A nineteenth-century
Spanish-style dining room is the centerpiece of the complex, which
also includes an outdoor terrace bar, swimming pool, and motel-

style guest rooms. The inn is less than an hour's drive from Ponce, a city with a strong cultural tradition and many old buildings."

—*B.C.*

Open all year.
48 rooms, all air conditioned and with private bath and porch or
   balcony.
Rates $30 single, $35 double.
Credit cards: American Express, Carte Blanche, Diners Club, MasterCard, Visa.
Innkeeper: Joaquin Colon.

_____*Jayuya*

Hacienda Gripiñas
Route 527 (P.O. Box 387)
Jayuya, Puerto Rico 00664
Telephone (809) 721-2884 or toll-free (800) 223-6530

"This lovely hacienda high in the mountains near the center of the island was a coffee planter's house. In this area the Taino Indian culture flourished, and there are several sites of archaeological and artistic interest to be enjoyed by the visitor to this remote part of Puerto Rico. Life here is pleasant and quiet, and an evening can be spent on the hacienda's wide verandas listening to nothing but tree frogs—the island's beloved *coquis*. Gripiñas's interior has been furnished with elegant simplicity, emphasizing the local culture and maximizing the use of the island's rich woods. A visit here is an introduction to a Puerto Rico few mainlanders know."

—*B.C.*

Open all year.
19 rooms, all with private bath.
Rates $25 single, $30 double.
Credit cards: MasterCard, Visa.
Restaurant featuring local cuisine; bar.
Innkeeper: Edgardo Dedos.

_____*San Juan*

El Convento
100 Cristo
San Juan, Puerto Rico 00903
Telephone (809) 723-9020

"There are two San Juans: 'new' San Juan, with its brassy Condado Beach, framed by skyscraper hotels and accompanied by disco sounds, and Old San Juan, as graceful and beautiful a Spanish city as you will find anywhere in the Caribbean or Central America. Old San Juan has most of Puerto Rico's museums, many of its best restaurants, and much of its history. At the heart of the old city is this compelling hotel, which was built as a convent in the seventeenth century, when San Juan was a walled administrative outpost of Spain's American empire. From El Convento, most of the historic area is within walking distance. So are many streets of lovely Spanish-style houses, and small shops and restaurants with a more relaxed island pace.

"El Convento is built around a cloister, with rooms opening onto wide, tiled verandas, furnished with deep, dark woods and tropical plants. Here and there is an unexpected porch from which to watch the sunset in the harbor. A terrace bar and restaurant at the center of the building is a nice place to loiter."   —B.C.

Open all year.
100 rooms and suites, all with air conditioning and private bath.
Rates $55–$90 single, $60–$110 double, $125 suites.
Credit cards: American Express, Carte Blanche, Diners Club, MasterCard, Visa.
Restaurant and bar.
Manager: Juan Bonini.

_____ *Vieques Island*

La Casa del Frances
Barrio Esperanza
Vieques, Puerto Rico
Telephone (809) 741-3751

An offshore island of fifty beaches, mountains, and a history that is part plantation, part piracy, Vieques has a loyal following.

"La Casa del Frances is a former plantation house now functioning as a small hotel. It displays a hacienda splendor, from its atrium garden to the well-tended jungle of tropical plants beyond the porch. The owner played Beethoven when he served chicken, and Mozart with the fish."   —David Binder

Open all year.
19 rooms, all with private bath.
Rates $49–$54.
No credit cards.
Innkeeper: Irving Greenblatt.

Part Six

Canada

New Brunswick
Nova Scotia
Ontario
Prince Edward Island
Quebec

Part
Six

New Brunswick

Grand Manan

The Marathon Inn
North Head, Grand Manan
New Brunswick EOG 2MO
Telephone (506) 662-8144

"The inn stands on a hill overlooking the fishing village of North Head on Grand Manan Island, about twenty miles off the coast of New Brunswick in the Bay of Fundy. The bright, spacious front parlor with a Franklin stove and bay windows, the antique furnishings and decorations in every room, and the cheerful ambience of the service all help to recall the Victorian origins of this hotel. The Marathon was built in 1871 by a retired sea captain. The bedrooms are unaffectedly quaint and the bill of fare—especially the seafood—is authentic and tasty. The proprietors, Fern Leslie, her son Jim and his wife, Judy, will welcome you and assist you in any way they can from filling you in on local customs and geography to helping you plan a day trip to Machias Seal island to view the puffins and other seabirds that nest there. The Leslies introduced a new attraction to the Marathon: the summer Dulse Festival, a folksy-artsy musical show and all-around good time. Dulse, by the way, is an

323

edible—in fact delicious—seaweed indigenous to Grand Manan and good for what ails you.

"Grand Manan is a special place, not simply because it is an island: it is special even as islands go. Visitors find themselves yearning to return without really understanding why. Willa Cather, for example, came year after year to her cottage overlooking Whale Cove, and flourished there in creative privacy. Ever since the island was first settled nearly 200 years ago, writers and painters have found Grand Manan strangely inspirational, as have countless bird watchers from Audubon himself to the annual flock of purest amateurs. Helen Charters, an artist and friend of mine who lives on the island, says that Grand Manan is a 'primal point.' Extremes are possible here. Powerful rhythms are present. The beauty—and the danger—of Grand Manan is indestructible. The people, and whatever it is that shapes them and compels them, will not be undone by visitors."

—*Michael Brian Oliver*

"Whether balsam-scented from the highland woods to the west, or from the east with a damp chill of fog and the smell of herring smokehouses, the breeze is always there to remind you of the sea and its dominance over all island activities. Everywhere there are birds in great variety and staggering quantity. Proprietors of several herring smokehouses welcome visitors, and you will have a chance to sample this distinctive product. One should keep in mind the formidable logistics of food shopping for the inn, most of which must be done on the mainland. The menu will occasionally be limited and may feature some improvisations or 'standbys,' but these are always well prepared and tasty. If the beds leave something to be desired from the standpoint of comfort, your vigorous day and the sea air will ensure you a sound night's sleep."

—*Mr. and Mrs. William G. Sayres*

Open May 1 to October 31

34 rooms, 5 with private bath.

Rates $45–$54 single, $34–$43 double per person, including breakfast and dinner. Lunch on request. Children under 10, half rate. Weekly rates available.

Credit cards: MasterCard, Visa.

Grand Manan Ferry Service connects island with Black's Harbour, New Brunswick. For schedules call (506) 662-3606 or (506) 456-2465.

Innkeepers: James and Fern Leslie.

Rates for Canadian entries are quoted in Canadian dollars.

Sackville

Marshlands Inn
73 Bridge Street (Box 1440)
Sackville, New Brunswick EOA 3C0
Telephone (506) 536-0170

Since Sackville is about midway between the Bay of Fundy and Northumberland Strait, it usually has a warmer temperature in winter and a cooler temperature in summer than the rest of New Brunswick. It is on the edge of the Tantramar Marshes and about an hour's drive from beaches and a few miles from Fort Beausejour and its museum.

"We visited the inn in the first week of October because we wanted to look at the changing leaves. The inn is an old white house surrounded by trees; our room was large and quaint, with soft beds, embroidered hand towels, and a footed bathtub. The meals were excellent—we met for drinks in the parlor before dinner (I had lamb curry) and then moved back into the parlor for coffee. Before bedtime, we were offered hot chocolate. There is a wildlife preserve nearby and we watched the 'tidal bore'—the tide rises quickly in a narrow river, about 40 feet in one hour."

—_Mrs. Yetta G. Samford, Jr._

Open late February to late November.
12 rooms, 6 with private bath.
Rates $35–$50.
Credit cards: MasterCard, Visa.
Bus depot within 5-minute walk. Train station less than 1 mile from
inn.
French spoken.
Innkeeper: H. C. Read.

Details of special features offered by an inn or hotel vary according to information supplied by the hotels themselves. The absence here of a recreational amenity, a bar, or a restaurant doesn't necessarily mean one of these doesn't exist. Ask the innkeeper when booking your room.

Nova Scotia

Mahone Bay

Sou'wester
Box 146
Mahone Bay, Nova Scotia, 80J 2EO
Telephone: (902) 624-9296

"The tourist homes of Canada offer a surprisingly economical opportunity for travelers to soak up local color while enjoying accommodations that innkeepers can provide only in their own homes. One of them, the Sou'wester, is in the quietly elegant town of Mahone Bay. With its many small shops offering handcrafts and collectibles, the town has been described as an artists' and photographers' paradise.

"The Mahone Bay experience would be incomplete without a stay at the Sou'wester. This beautifully constructed and immaculately maintained turn-of-the-century home was built by one of Nova Scotia's famous shipbuilders, and everything about it, from the porch to the library, suggests tranquillity. Visitors can sail, picnic, and use a dory, canoe, or bicycles. Breakfast is prepared for guests every morning. For lunch and dinner one can do no better than to visit the nearby Zwicker Inn.

"We would advise the world's lovers of dining to make quick tracks to the Zwicker Inn. Anything you order, from the halibut fillet to the heavenly chicken, from the fish chowder to the leek-and-potato soup, will be of such quality that dining in the old city of Quebec will seem like a soup line by comparison."

—Carl and Barbara Semencic

Open May to mid-October.
3 rooms, with shared baths.
Rates $18 single, $25 double; breakfast $1.50 to $3 extra.
No credit cards.
No restaurant.
Innkeepers: Mable and Ronald Redden.

—————————————————————————— *Wolfville*

Blomidon Inn
127 Main Street (Box 839)
Wolfville, Nova Scotia B0P 1X0
Telephone (902) 542-9326

"In renovating this old mansion the owners, Gale and Peter Hastings, have turned back the clock to a time when quiet and graceful living were the order of the day. We were fortunate to be among the first guests of the inn in the summer of 1981. Located along the Evangeline Trail in Nova Scotia's Annapolis Valley, the inn has rooms named for places or people famous in the region. Most of the rooms have quilt work done by Mrs. Hastings; many have private baths and fireplaces. Breakfast is served in a beautifully decorated morning room while the music of Mozart and Haydn plays softly in the living room." *—Barbara and Philip Kane*

"The Kanes didn't say enough! We traveled for three weeks in New England and the Maritimes and this was the most outstanding inn of all. The bedrooms are beautifully furnished (mahogany beds) and decorated (small prints and quilts). The inn now has a dining room and although the hostess claims it is simple country cooking, our three dinners were hardly simple. Wonderful bread and oatcakes, homemade applesauce with roast pork, fresh fish with real hollandaise, fresh fruit desserts.

"We felt at home but in surroundings that most homes never achieve. This is a first-class inn with a first-class dining room."

—Morton McMichael

Open all year.
11 rooms, 10 with private bath.

Rates $30–$35 shared bath, $45–$49 private bath, $30–$35 single, including continental breakfast and afternoon tea.

Credit cards: MasterCard, Visa.

Some French spoken.

Train and air service to Halifax. Limousine service to airport. Acadian Bus Lines from Halifax, Yarmouth, or Digby.

Innkeepers: Peter and Gale Hastings.

Would you be so kind as to share discoveries you may have of charming, well-run places to stay in Europe? Please write to *Europe's Wonderful Little Hotels and Inns,* c/o Congdon & Weed, 298 Fifth Avenue, New York, New York 10001. (By the way, a new and greatly expanded edition of this splendid guide is now available at your bookseller's.)

Ontario

Algonquin Park

Arowhon Pines
Huntsville P.O.
Ontario P0A 1K0
Telephone (705) 633-5661

"The Pines, as friends call it, rarely advertises in any medium more international than _The Toronto Globe and Mail,_ but Europeans and North Americans who find it learn about it through word of mouth. Innkeepers Eugene and Helen Kates adhere to one of Eugene's gruff-voiced tenets: 'Look,' he rumbles, 'we're in the business of selling three things: a bedroom, a dining room, and a setting. The setting is superb . . .'—he's right: the Pines adjoins a lake near the southern corner of a 3,000-square-mile provincial park that is a favorite of Canadian naturalists, canoe-trippers, and landscape painters—'. . . but that's beyond our control, so we have to do our best with the other two.'

"The broad, hexagonal dining room, jutting over the lake, was built in the late 1930s by two brothers, Paul and Jack Lucasavitch. Of necessity they used only hand tools, plus a team of horses to winch into place the enormous central cast-iron chimney. Still solid as Canadian Shield granite, their construction has been applauded in several books on fine log buildings. As for its wares, the Pines' baker produces fresh breads and cakes daily, and each summer the Kateses have managed to steal yet another bright young chef from some major Toronto restaurant: their reputation for food has gone consistently up. (N.B. The sale of alcohol is forbidden in Ontario's parks. If you want wine with your meals—and they deserve it—you must bring your own. The hotel provides stemware, mixers, and corkscrews.) Fifty bedrooms are clustered in small buildings scattered through the densely wooded grounds. Each cabin has a common lounge area with a fireplace, comfortable chairs and sofas, a small refrigerator, and an eclectic collection of books. Helen Kates is a compulsive antiques hunter, so many of those stripped-pine pieces are authentic 'old Canada.'

"Canoeing is our recreation of choice. There's an easy but fun white water creek leading to the Pines' lake from one to the north. There are wolf howls at night, loon calls at dawn. We've seen dozens of bird species, bear on almost every trip, and a moose twice. The canoes are free. So are the tennis and shuffleboard courts, rowboats, small sailboats, swim docks, picnic lunches, and well-marked trails through the bush. There is a small charge for outboard motor-equipped fishing boats and for baby-sitting. No tipping: *servis compris.*"   —*Mechtild Hoppenrath and Charles Oberdorf*

Open mid-May to mid-October.
49 rooms, all with private bath.
Rates $82.50–$165 single, $66–$126.50 double per person, AP.
   (Prices quoted are Canadian dollars.)
No credit cards.
Winter address for correspondence: 147 Davenport Road, Toronto
   M5R 1J1. Winter telephone: (416) 923-7176.
Innkeepers: Eugene and Helen Kates.

Alton

The Millcroft Inn
John Street (Box 89)
Alton, Ontario L0N 1A0
Telephone (416) 791-4422

"Toronto's most elegant country retreat was created several years ago out of an old knitting mill, $3 million, and a lot of imagination. To ensure quality, the hotel is managed—though not owned—by the people from the Windsor Arms Hotel, in Toronto. Rooms in 'the Mill,' all twenty-two of them, are furnished with Canadian antiques. The twenty crofts on the hill are a longer walk from the heart of things—from the tennis courts, the outdoor pool, the bar, and the dining areas. Management by the Windsor Arms Hotel guarantees above all fine food imaginatively prepared: homemade sherbets and ices, salads of such uncommon ingredients as celery root, perfect drinks, vegetables grown in the inn's own garden and often picked moments before serving. Meals are not cheap. But many Toronto food fanatics drive two hours for the pleasure of eating there, without even spending the night." —*Mechtild Hoppenrath and Charles Oberdorf*

Open all year.
42 rooms, all with private bath.
Rates $90–$100.
Credit cards: American Express, Diners Club, MasterCard, Visa.
French, German, and Spanish spoken.
Gray Coach buses to Orangeville, taxis to Alton.
Innkeeper: Peter Chlup.

_____*Elora*

The Elora Mill
77 Mill Street West (Box 218)
Elora, Ontario N0B 1S0
Telephone (519) 846-5356

"Until 1973 this hotel was known as Drimmies Mill, a gristmill powered by the thundering waterfall that now crashes past the best tables in the cocktail lounge. Two families bought and refitted the old mill, transforming it into the crown jewel of this town of 2,500, which had already attracted a fair number of Sunday drivers with its artists' and craftsmen's workshops, its natural setting (hard by a deep limestone gorge full of caves, waterfalls, and rapids), and the beautiful surrounding countryside, largely farmed by buggy-driving Mennonites. We prefer the food at the less expensive, Basque-style Café Flore, just down the street, to dinners at the Mill. Or we go on a Saturday and assemble lunch from the Mennonite farmers' markets in nearby Kitchener and Elmira. In August, the town of Fergus, just down the road, stages one of Canada's more important festivals of 'highland games,' complete with bagpipes and flying cabers. In winter the Elora Gorge Conservation Area becomes one of the

province's best cross-country skiing areas, the better for knowing
that the Mill will have a nice hot buttered rum on hand at the end
of the run."   —*Mechtild Hoppenrath and Charles Oberdorf*

Open all year.
20 rooms, all with private bath.
Rates $60–$80.
Credit cards: American Express, MasterCard, Visa.
Train and bus service to Guelph, 11 miles away.
Innkeeper: Crozier Taylor.

_____ *Hamilton*

Royal Connaught Hotel
112 King Street East
Hamilton, Ontario L8N 1A8
Telephone (416) 527-5071

"The hotel is centrally located on King Street. It has a nice atmosphere; spacious, modern, well-appointed rooms. The staff is attentive, particularly in the dining room and at the reception desk."
                                        —*H. C. Beddington*

Open all year.
215 rooms, all with private bath.
Rates from $60 single, $66 double.
Credit cards: American Express, Carte Blanche, Diners Club, En
    Route, MasterCard, Visa.
Manager: Barry Massey.

_____ *Niagara-on-the-Lake*

The Pillar and Post Inn
48 John Street (Box 1011)
Niagara-on-the-Lake, Ontario L0S 1J0
Telephone (416) 468-2123

"This inn is less historically authentic than others in the town. It's
a fairly recent recycling of an old industrial building, with all the
modern conveniences like sauna and outdoor pool and mostly 'reproduction antiques' in the rooms. But it does have pretty quilts and
fireplaces in some bedrooms."
                        —*Mechtild Hoppenrath and Charles Oberdorf*

"A nice pool, pretty flowers, and an excellent breakfast buffet. A special treat for us was that it was across from the yacht boatyards."
—*Dr. and Mrs. Michael Durishin*

Open all year.
91 rooms, all with private bath.
Rates $80–$90.
Credit cards: American Express, MasterCard, Visa.
Innkeeper: Neil O. Foster.

Prince of Wales Hotel
6 Piton Street (Box 46)
Niagara-on-the-Lake, Ontario L0S 1J0
Telephone (416) 468-3246

"Dining adequately is no problem anywhere in Niagara-on-the-Lake, but dining splendidly is impossible. To the extent that it still reflects some excellent past management—by the Toronto consultants Nicholas Pearce and David Barrette—the Prince of Wales remains the best place to eat. A restored and enlarged hotel of Victorian vintage, the closest one to the Shaw theater, it is also a reasonable place to sleep. In any town this size, it would be a treasure."   —*Mechtild Hoppenrath and Charles Oberdorf*

"I agree with your evaluation of dinner."   —*Mary Jane Durishin*

Open all year.
87 rooms, 7 suites, all with private bath.
Rates $65–$70 single, $70–$80 double, $85–$135 suites.
Credit cards: American Express, MasterCard, Visa.
French and German spoken.
Innkeepers: Henry and John Wiens.

Toronto

King Edward Hotel
37 King Street East
Toronto, Ontario M5C 1E9
Telephone (416) 863-9700

"If you are headed for the center of the business district, there is no better hotel than the King Edward. The solid grandeur has been strikingly updated in a counterpoint that plays the freshness and openness of modern taste against the muted background of elaborate ornamentation. Decor is a triumph. Service is a close second."

—*George Herzog*

Open all year.
290 rooms, 30 suites, all with private bath.
Rates $98–$155 single, $118–$175 double (Canadian currency).
Credit cards: American Express, Diners Club, En Route, Master-Card, Visa.
Eight languages spoken by the concierge.
General Manager: Mr. I. Fahmy.

Park Plaza Hotel
4 Avenue Road
Toronto, Ontario M5R 2E8
Telephone (416) 924-5471

"The Park Plaza is of the same chain as the Inn on the Park in London. No rooms, only suites. The hotel has a delightful atmosphere, is well appointed and well located."   —*H. C. Beddington*

Open all year.
340 rooms, all with private bath.
Rates $80–$90 single, $95–$105 double.
Credit cards: Air Canada, American Express, Diners Club, Master-Card, Visa.
French and many other languages spoken.
Manager: Konrad Steger.

The Windsor Arms Hotel
22 St. Thomas Street
Toronto, Ontario M5S 2B9
Telephone (416) 979-2341

"Booking into the Windsor Arms means shring the taste of Pierre Trudeau and Katharine Hepburn. A little gem of a Tudor-style palace, it nestles quietly off the trafficked streets, yet is just a block from the most elegant shopping of Yorkville and the Royal Ontario Museum. Rooms have been restored and redecorated in warm colors. Furnishings range from late Regency to a 1920s variety of English Renaissance, with an occasional brass bed. My room was graced with a sitting alcove that had a charming settee and a beautiful wall of cupboards with leaded-glass fronts. The cupboards, alas, were bare—but bare was the last thing that could be said of the garden that provisions the hotel's several fine restaurants, among the best in Toronto. If you want a small taste of British-Canadian tradition, treat yourself to kippers at breakfast." —*George Herzog*

Open all year.
81 rooms, 25 with shower, 56 with bath and shower.
Rates $65–$275.
Credit cards: American Express, Carte Blanche, Diners Club, MasterCard, Visa.
French spoken.
Near train and bus stations.
Innkeeper: Norbert Ackerman.

If you would like to amend, update, or disagree with any entry, write *now*.

Prince Edward Island

Brackley Beach

Shaw's Hotel
Brackley Beach
Prince Edward Island C0A 2H0
Telephone (902) 672-2022

"Different guests have different reasons for cherishing Shaw's Hotel. For most it appeals as a happy family inn, managed without needless and stuffy formalities, containing a main building of twenty-three rooms in a Victorian-style residence, supplemented by nearby cottages of various sizes, accommodating from two to ten guests. The spacious ground and large farm buildings are a conspicuous advantage, and offer an admirable playground for adults and children alike. Appetizing food, much dependent on the sea and local produce, is another obvious asset. An important feature is the warm and charming staff who provide excellent service in the hotel's dining room and other departments where a high standard of cleanliness is always maintained.

"Unlike so many of the guest families, I may seldom bathe in the temperate surf of the neighboring Gulf of St. Lawrence (summer temperatures average 65 to 75 degrees), but I frequently tramp on the sand and in the woods. I derive constant delight from the charm of the varying scenes in the shifting light from morning to night. Here telescoped within a few acres are cardinal features that give Prince Edward Island in general an impressive beauty. They explain why for many years I have returned to Shaw's each summer. The warm, friendly atmosphere provides an environment that permits one to do whatever the inclination dictates: read, meditate, write, exercise muscles, or simply relax. Shaw's is a vacation haunt in the best and widest sense of the term."   —*Alexander Brady*

"Shaw's is a place where children can and do have fun in the fields and gardens as well as on the beach, while their parents go on walks or sightseeing, or go about their swimming, tennis, golf, or reading, or just sit and chat on the broad veranda. Privacy is respected, but people meet and mingle comfortably, talking over the events of the day over coffee or a visit to the Lobster Trap, the hotel's unassuming and delightful bar. It is no wonder that many guests return to Shaw's frequently over the years. In some cases, members of a family have come for three or four generations. Others simply come upon the hotel in their travels, stop for a night—and stay for a week.

"Visitors will find guests of all shapes and sizes, and from all walks of life. It is pleasantly littered with chief justices, premiers, doctors, authors, architects, professors, plumbers, and tycoons, who find common ground in its way of life. Many Canadians regard Shaw's as a national institution. Certainly it is a national asset."

                    —*Tom Symons*

Open mid-June to mid-September.
23 rooms, 1 suite, 11 cottages, 20 with private bath.
Rates $45–$75 per person, including breakfast and dinner.
No credit cards.
French spoken.
Prince Edward Island airport is 20 miles from the hotel.
Innkeeper: Robbie Shaw.

Rates for Canadian entries are quoted in Canadian dollars.

Quebec

Como

Auberge Willow Place Inn
208 Main Street (Box 100)
Como, Quebec J0P 1A0
Telephone (514) 458-7006

"This inn has a perfect name, as there are many willow trees in the area. It is about thirty-five miles west of Montreal. The grounds behind the inn go down to the Lake of Two Mountains, and from your table you can see sailboats passing by in the summer. In winter you can watch cross-country skiers. The inn has quite a few antiques and is decorated with good taste. Some of the bedrooms have four-poster beds, and everything is spotless." —_Britt Rottboll_

Open all year.
8 rooms, all with private bath.
Rates $25–$30 single, $35–$40 double, including continental breakfast.
Credit cards: American Express, MasterCard, Visa.
French spoken.
Innkeepers: David Crockart and Michael Dobbie.

———————————————————————*North Hatley*

Hovey Manor
Box 60
North Hatley, Quebec J0B 2C0
Telephone (819) 842-2421

"The rooms in the main building are furnished in simple early North American style and are very comfortable, if not soundproof. The lovely sitting room–library with its fine fireplace is a charming room in which to relax, read, chat with old and new acquaintances and friends, or share a drink before dinner. Nearby, the Carriage House, with its enormous fireplace, is full of antiques. Here (and in the beautiful old gardens as well) are served drinks throughout the week and marvelous steak dinners on Saturday nights. The Carriage House also has some very small guest rooms that are less expensive than those in the main house. Cottages are also provided for families. At Hovey Manor one can be active or inactive, according to one's own inclination. Some come to rest, some to write, and some for the variety of activities on and off the premises. Summer stock may be enjoyed at the nearby Piggery and at Bishop University. The works of artists and artisans may be seen in town."

—*Clara Loomanitz*

Open all year.
30 rooms, all with private bath.
Rates $48–$75 single, $80–$100 per couple, MAP (U.S. dollars).
Credit cards: American Express, MasterCard, Visa.
French spoken.
Bus service from Montreal.
Innkeepers: Steve and Kathryn Stafford.

———————————————————————*Quebec City*

Château Frontenac
1, Rue-des-Carrières
Quebec City, Quebec G1R 4P5
Telephone (418) 692-3861

"Located in the very heart of the old town of Quebec, the Château Frontenac is a striking structure overlooking the St. Lawrence. On arrival new guests are often puzzled by the architecture because the entrance is in the courtyard. They shouldn't drive around looking for the door but rather drive right into the courtyard to unload.

Once through the gleaming copper doors, guests find themselves in a beautiful lobby renovated in the original style. However, while the public rooms are all newly renovated, some guest rooms are not. Thus, the quality of rooms can vary quite widely, and prospective guests might wish to ask about this before registering. Room service is a bit spotty, but service in the dining room and bar is excellent. In keeping with the location, the dining room offers several delicious French-Canadian specialties and a drink in the circular bar overlooking the St. Lawrence is an experience not to be missed. The Château Frontenac is within walking distance of the Citadelle and the lovely Parc des Champs de Bataille. Also many fine restaurants, in varying price ranges, are only a short stroll away."

—Raymond Sitton and June Wright

Open all year.
500 rooms, all with private bath.
Rates $80–$98 single, $96–$114 double.
Credit cards: American Express, Carte Blanche, CP, Diners Club, En Route, MasterCard, Visa.
French and Spanish spoken.
Manager: Gustav Bamatter.

St. Jovite

Gray Rocks Inn
Mt. Tremblant (Box 1000)
St. Jovite, Quebec J0T 2H0
Telephone (819) 425-2771

"We wanted a place to take a ski vacation in the Northeast and chose Gray Rocks on the advice of friends, some of whom had visited there two or three times. The inn is in the Laurentian Mountains and both skiing and skiing instruction are offered throughout the winter. We wanted a room in the inn itself (one may also stay in separate chalets) and were pleased to find large, comfortable accommodations. The food was served family style and was delicious and plentiful. The owners even joined us for dinner one evening and, as a friendly gesture, provided our table with our choice of wines from their well-stocked cellars. The inn, which has several bars, offers game rooms at night for cards and chess. There are some organized activities for those interested." *—Philip and Debbie Fretz*

Open mid-May to mid-October, mid-November to mid-April.
127 rooms, 110 with private bath; 8 cottages, 7 with private bath.
Rates $67.50–$100.50 per person, AP.

Credit cards: American Express, Carte Blanche, Diners Club, MasterCard, Visa.
French spoken.
74 miles northwest of Montreal. Taxis can be hired from Montreal
   airport to inn for about $75; reserve at inn in advance. Rail
   service on weekends from January to mid-March. Bus service to
   door three times daily by Voyager Bus Lines.
Innkeeper: Bob Earl.

Would you be so kind as to share discoveries you may have of
charming, well-run places to stay in Europe? Please write to *Europe's
Wonderful Little Hotels and Inns,* c/o Congdon & Weed, 298 Fifth
Avenue, New York, New York 10001. (By the way, a new and greatly
expanded edition of this splendid guide is now available at your
bookseller's.)

_____ *Maps*

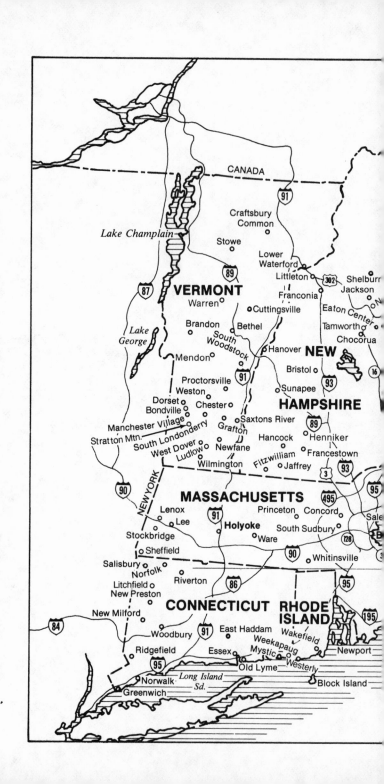

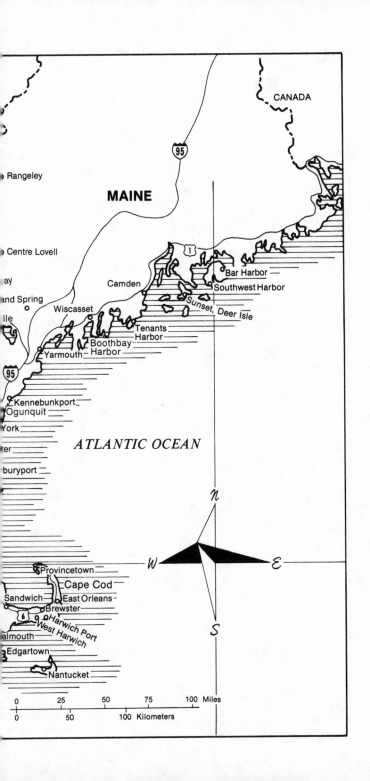

CANADA

Rangeley

MAINE

95

Centre Lovell

ay

and Spring

lle

Camden

Bar Harbor

Southwest Harbor

Wiscasset

Sunset, Deer Isle

95

Tenants
Harbor

Yarmouth

Boothbay
Harbor

Kennebunkport

Ogunquit

York

ATLANTIC OCEAN

ter

buryport

N

Provincetown

Cape Cod

W

E

Sandwich

East Orleans

Brewster

6

Harwich Port

West Harwich

almouth

S

Edgartown

Nantucket

| 0 | 25 | 50 | 75 | 100 Miles |

| 0 | 50 | 100 Kilometers |

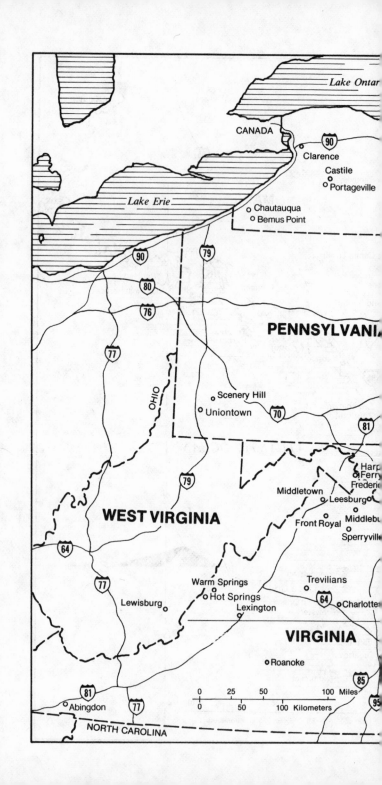

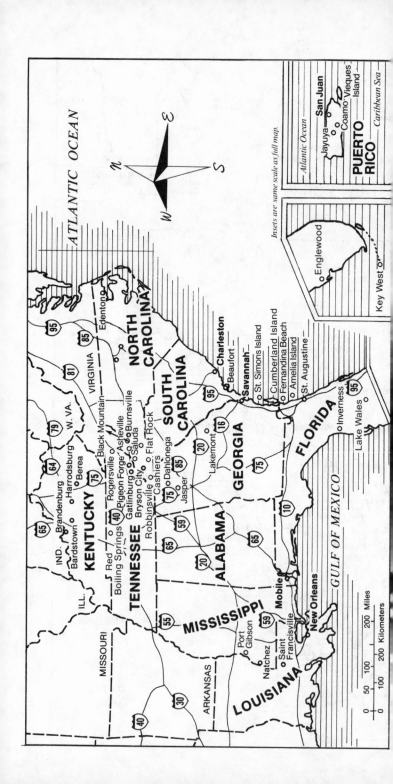

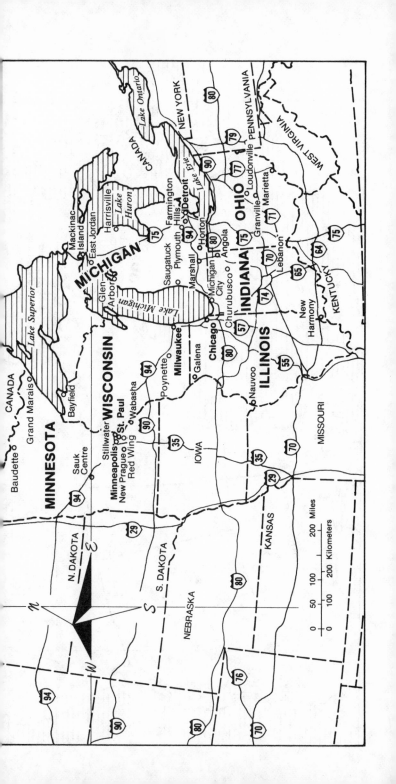

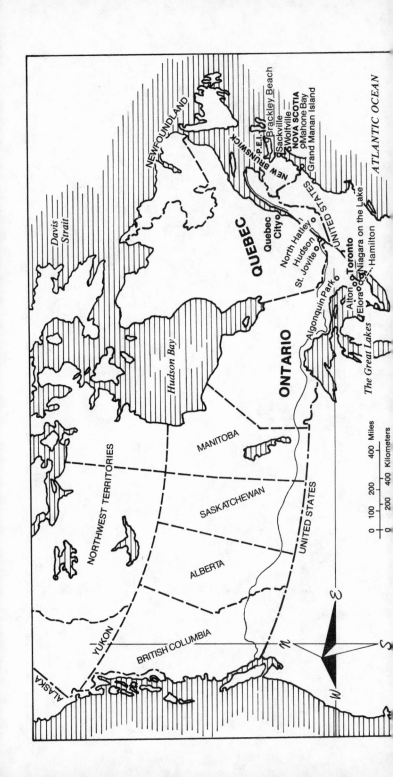

Hotel
Reports
_____

The pages that follow are for you to use to amend, criticize, or update entries in this book, or to suggest new entries for our next edition. When you nominate a hotel or inn, please tell other travelers about the region or neighborhood as well as the hotel itself; this is particularly helpful when you write about areas of the country not familiar to many people. There is no need to include a lot of factual information (prices, number of rooms, etc.) with your entry; this is supplied by the hotels and inns. What you will give us is the spirit and character of the places you find. There is no need to confine your comments to a single page. It is important that you send your comments soon, so that this guide can be kept as up-to-date as possible. And thank you for sharing your finds with other people like yourself.

To:
   The Editor
   America's Wonderful Little Hotels and Inns
   Congdon & Weed, Inc.
   298 Fifth Avenue
   New York, N.Y. 10001

Name of Hotel _____

Address _____

_____

Date of most recent visit _____ Duration of visit_____
☐ New recommendation   ☐ Comment on existing entry

In addition to a description of the inn and its setting, your room, the food, and some of the nearby sights, we'd like to hear about your comfort (or discomfort) during your stay—cleanliness, service, lighting, plumbing, parking, quiet, etc.—and the quality of the welcome and hospitality you received.

Report:

Signed _____

Name and address (please print) _____

_____

_____

To:
The Editor
America's Wonderful Little Hotels and Inns
Congdon & Weed, Inc.
298 Fifth Avenue
New York, N.Y. 10001

Name of Hotel _____

Address _____

_____

Date of most recent visit _____ Duration of visit_____

☐ New recommendation   ☐ Comment on existing entry

In addition to a description of the inn and its setting, your room, the food, and some of the nearby sights, we'd like to hear about your comfort (or discomfort) during your stay—cleanliness, service, lighting, plumbing, parking, quiet, etc.—and the quality of the welcome and hospitality you received.

Report:

Signed _____

Name and address (please print) _____

_____

_____

To:
The Editor
America's Wonderful Little Hotels and Inns
Congdon & Weed, Inc.
298 Fifth Avenue
New York, N.Y. 10001

Name of Hotel _____

Address _____

_____

Date of most recent visit _____ Duration of visit_____

☐ New recommendation   ☐ Comment on existing entry

In addition to a description of the inn and its setting, your room, the food, and some of the nearby sights, we'd like to hear about your comfort (or discomfort) during your stay—cleanliness, service, lighting, plumbing, parking, quiet, etc.—and the quality of the welcome and hospitality you received.

Report:

Signed _____

Name and address (please print) _____

_____

_____

To:
The Editor
America's Wonderful Little Hotels and Inns
Congdon & Weed, Inc.
298 Fifth Avenue
New York, N.Y. 10001

Name of Hotel _____

Address _____

_____

Date of most recent visit _____ Duration of visit_____
☐ New recommendation   ☐ Comment on existing entry

In addition to a description of the inn and its setting, your room, the food, and some of the nearby sights, we'd like to hear about your comfort (or discomfort) during your stay—cleanliness, service, lighting, plumbing, parking, quiet, etc.—and the quality of the welcome and hospitality you received.

Report:

Signed _____

Name and address (please print) _____

_____

_____

To:
The Editor
America's Wonderful Little Hotels and Inns
Congdon & Weed, Inc.
298 Fifth Avenue
New York, N.Y. 10001

Name of Hotel _____

Address _____

_____

Date of most recent visit _____ Duration of visit_____
☐ New recommendation   ☐ Comment on existing entry

In addition to a description of the inn and its setting, your room, the food, and some of the nearby sights, we'd like to hear about your comfort (or discomfort) during your stay—cleanliness, service, lighting, plumbing, parking, quiet, etc.—and the quality of the welcome and hospitality you received.

Report:

Signed _____

Name and address (please print) _____

_____

_____

To:
  The Editor
  America's Wonderful Little Hotels and Inns
  Congdon & Weed, Inc.
  298 Fifth Avenue
  New York, N.Y. 10001

Name of Hotel _____

Address _____

_____

Date of most recent visit _____ Duration of visit_____
☐ New recommendation   ☐ Comment on existing entry

In addition to a description of the inn and its setting, your room, the food, and some of the nearby sights, we'd like to hear about your comfort (or discomfort) during your stay—cleanliness, service, lighting, plumbing, parking, quiet, etc.—and the quality of the welcome and hospitality you received.

Report:

Signed _____

Name and address (please print) _____

_____

_____

To:
   The Editor
   America's Wonderful Little Hotels and Inns
   Congdon & Weed, Inc.
   298 Fifth Avenue
   New York, N.Y. 10001

Name of Hotel _____

Address _____

_____

Date of most recent visit _____ Duration of visit_____

☐ New recommendation   ☐ Comment on existing entry

In addition to a description of the inn and its setting, your room, the food, and some of the nearby sights, we'd like to hear about your comfort (or discomfort) during your stay—cleanliness, service, lighting, plumbing, parking, quiet, etc.—and the quality of the welcome and hospitality you received.

Report:

Signed _____

Name and address (please print) _____

_____

_____

Index by State

_Index by Inn Name